A C T S

Life in Action

ACTS

Life in Action

Roy L. Laurin

**Foreword by
Billy Graham**

KREGEL PUBLICATIONS
Grand Rapids, Michigan 49501

Acts: Life In Action by Roy L. Laurin
Published in 1985 by Kregel Publications,
a division of Kregel, Inc. All rights reserved.

Library of Congress Cataloging in Publication Data

Laurin, Roy L. (Roy Leonard), 1898-1966.
    Acts: Life In Action.

    Reprint. Originally published: Findlay, Ohio:
Dunham Pub. Co., c1962.
    1. Bible. N.T. Acts—Commentaries. I. Title.
II. Title: Life in action.
BS2625.3.L38   1985   226'.607   85-8158
ISBN 0-8254-3127-1 (pbk.)

Printed in the United States of America

CONTENTS

Foreword by Billy Graham 9

Preface 11

Introduction 15

1. Young Churches in Action (1:1) 19

2. Power for Witnessing (1:1-8) 26

3. The Ascension and Its Meaning (1:9-11) 32

4. Peter and the Others (1:12-26) 40

5. Tongues on Fire (2:1-13) 47

6. This is That or The Explanation of
   Pentecost (2:14-21) 57

7. The Divine Break-through or The Reason for
   Pentecost (2:22-36) 64

8. Continued Story or The Results of
   Pentecost (2:37-47) 71

9. Such as I Have (3:1-11) 78

10. The Power of Faith (3:12-26) 85

11. No Other Name (4:1-12) 91

12. Christianity Facing New Challenges (4:13-31) 97

13. Them That Believed (4:32—5:11) 103

14. Works of Wonder (5:12-16) 108

15. The New Way of Life (5:17-42) 114

16. The Church at Work (6:1-8) 121

17. How Long Is a Full Life? (6:8—7:53) 127

18. The Christian Looks at Death (7:54-60)............134

19. The Expulsive Power of a
     Great Compulsion (8:1-14)....................141

20. The First Missionary (8:5-13) 147

21. The Relation of the Holy Spirit to the
     Believer (8:14-25) 154

22. A Distinguished Convert (8:26-40) 162

23. Christian Baptism (8:36) 169

24. Christianity's Most Remarkable
     Conversion (9:1-19)..........................175

25. Jesus Christ the Son of God (9:20)...............182

26. Why Do Christians Suffer? (9:21-31) 188

27. The Healing Ministry of the Church (9:32-43) 195

28. The Yielded Value of Little Things (9:36-43) 201

29. Who Can Belong to the Church? (10:1-48; 11:19-30) .207

30. What Do We Mean by the Church? (11:19-30) 214

31. Faith Takes a Name (11:26) 220

32. The Power of Prayer (12:1-25)...................227

33. Fidelity in Service (13:1-3) 233

34. The Saving Message (13:4-43)...................240

35. Trial and Triumph (14:1-18) 248

36. What Heaven Is Like (14:19-20; 2 Cor. 12:1-12).....254

37. Religious Controversy in the Church (15:1-35) 262

38. Personal Controversy in the Church (15:36-41) 271

39. The Man in Your Life (16:1-24) 278

40. Question and Answer (16:25-40) 285

41. The Tale of Two Cities (17:1-14) 291

42. Turning the World Upside Down (17:6) 298

43. The Unknown God (17:15-34) 305

44. Paul, His Life and Letters (18:1-28) 312

45. Christianity and the Unusual (19:1-20) 320

46. Is Christianity the Only Way? (19:9) 327

47. Christianity's Conflict with Religion (19:21-41) 334

48. Is Sunday the Right Day of Worship? (20:1-12) 341

49. The Ideal Christian Servant (20:13-38) 349

50. Divine Providence and Human Events (21:1-17) 358

51. Church and State (21:18-40) .365

52. Christianity's Best Apologetic (22:1—23:35) 371

53. When Is the Best Time to Be Saved? (24:1-25) 378

54. Almost or Altogether (25:1—26:32) 384

55. The Contrary Winds of Life (27:1—28:10) 391

56. The Triumph of a Well-lived Life (28:11-31) 399

FOREWORD

Dr. Roy Laurin has one of the most unique and incisive ways of expressing spiritual truth of any clergyman I know. I have read every book he has ever written and some of them several times. In fact, many of the thoughts which I use in my preaching have come from this great West Coast preacher's writing.

In LIFE IN ACTION, Dr. Laurin has given us something long needed in evangelical literature — a scholarly, evangelistic and warm exposition of the Book of Acts. I have already seen two or three outlines that I am tempted to "borrow," and I believe this book will enhance and deepen our private devotions.

Dr. Laurin's research on this book is the work of several years. I get the impression that he is giving us the very cream of his rich preaching ministry in LIFE IN ACTION.

As I enter the middle years of my ministry, the Book of Acts is becoming an increasing challenge to me. I search it zealously for any clues of fire and power, the two elements so sorely missing in the pulpit in this decade of the Sixties.

The world about us seeks self-transcendence by artificial and chemical means. In one recent year doctors wrote prescriptions for 40 million tranquilizers. The record consumption of alcohol is a crude attempt at self-transcendence. But the Book of Acts shows how God transcends men and enables them to live beyond themselves by the power of the Spirit. In the Book of Acts we see men with cool heads and warm hearts in contrast to the prevalence of hot heads and cold hearts today. In Dr. Laurin's exposition we feel something of the glow and thrilling dynamic of those early Christians. It is my prayer that this book will help Christian leaders all over the world to recapture some of the magnificent triumph of the Early Church.

As I commend this book to you, I pray that you will not only read it, but study it. May the Spirit which motivated the lives of those heroes of the Book of Acts make us equally adequate for the times in which we live.

BILLY GRAHAM

PREFACE

The disciples of the early church whose acts are recorded in this book of action were not merely men of words and ideas; they were men of action. There is bold and dramatic movement from Jerusalem and its upper room to Rome and its prison. We see a growing group of men and women, filled with the dynamic power of a new life. Here are heroic deeds done for Christ. In the account which describes these things there are few descriptive adjectives. It is filled with nouns and verbs that tell of exploit and adventure. All of this stems from Pentecost and the Book of Acts becomes the story of the Holy Spirit in the church in terms of faith and life, doctrine and action.

ACKNOWLEDGMENTS

On the menu of an old restaurant in Amsterdam the author read that many of the recipes from which "specialties" were prepared were three and four hundred years old. While no such claim of extended age can be made for the literary recipes of this book, it remains as a fact that much of its contents is the fruit of a lifetime of reading, preaching and living.

Beyond this is an area of special research which gave invaluable help. This help came chiefly from the following three sources: *The Young Church in Action,* J. B. Phillips; *The Acts of the Apostles,* R. B. Rackham; *The Book of the Acts,* F. F. Bruce. Grateful acknowledgment is made to these superlative authors, and to my son, Robert B. Laurin, Professor of Old Testament at California Baptist Theological Seminary for manuscript counsel.

INTRODUCTION

The Acts of the Apostles is the only unfinished book in the Canon of Scripture. It is not unfinished in the sense of revelation, but accomplishment. The last chapter does not conclude what the first chapter commences, for the chapters continue in the experience of the continuing church.

No one will ever understand the New Testament or profit fully from its reading unless he sees the Gospels in their relation to the Epistles with the Acts of the Apostles as a bridge connecting the facts of gospel history with the principles of Christian truth.

"To see how necessary the Book of Acts is to the place accorded it, it is only required in reading to close the book at the Gospel of John and open it again at the Epistle to the Romans. In John you close with Jesus on the shores of Galilee, but in Romans you find Him gone from the earth and the church in His place, but no account of the origin or constitution of that church. Without the Book of Acts you cannot assist at the birth of the church and the inauguration of the dispensation of the Holy Ghost."

In the Acts of the Apostles we have a framework created by these events of the early church into which we can put the devotional content of a life of action for modern Christians. We are confronted here with heroic men and women who hazarded their lives for Christ. Here is shed the first martyr's blood which became the seed of the church. Here the lines of gospel communication run out to the then civilized world. Here is the progressive development of revealed truth. Here is the laboratory of faith and life in which theories of faith are proved by experiences of life.

The Acts of the Apostles is important because it is the arena in which we see the Apostle Paul in action. His dramatic conversion on a Damascan highway is followed by seclusion in the desert. He emerged to become Barnabas' assistant at Antioch. He boldly and unflinchingly proclaimed his new found faith in the synagogues of Jewry. He became the greatest missionary of all time. After fifteen years of turbulent crusading, traveling and preaching, he had firmly established the church in the midst of both paganism and Judaism. He had at the end of his brief writing career shaped Christianity with his pen. In the light of these things Acts becomes the great workshop of the Apostle Paul whose dynamic and fruitful life dominates its pages.

Perhaps the greatest contemporary significance of the Acts of the Apostles is its use as a source book for the doctrines of our Christian faith. Here the disciple can nourish his faith on the great truths that became the foundation of the church. Here the preacher can find practically every major item of the Christian faith. He can preach on such items of faith as the deity of Jesus Christ, the Holy Spirit, the church, the Kingdom of God, the return of Jesus Christ, Christian witnessing, the gospel, baptism, the Lord's supper, the ascension of Jesus, divine election, healing of the sick, the power of faith, miracles, the problem of death, evangelism, missions, conversion, human suffering, prayer, heaven, the Scriptures, Sunday worship, divine providence, church and state, adversity and life fulfillment.

ACTS
Life in Action

1

YOUNG CHURCHES IN ACTION

Acts 1:1

The story of the church which unfolds in the Acts of the Apostles is one of the most fascinating stories of the Bible. It is the story of young churches in action—not in meditation, contemplation or worship—but action. In fact, action is the theme as well as the name of the Book of Acts. It is its atmosphere, story, movement and inspiration.

We will look at young churches in action in at least five ways.

I. THE RECORD OF YOUNG CHURCHES

This record is found in what is called the Acts of the Apostles, the fifth book of the New Testament and its last book of history, four of which have preceded in the four Gospels. We are not to suppose that this Acts of the Apostles contains all the acts of all the apostles. It is more properly understood as "some of the acts of some of the apostles" (Phillips).

This book is otherwise known to us as the acts of the Holy Spirit, for it describes the deeds and exploits of the apostles under the power of the Spirit, whose coming is recorded as one of the major events of the book. This book is likewise the record of the birth, founding and deeds of young churches revolving around two centers, the Church at Jerusalem and the Church at Antioch.

The writer of this record of young churches in action is without question the same as the writer of the third gospel, Dr. Luke. He is so identified in the opening statement of the book—"The former treatise have I made, O Theophilus . . . ."

What Luke wrote about in the third Gospel were the things "Jesus began both to do and teach." You have here the relation of teaching to action and faith to life. And now in this history of the Acts there is a continuation of Jesus' teachings and actions in the record of young churches. You have the same writer, the same readers and the same subjects in extended form.

In the picturesque Bantu language the title of the Book of Acts is "Words Concerning Deeds." Indeed, nothing could be more aptly descriptive of what Acts contains than this title, the deeds of young churches put into words.

One of the things that Acts and the Gospels have in common is that they were written some time after the transpiration of the events which they record. Acts is considered to have been written about thirty years after the ascension, and three years after the concluding events of its final chapter, or somewhere around 65 A.D. This means that you have a remarkable case of events recorded through the Holy Spirit. These are taken from the natural sources available to Luke from the many who were present on the Day of Pentecost, as well as from his close association with Paul around whom much of the record is written.

II. THE BIRTH OF YOUNG CHURCHES

You could not have imagined a more turbulent time in which to give birth to the church than the time described in Acts. There were only a few more than eleven Christians on record when Jesus' ascension took place. A twelfth was later chosen and these twelve were multiplied ten times to increase the original company to one hundred and twenty, who tarried in Jerusalem to await the coming of the Holy Spirit. Jesus had appeared to upwards of five hundred during the forty days between the resurrection and the ascension. What happened to the three hundred and eighty we do not know, but undoubtedly they were later identified with the stirring events which followed Pentecost.

This handful of Christians was besieged by bigoted Jews on the one hand and fanatical pagans on the other hand. Considering the disparity of their number the successful survival of this new sect could scarcely be predicted with confidence by anyone who lived at that time.

The church was not only born in a crisis time; it has lived and thrived in repeated crises times. Furthermore, it will come to its climax and grand finalé in a time of crisis.

Historical perspective reveals crises in most all periods, and ours is no exception. One modern observer says this, "Our world is crumbling. There is no return to normalcy. Conditions are bad but they will worsen. Our world has seemed good to us, but it has not seemed so to 75% of the globe's population, which lives in underprivileged areas. Peace and prosperity for us have rested in part upon oppression, exploitation and injustice for residents of under-developed countries." A West Point Academy professor told military and civil defense leaders recently, "We of the West are a diminishing minority in an awakening world." Crisis has always been with us in one form or another and the church has had to live as it was born. But whatever dangers threatened, and still threaten the church, we remember the words of our Lord, "the gates of hell shall not prevail against it."

In spite of the times existing at the birth of these young churches we must conclude that "never before has any small body of ordinary people so moved the world that their enemies could say, with tears of rage in their eyes, that these men 'have turned the world upside down' " (Phillips).

In spite of the times and their persecutions with the loss of all their possessions, and sometimes their lives, this small company of Christians, by their own personal witness and communication, took the message of salvation and distributed it to their world within the short span of a few generations. The significance of this is that these people survived because they were young churches in action. They did not vegetate or fossilize. They multiplied by self-propagation. And they did all this without benefit of a written New Testament, college or seminaries, printing press, radio or newspaper, railroad or airplane, money, television, church buildings, ecclesiastical organization or public favor. They did it in the face of hostility, danger, persecution, deprivation and impending death. But they did it. So must we if we are to survive as a church militant in a crisis time.

III. THE FAITH OF YOUNG CHURCHES

There is no doubt that the survival and success of these young churches stem from their faith. They believed something profoundly and passionately enough to proclaim it and die for it.

In making an observation on the sterility of modern television preaching the editor of a secular trade magazine said this: "The fault lies in a kind of creative sickness which seems to be characteristic of most religious organizations. . . . Recently I talked with an important executive at one of the TV networks who cited three reasons for the current state of religious programming. The first of these was to the effect that most churches and churchmen are surprisingly vague about what they really believe. Before they try to tell others about their faith, they should indulge in some real intellectual housecleaning."* This was not true of these young churches. Of one of them it was said, "they accepted the message most eagerly and studied the Scriptures every day to see if what they were now being told were true" (Phillips).

The faith of these young churches was capable of survival because it was faith in action. Not until our faith becomes faith in action will it be an adequate faith. What we believe must become how we live and what we do.

These young churches believed profoundly in two things, the crucifixion and the resurrection. Everytime they preached or witnessed, these two things were either explicit or implicit in what they said. In fact, there could be no salvation apart from belief in these two things. Paul would later record it in these words to the Romans, "That if thou shalt confess with thy mouth the Lord Jesus, and shalt believe in thine heart that God hath raised him from the dead, thou shalt be saved. For with the heart man believeth unto righteousness; and with the mouth confession is made unto salvation" (Romans 10:9, 10).

---

*The Churchman, January 1960.

When the New Testament epistles were later written, and many of them were written within the span of time involved in the Book of the Acts, they amplified these two items of faith to include justification, the deity of Christ, the inspiration of the Bible, the resurrection of the body and many other concepts included in the Christian faith.

The key to the faith of these churches is in Acts 1:8, "Ye shall receive power, after that the Holy Ghost is come upon you: and ye shall be witnesses unto me both in Jerusalem, and in all Judaea, and in Samaria, and unto the uttermost part of the earth." Their faith was faith in a person. It was the person of Jesus Christ, the Son of God, crucified for our sins, risen from the dead and ascended into heaven as High Priest. The evidence of these facts was found in the Holy Spirit, whom Jesus had promised to send in His stead. Having ascended and occupied His heavenly ministry the Holy Spirit came as the personal presence of the Godhead in the church.

IV. THE SIMPLICITY OF FAITH AND WORSHIP IN YOUNG CHURCHES

All things are simple at their beginning. God began the complex creation, with its innumerable materials and forms of existence, with a comparatively simple atom consisting of a nucleus and its electronic field. The nucleus was made up of protons and neutrons in cohesion, and swinging around it was the electronic field. Out of this came the entire creation. While a newly born baby is a complex human machine yet its needs and functions are very simple, consisting of a few plain clothes and a simple form of food. It is when that baby grows up that things become complex and involved, as for instance, its wardrobe, its food and its modern form of life.

The church was very simple in its faith, government and worship following Pentecost. Later under church-statism it became very complex. Its faith was expressed in many creeds. Its government was pre-empted by a privileged class known as a hierarchy. Its worship became cluttered and corrupted with pagan symbols and customs until now some church systems are half-Christian and half-pagan with worship no longer spiritual but expressed by the five senses of the body. We have a tradition-choked church which has all but lost its way in the complexity of its own arrangements and is unfit to show any sinner the way to God.

The Christians who live and breathe in the Book of the Acts were known as "followers of the way." They knew few ceremonies for they had just become rid of the now outmoded temple worship with its priests and sacrifices. They could tell their mission to the world in one simple sentence — "I am the way, the truth, and the life: no man cometh unto the Father, but by me."

While for some time Christian converts continued to worship in synagogues and Christian preachers continued to use them as their forums, the essential elements of Christian worship were very simple. They were the Lord's supper, the love feast, baptism, but not much more. There were no rich vestments, nor elaborate rituals, for there were no church buildings in which these could be properly used. All of this came as the accretion of time. The early observances of worship took place in private homes, without churches or cathedrals, and without clergy or established ritual.

V. THE POWER OF YOUNG CHURCHES

Just before His ascension the founder and head of these young churches said, "But ye shall receive power, after that the Holy Ghost is come upon you: and ye shall be witnesses unto me both in Jerusalem, and in all Judaea, and in Samaria, and unto the uttermost part of the earth" (Acts 1:8). The manifestation of this power was like a "rushing, mighty wind" or as Phillips translates it, "the rushing of a violent wind." Here was something spiritually cyclonic with revolutionary and irresistible effects. No wonder the handful of people of these young churches could "turn the world upside down."

What kind of power did this first generation of Christians have? In some instances it was power to heal; but this apparently became a diminishing power subject to the discretionary will of God, for when you get past Acts only four instances of sickness are dealt with and each in a different way. In other instances this power was the power to open prison doors, raise the dead, resist persecution and endure death with glory. But in the facts of this case the chief power possessed by these young churches was the power of evangelizing by witnessing. Through this power these churches turned the world upside down and changed the course of history.

2

POWER FOR WITNESSING

Acts 1:1-8

It is evident from what we read in Acts that its chief characteristic is action. Supporting this action was a unique power that gave thrust and movement to the early church. It is true to say that the ethic of Christianity is in its gospels and epistles while the dynamic of Christianity is in its Acts of the Apostles.

The text will supply us with the story of this thrilling action.

I. THE FORTY DAYS (verses 1-3)

The period of forty days between the resurrection and ascension of Jesus was not a vacuum. It was filled with quiet but thrilling activity when Jesus was doing two things.

1. Giving Commandments (verse 2). ". . . after that he through the Holy Ghost had given commandments unto the apostles whom he had chosen."

Undoubtedly Jesus had many things to tell His diciples during these days, but one thing was more important than all the rest. It was what we call the Great Commission in which Jesus turned the faces of His disciples toward the world, and charged them to preach the Gospel to every creature.

2. Confirming the Resurrection (verse 3). "To whom also he showed himself alive after his passion by many infallible proofs. . . ."

This was done through personal appearances under every conceivable condition and circumstance, so there could be no doubt of the reality of His resurrection. The entire thrust of the church depended on this confirmation and no evidence of it would be neglected.

An amplified record of these post-resurrection appearances is found in Paul's great chapter on the believer's resurrection in his First Epistle to the Corinthians, Chapter 15, verses 3 to 8: "For I delivered unto you first of all that which I also received, how that Christ died for our sins according to the scriptures; and that he was buried, and that he rose again the third day according to the scriptures: and that he was seen of Cephas, then of the twelve: after that, he was seen of above five hundred brethren at once; of whom the greater part remain unto this present, but some are fallen asleep. After that, he was seen of James; then of all the apostles. And last of all he was seen of me also, as of one born out of due time." Lacking precise details of these appearances our imagination must lead us to reconstruct some of the thrilling and wonderful things which transpired during Jesus' reunion with His disciples.

There is an important lesson for modern disciples in these appearances. The only way the disciples could have been sustained in their faith after the crucifixion was through fellowship. The only way any modern disciple can be sustained, after his acceptance of Christ, is through fellowship with the risen and ever present Savior.

This period of the forty days is the sequel to the crucifixion when the hopes of the disciples were crushed and beaten to earth. Now they were convinced that Jesus was indeed the Messiah and in this conviction, sustained by fellowship, they could stand fearlessly before the world.

Imagine the thrilling experience of having someone return from the dead. The joy of these disciples knew no bounds. Their hopes took wings. They felt that they could endure any adversity for they were going to live forever. They now had something to live and die for and it would not be long before the great test of what they possessed would be upon them.

There need be no doubt about the reality of the resurrection when one considers the "many infallible proofs" produced during these forty days. The appearances of Jesus were under every conceivable circumstance, — sometimes at night, then again at dawn and at another time in the blazing light of noon. They were sometimes to one, sometimes to a few and sometimes to hundreds. It was on one occasion by the sea, then in the city, again in the mountains or on the highway and then in a room.

The resurrection is without doubt the best attested, scrutinized and documented fact of history. And after all the evidence has been gathered there remains the greatest evidence of all, personal experience. "You ask me how I know He lives? He lives within my heart."

It was during these forty days that Jesus spoke to His disciples "of the things pertaining to the Kingdom of God." From what we can put together of the various occasions of Jesus' appearances to His disciples these things consisted of the following:

1. A summary of the Gospel — the crucifixion and resurrection.
2. A command of service — the Great Commission.
3. A commission to represent Christ during the ten-day interval between Jesus' ascension and the Holy Spirit's coming (John 20:21-23).
4. An equipment to carry out both the command and the commission, namely, the Holy Spirit.

A tourist was making his first visit to the national capitol, and a friendly cab driver was driving him around to see the beautiful buildings. As they rode past the government archives building, the tourist noticed the carved words across the huge building, "What Is Past Is Prologue." "Just what does that mean?" the tourist asked. "It means," said the driver, "that you ain't seen nothin' yet." All of these appearances, commands, commissions and equipment were prologue.

II. THE ASCENSION (verses 4-8)

Here is recorded the last earthly meeting between Jesus and His disciples. A number of things transpired.

1. The Place. The place of the meeting and ascension is

described in Luke 24:50. It was Bethany, on the eastern slope of the Mount of Olives. It was where Lazarus was raised from the dead and where his sisters had lived. The place was significant also because it had been predicted by the Prophet Zechariah that the Messiah should ascend from this Mount (Zech. 14:4). There is also an added prophetic significance because it is the place to which Christ shall return at His second coming.

2. The Promise of the Holy Spirit. The ascension was to be part of the fulfillment of a promise Jesus had previously made when He had told them it was expedient for Him to go away that the Comforter might come. This coming of the Holy Spirit would be the crucial event of the entire Book of Acts because it would complete the redemptive purpose of God. It would be the source of individual power. It would be the great unifying event for it would unite believers into the Body of Christ.

This event of the coming of the Spirit would be as Jesus says in verse 5, a baptism. This was not of water but of spirit. It would be an immersing in a body. It would be a fusing or uniting in an indissoluable union.

3. A Question Would be Answered. The disciples were not yet aware of the full implications of what was happening. They were still immersed in their dreams of a material kingdom and they asked, "Lord, wilt thou at this time restore again the Kingdom of Israel?" (verse 6). Jesus gave them an answer which is a key to the whole historical and prophetical area in which we are living. He said, "It is not for you to know the times or the seasons, which the Father hath put in his own power" (verse 7). This is a plain and conclusive answer to any date setting. Even Jesus did not know or could not reveal the answer under His kenotic submission to the Father's authority through the Holy Spirit.

4. The Promised Power. This is described in verse 8. "But ye shall receive power, after that the Holy Ghost is come upon you: and ye shall be witnesses unto me both in Jerusalem, and in all Judaea, and in Samaria, and unto the uttermost part of the earth."

The New Testament speaks of two kinds of power. First, there is *the power of authority* such as is described in John 1:12, "but as many as received him, to them gave he power to become the sons of God, even to them that believe on his name." This was not the kind of power promised at Pentecost. This is the power which was manifested toward us at conversion when we became the sons of God. Second, there is the *power of ability*. It is this kind of power which came with the Pentecostal gift of the Holy Spirit. It was not specifically the power to heal or raise the dead. It was the power of ability to evangelize through witnessing.

This power of witnessing would prove to be the power of personal excellence in the individual believer. It would also be the cause of the growth and multiplication of the corporate Body of Christ — the Church.

Jesus said, "Ye shall receive power *after* . . . ." It would be after Pentecost which would be ten days hence. That event is a fact and this power is available to the modern disciple.

It was to be the power of a person. The person would be the Holy Spirit, whose coming Jesus anticipated by His upper-room promise.

It was also to be the power for witnessing to a person, not just an idea or a philosophy. This was a way of life, not just a system of thought or an exercise of religion. The witnessing would be to the person of Christ. He said, "Ye shall be witnesses *unto me*." The disciples were therefore not witnesses to, or mere guardians of, creeds, ideas or law; but to a person, Jesus Christ.

But who would receive this power which would account for the commencement and continuity of Christianity? It would be for the individual disciples who tarried in Jerusalem, and the individual disciples who succeeded them in the Body of Christ.

This power which emanated from Pentecost did not create a hierarchy of special caste and privilege to impose its will on others. It was power for individual Christians who were to function as witnesses and to multiply the body of believers. The ecclesiastical monstrosities of hierarchical form that exist today are historical accretions which have no basis of being in the original founding of the church. The New Testament church which began at Pentecost was a church of the people whose individual members partook of fellowship, power and blessing directly from the Head of the church Himself.

What we are considering are the last words which Jesus spoke on the earth.

They are words of challenge. They speak to everyone of the challenge of Christian discipleship. In Masefield's play, "The Trial of Jesus," Longinus, the Roman centurion, who stood at the foot of the cross, is heard talking with Proculo, Pilate's wife, just after the crucifixion. "Do you think he is dead?" she asks him. "No lady, I don't." "Then where is he?" "Let loose on the world, lady," replies Longinus, "where neither Roman nor Jew can stop his truth."

They are words of preparation. They tell us the source and extent of the preparation available to us in the person of the Holy Spirit.

They are words of responsibility. When we consider the effect on the world of the handful of dedicated and empowered Christians in this early church, we cannot escape the sense of responsibility that rests upon us who face this generation. Ours is the responsibility of witness. Unless conditions greatly change we will never have to pay the fearful price this first generation of Christians paid. But even if we do our responsibility is still valid.

One stormy day a coast guard crew was ordered to the rescue of a liner wrecked off the coast of New England. An old and tried seaman was in charge, but the members of the crew were for the most part young, untested men. When one of them comprehended the situation, he turned white-faced to the captain and said, "Sir, the wind is off-shore, the tide is running out. We can go out, but against this wind and tide we cannot come back." The grim old captain faced the young man and said, "Launch the boat; we go out." "But, sir—," protested the young man. "We don't have to come back," replied the captain.

3

THE ASCENSION AND ITS MEANING

Acts 1:9-11

It was now forty days after the triumphant and thrilling experience of the resurrection when Jesus overcame the forces of death and walked out of the tomb in the full powers of His resurrected life. From that moment "he showed himself alive after his passion by many infallible proofs." He appeared to Mary at the entrance of the garden tomb; to the disciples on the Emmaus road; to the disciples in the upper room with Thomas missing; to the disciples at the Sea of Tiberias; and again to the disciples in the upper room with Thomas present.

Now in the company of some five hundred disciples who came from various places, in and near Jerusalem, He went out to Bethany, a small town on the eastern slope of the Mount of Olives. It was about fifteen furlongs, or a Sabbath day's journey from Jerusalem, on the Jericho road. It was the town where Lazarus lived. And here near Bethany, Jesus met with His disciples for the last time.

Who of us can fathom the depths of emotion plumbed at that moment? Who can imagine the drama of this last meeting? Who can feel what they must have felt as they gathered on the slopes of the Mount of Olives? Perhaps they did not fully realize what was about to take place until the feet of Jesus slowly lifted from the rocky sides of that eminence. If so, then it would just begin to dawn upon them. Then, perhaps, panic seized them and they rushed forward to restrain the ascending Christ, grasping His tunic and clutching at His feet.

It must have been an awesome but wonderful moment to have

seen Jesus gradually rise from the earth and almost imperceptibly ascend toward heaven. After the first panicky moments they must have fallen to the ground to watch their Lord ascend into the heavens until a cloud wafted across the sky, slowly enveloped Him in its billowy, gossamer glory and they saw Him no more.

But what, on the other hand, must have been the scene on the other side of the enfolding cloud, beyond the sight of the disciples, when with accelerated swiftness and in a flash of time, without being susceptible to gravity or the cold of space, Jesus went beyond the separating spheres into the presence of God and the angels.

Can anyone imagine—no, no one—the welcome in heaven to the returning Son of God? There was the music, the hosannas, the acclaim and the triumph of His return. He returned to the glory of the Father whence He left to be incarnated. He returned to heaven to be reinstated in all the majesty and glory which He had voluntarily surrendered in His *kenosis.* He returned to heaven to become the potential possessor of universal dominion. He returned to heaven to be the omnipresent object of our worship.

Hardly had Jesus gone, and while the disciples were still beholding, "suddenly two men stood by them in white apparel: which also said, Ye men of Galilee why stand ye gazing up into heaven? This same Jesus, which is taken up from you into heaven, shall so come in like manner as ye have seen him go into heaven" (verse 11). This sets before us both a going and a coming of Jesus and in between there has stretched an interval of almost twenty centuries. During this interval, with the continuing generations of disciples on earth and the Savior in heaven, there have been the practical effects of the ascension. Though time and space separate them, yet they are not divided for there is the mystical union between disciple and Lord in the Body of Christ.

While there is separation there is no isolation for our Lord is omnipresent among us. The ascension has become another link in the chain of redemptive events which include incarnation, crucifixion, resurrection and return. The incarnation meant *God with us;* the crucifixion meant *God as us;* the ascension means *God for us;* and Pentecost means *God in us.*

The relation of the ascension to redemption is observed in the following:

I. A FINISHED REDEMPTION

"He was received up into heaven and sat on the right hand of God" Mark 16:19).

When Jesus sat on the right hand of God it meant a finished and completed redemption. It did not necessarily mean a literal physical act, but rather a symbolic fact. It signified, what was never true at any time prior to the cross, that no high priest of Israel had ever offered a conclusive and perfect sacrifice. "But this man when He had offered one sacrifice for sins forever, sat down on the right hand of God" (Heb. 10:12). This was the first time a sacrifice was concluded by the offerer sitting down to contemplate the finished and conclusive nature of his offering. This was the first time a high priest ever sat down after offering his sacrifice. The practical spiritual implication of this fact is that faith in Him as Savior brings us under this perfected and finished redemption.

II. A SECURE REDEMPTION

" . . . We have as an anchor of the soul, both sure and stedfast, and which entereth into that within the veil; whither the forerunner is for us entered, even Jesus, made an high priest for ever after the order of Melchisedec" (Heb. 6:19, 20).

The ascension is this "anchor of the soul." Our salvation is not anchored to our feelings, nor to our ability to hold on; but to the present intercessory work of the ascended Christ at the throne of God. This is anchorage enough.

I stood above that breath-taking crevice in Colorado known as the Royal Gorge through which the Arkansas River runs. Across this gorge engineers have built a great suspension bridge, the highest of its kind in the world. The strength of this bridge is in the suspension cables which are anchored in great blocks of concrete, which in turn are imbedded in the subterranean rock of the mountains. The security of the bridge is not in what is seen of steel and cable, but in what is not seen in its invisible anchorage that cannot be either scrutinized or assessed by human sight. So it is with the believer's salvation. It is secured to the immutable throne of the eternal God by the invisible anchorage of the ascension.

III. A CONTINUING REDEMPTION

"Wherefore he is able also to save them to the uttermost that come unto God by him, seeing he ever liveth to make intercession for them" (Heb. 7:25).

While the work of redemption in relation to God is finished, the work in relation to man is unfinished. It is in this context of man's continuing spiritual need that I John 2:1 is written, ". . . And if any man sin, we have an advocate with the Father, Jesus Christ the righteous." Jesus Christ is our advocate or counsellor, to meet the redemptive needs of man by answering the accusations and condemnations of Satan, as well as to propitiate the sins of the believer.

The believer has continuous need of the advocacy of Jesus. On the cross He was the finished and satisfying sacrifice. At the throne He is the propitiating advocate and the interceding high priest. The God-ward redemption is an accomplished fact. The man-ward redemption is a continuing experience. The believer's salvation is both finished and unfinished. It is finished in our eternal relationship to God. It is being finished in the experience of the believer's daily life. It is finished in its justification aspect. It is being finished in its sanctification aspect. It is finished in relation to the believer's position. It is being finished in relation to the believer's condition.

IV. A SUPREME REDEMPTION

"Wherefore God also hath highly exalted him, and given him

a name which is above every name: that at the name of Jesus every knee should bow, of things in heaven, and things in earth, and things under the earth" (Phil. 2:9, 10).

The ascension placed Jesus not only upon a throne of grace as our advocate, but also upon a throne of sovereignty as the ultimate ruler of the world as King of kings and Lord of lords. It is from this position of sovereignty that He awaits His Father's pleasure to assume control of men and institutions. This is the hope of both the church and the world. From this the church can move in a position of strength to conduct its ministry to the world. From this also the world can endure its changing fortunes as it considers the ultimate solution and answer to life's vexing problems.

V. An Exalted Redemption

"And hath raised us up together, and made us sit together in heavenly places in Christ Jesus" (Eph. 2:6).

This points to the spiritual exaltation of every believer whose positional relationship to Jesus Christ puts him in the sphere of potential power and blessing equivalent to his exalted place at God's right hand. Not only is this true, but what is positionally true *of us* should be made experimentally true *in us*. The admonition of the Scripture is exactly this, "If ye then be risen with Christ, seek those things which are above, where Christ sitteth on the right hand of God" (Col.3:1).

I once watched a number of blackbirds attacking another bird. One after another they would dart down and strike the hapless bird whose strategy, I noticed, was not to try and dive down and away from its attackers, but to gradually fly higher and higher in ever widening circles of flight. As it did there were fewer enemies to attack it until at last it was alone in the higher reaches of the sky and safe. The Christian's safety under attack from his spiritual and natural enemies is to move higher in spiritual altitude. His enemies cannot live in the atmosphere of the believer's spiritual life in the heavenlies. The level of our defense is in the higher levels of fellowship with Christ. "For though we walk in the flesh, we do not war after the flesh: (For the weapons of our warfare are not carnal, but mighty through God to the pulling down of strong holds;) Casting down imaginations, and every high thing that exalteth itself against the knowledge of God, and bringing into captivity every thought to the obedience of Christ (II Cor. 10:3-5).

VI. A Sufficient Redemption

"But ye shall receive power, after that the Holy Ghost is come upon you: and ye shall be witnesses unto me both in Jerusalem, and in all Judaea, and in Samaria, and unto the uttermost part of the earth" (Acts 1:8).

The ascension meant a new power for every Christian. Prior to His ascension Jesus indicated the coming of the Holy Spirit. His coming was related to the needs of the individual believer. It had to do with the knowledge of truth, the facility of witnessing and the conviction of sin. In fact, it related to every need of the individual believer's life.

Meredith Wilson tells a fable about the band whose music so pleased a king that he opened to the musicians his royal treasury. With an expansive gesture he invited them to walk in and fill up their instruments with as much gold as they could hold. For the bass tuba player and the drummer that was lovely. But one man dejectedly departed, saying, "And there I stood with my piccolo!" Far too many Christians meet life with a piccolo response. We appropriate altogether too little of the vast resources of grace which are available to us through our position in Christ and through the power of personal living which was released at Pentecost.

VII. An Active Redemption

When Jesus ascended into heaven He left the task of world evangelism in the hands and under the responsibility of His disciples. His last meeting with them was a commissioning service in which He sent them to the whole world with a whole gospel for the whole man.

No one who understands the significance of the ascension will minimize or neglect the missionary program of the church. It is the church's life-blood without which the church will become ineffectual.

VIII. AN ULTIMATE REDEMPTION

In the ascension of Jesus we have the assurance of the ultimate redemption of all things through the return of Christ.

At His ascension Christ was put in a position to achieve this ultimate purpose of His return. The language of Matthew 26:64 puts the ascension and the second coming in juxtaposition. ". . . Hereafter shall ye see the Son of man sitting on the right hand of power, and coming in the clouds of heaven." In fact, the second coming of Jesus is consistently based upon the ascension of Jesus.

John 14:3 declares His intention to "go" and prepare a place. But it also declares His intention to "come again." His going is to prepare a place and His coming is for those for whom the place is prepared. The certainty of the coming is based upon the actuality of the going.

Acts 1:11 declares the same thing. It was "while they looked stedfastly toward heaven as He went up" that two men stood among them to say, "Ye men of Galilee why stand ye gazing up into heaven? this same Jesus, which is taken up from you into heaven, shall so come in like manner as ye have seen Him go into heaven." This is the promise, that as certainly as Jesus was taken up so certainly would He return. It was promised further that the return would not only be *because* He went away, but *as* He went away. It would be in "like manner" which means visibly, physically, bodily and personally. Therefore in the ascension we have the assurance and guarantee of the ultimate and final redemption of the world. This means the redemption of the world's institutions, cultures, systems and nations.

The ascension is behind us by almost twenty centuries. How far ahead of us the second coming may be none can tell, but it is always later than we think. In between these two pivotal events the believer contemplates the one and anticipates the other in the knowledge that his Lord is available for every need of his life. All of this has been made true by the ascension for through the ascension, Christ is our high priest and advocate, our forerunner and anchor, and our sovereign Lord. Through the ascension we are seated with Him in the heavenlies in all the privileges, powers and advantages of His resurrection life. His power is in us through the Holy Spirit whom He sent in His stead. And to crown it all Christ is coming again to complete the ultimate redemption of the world.

4

PETER AND THE OTHERS
Acts 1:12-26

The events described in the first chapter of the Book of Acts are prologue. They precede the formation of the church. These things include the promise of power for the propagation ministry of the church, the ascension of Jesus and the promise of His return. Added to these we now have the composition of the company of disciples who would be formed into the Body of Christ at Pentecost.

The church is made up of people. It is the people who constitute the church and not an ecclesiastical super-structure called a hierarchy. Just what kind of people made up this early church? Generally speaking we can properly use the phrase, Peter and the others.

First there was *Peter*. There is no doubt that he was the leader of both the apostles and the disciples following the ascension of Jesus. His name heads the list of the eleven. It was Peter who "stood up in the midst of the disciples" and led the proceedings in the upper room when they chose one of their own to take the place of Judas.

There is also no doubt that while Peter was the leader, his leadership was not that of a prelate, primate or pope. There is no evidence that there was even any such intent to give Peter any kind of papal primacy. All this was invented centuries afterward and made retroactive to these beginning events.

There is also no doubt that Peter's position as head of the apostles was a diminishing one. This diminishing place of Peter is revealed in a number of incidents related to the events of the early church, all of which indicate that the claim of his being the first pope is fictitious, extra-scriptural, unbiblical and pure imagination.

1. If Peter had any such primacy it would have equally applied to Paul for, while Peter was considered the apostle to the Jews, Paul was considered the apostle to the Gentiles. This would have meant a dual leadership if there was ever any intent of hierarchical primacy.

2. At the time of the first ecumenical council of the church at Jerusalem (Acts 15) the moderator of that council was not Peter but James, the brother of Jesus, and a layman. Peter was one of the spokesmen along with Paul, Barnabas and others. But he was not the leader.

3. Peter was sent by the apostles to Samaria to investigate certain reports reaching Jerusalem concerning Philip's ministry in that country (Acts 8:14). He is sent with John who was considered his equal. If Peter was the primate how could he be "sent" by those lesser than he?

4. When Peter entered the house of Cornelius at Caesarea, Cornelius fell down at his feet and paid him homage as a god, but Peter rejected this behavior and said, "I myself also am a man" (Acts 10:26). If Peter was the first pope he did not act like modern popes for he refused to allow people to kneel and genuflect before him.

The allegation that Peter was the first pope belongs neither to history nor to scripture, for in scripture Peter had a diminishing place just as Mary had a diminishing place. In fact, when the time came for the church to burst its local bounds at Jerusalem and become catholic it was not Peter who led the catholic party, but Paul. Peter wanted the church to remain an isolated island of Jewish tradition and not become catholic in nature.

Second, there were *the others*. These are described as "the disciples" or brethren who "were about an hundred and twenty." This is the total number at this time of those who were determined to follow Jesus by waiting at Jerusalem for the Holy Spirit.

This number included the following:

1. *The Eleven.* These included Peter and those listed in verse 13. These were the original men whom Jesus called to surround Him, minus Judas.

2. *The Women, and Mary the Mother of Jesus, with His Brethren.* This is the last mention of Mary in the New Testament. There is no further account of her in the Bible. She is not held up anywhere for special favor or veneration. What has developed in the modern cult of Mary is something extra-scriptural and unbiblical. In fact, it is totally unchristian.

Mary has a diminishing place in the New Testament, just as Peter. Mary's place diminished at the moment Jesus appeared for the beginning of His public ministry at Cana of Galilee. Here Mary's influence over her son ended. A new era had arrived for now Jesus was acting as the Son of God and not as the son of Mary. Mary is subordinated at the very outset of Jesus' ministry to religious insignificance. She still remains His mother, but she has nothing to do with His work of redemption. When Jesus said to Mary, "Woman what have I to do with thee? Mine hour is not yet come," He reminded Mary and all modern devotees of the cult of Mary that henceforth their spheres lay inseparably apart. Henceforth He would act as God's Son without regard for His natural mother. In this incident, and in Peter's diminishing place among the disciples, is the death of the false claims that elevate Peter to papal primacy and Mary to practical religious supremacy over Jesus.

Mary was among the one hundred and twenty who tarried at Jerusalem. She was there as one of them; not as one above them. She needed the same power in the same manner that they needed it to overcome human sinfulness and weakness. And when the Holy Spirit came as "fire" it purged Mary of her sin as it did the others.

Included in these "others" were those who are called "his brethren," meaning the brethren of Jesus. There is no question at the level of responsible scholarship that the term "brethren" indicates an actual blood relationship to Jesus, revealing that Mary had other children after the birth of Jesus.

It is true that the term "brethren of Jesus" can be used of others apart from those of blood relation, such as the apostles (Matt. 28:10) or all Christians (Rom. 8:29). But at the same time there are various places in the New Testament where the "brethren" are not to be considered as sons of Joseph by a previous marriage, nor as cousins, nor as anyone else except His own blood brothers. This is clear, for example, from Luke 2:7. If Mary had borne no other children after Jesus, instead of "first-born son," the expression "only son" would have been used (as in John 3:16). Acts 1:14 also indicates this, for it makes a distinction between the Lord's brothers and the apostles (cf. also Matt. 12:46-47; 13:55-56; I Cor. 9:5).

The devotees of the cult of Mary and their fictitious idea of her perpetual virginity propounded this concept about the 4th Century through Epiphanius. There were others before Epiphanius who advanced this notion but it was given full status as a Romish doctrine in the 4th Century.

It is apparent that the brothers of Jesus did not acknowledge Him as Messiah before His crucifixion (John 7:5); but after His resurrection they are found among His followers as full-fledged believers. And together with the other members of this company of one hundred and twenty who tarried at Jerusalem the "brothers of Jesus" are here faithfully keeping their tryst and awaiting the coming of the Holy Spirit according to the promise of Jesus.

Let us now see what they were doing during this period of "waiting." It was not a period of inactivity by any means. What they were doing was in obedience to Jesus' command recorded at the close of Luke's gospel, "But tarry ye in the city of Jerusalem, until ye be endued with power from on high." This was, of course, a tacit recognition of their response and obedience to Jesus as Head of the church.

The principle of obedience to Jesus is primary in the Christian life. If the church had been obedient to Him it would not have become involved in all the superstitions, traditions and extra-scriptural practices which now obscure the true light of biblical Christianity.

Obedience to Jesus continues as the primary principle in the individual Christian life and is the secret of its success and reward. The greatest reward will be given for obedience and faithfulness. The Savior will say, "Well done, thou good and faithful servant." It will not be as the little boy is reported to have said in his Sunday school class where the teacher had been telling her class about crowns of glory and heavenly rewards. "Now tell me," she said at the close of the lesson, "who will get the biggest crown?" There was silence for a while then a little boy replied, "Him wot's got the biggest head." It will most likely be on the basis of the biggest heart; but it will surely be for faithfulness through the principle of obedience.

This period of "waiting" reveals:

1. The First Prayer Meeting (verses 12-14)

1st – The Occasion. The occasion was the return of the disciples to Jerusalem after the ascension of Jesus in obedience to the Lord's command to wait for the enduement of power.

2nd – The Place. It was in "an upper room" and persumably the same upper room where Jesus observed the Last Supper with His disciples. It is presumed also that this is the place where the Holy Spirit came upon the disciples at Pentecost, rather than in the temple which is often said to be the place of the pentecostal visitation.

3rd – The Attendance. Those who attended this first prayer meeting believed two important things. They believed in the coming of the Holy Spirit and they also believed in the coming again of Jesus. It was because of these stimuli that they met in such confidence in prayer.

It seems from this precedent that the one thing that will sustain the faith of the church is its prayer meetings. Those who attend its prayer meetings are just about the most important people in the church, as the most important people in Jerusalem during the ensuing ten days were "Peter and the others."

4th – The Duration. This prayer meeting lasted ten days, not continuously, for twenty-four hours each day, but for the extended period of the ten days.

5th – The Attitude. It is said that "these all continued with one accord." Their attitude was the unity of the spirit. It was the unity of obedience and expectation which was so essential to the fulfillment of Jesus' promise and to their later life and ministry as Christians amidst a hostile world.

2. The First Business Meeting (verses 15-17)

The business at hand was to elect another apostle to take the place of Judas who had not only defected, but who died at his own hand. As it subsequently developed, they elected Matthias and this is how they proceeded to conduct their business:

First, they appointed two from among the one hundred and twenty who had the qualifications described in verses 21, 22: "Wherefore of these men which have companied with us all the time that the Lord Jesus went in and out among us, beginning from the baptism of John, unto that same day that he was taken up from us, must one be ordained to be a witness with us of his resurrection." The first recorded public prayer of the church-to-be is found in connection with the choice of another apostle (verse 24). This prayer indicates the true purpose of all prayer, namely, to find out the will of God. They did not ask God to alter His will to fit their desires; but rather that they might know God's will in the matter before them.

Second, they cast lots (verse 26). "And they gave forth their lots; and the lot fell upon Matthias; and he was numbered with the eleven apostles." The word for lot is the Greek word *Kleros* from which we get our word *clergy,* to indicate the order of those divinely appointed or called. It is also used in I Peter 5:3 in the plural where it is translated *heritage* and refers to God's flock or all Christians. In this dual use the same word refers to a few leaders on the one hand and the flock of God on the other hand.

In the foregoing descriptions you see the personalities and proceedings involved in the founding of the church. In a sense every Christian was involved in these proceedings because we are all "baptized into one body." In Ernest Hemingway's story "For Whom the Bell Tolls," it is recorded as a town custom that the church bell be tolled on the death of a citizen. Often the people would come running to find out for whom the bell tolled. On one occasion, in answer to inquiry, this response was given: "No man is an island of itself; for every man is a piece of a continent, a part of the main: if a clod be washed away by the sea, Europe is the less. Any man's death diminishes me, because I am involved in mankind. . . . " Yes, we are involved with mankind but even more important as Christians we are involved with the church.

In the church we can find our most compelling reasons for living for here our identity is with God, the source and end and meaning of all life.

The most compelling human problem is the search for identity. Identity is to know who you are, where you are going, and what you are going to live and die for. That search ends when one is involved with the church.

5

TONGUES ON FIRE

Acts 2:1-13

On the fiftieth day after our Lord's resurrection and the tenth day after His ascension, there occurred a most singular phenomenon of God's dealings with man in respect to his salvation. This was the miracle of languages, or tongues on fire, on the day of Pentecost. Here is an event which was on the level of importance with the incarnation, the crucifixion, the resurrection and the ascension of Jesus.

Up to this moment in the brief record of church events we have had two of three important things in the church's redemptive program. *First,* we have had the *message.* This consisted principally of two items: the facts of the crucifixion and resurrection of Jesus. Faith in these things would result in forgiveness of sins, acceptance with God, the new birth and entrance into the kingdom of heaven. *Second,* there are already present *the men* who will take this message to the world. These consisted of one hundred and twenty disciples who tarried at Jerusalem to receive power and ability for this task. These one hundred and twenty consisted of the twelve apostles, the women who had followed Jesus, Mary the mother of Jesus, the brothers of Jesus, plus others who remain unidentified. So far we have the message and the men. One thing is lacking, *the method,* and this is supplied by Pentecost.

It has already been indicated that the method would consist of "witnessing." This task of witnessing would be committed to the entire community of believers and would not be confined to a special class of professionals, later to be known as the clergy, who would be fenced off from the laity by such things as celibacy, dress, titles or orders. It had likewise been indicated that there would be available a special power and ability for this witnessing (Acts 1:8). What happens at Pentecost is the fulfillment of this promise of power and ability. As it turns out, this power is the gift of the Holy Spirit and this ability is the gift of languages. This is one of the numerous gifts of the Holy Spirit. But it does not follow that the gift of languages is a continuing ability for succeeding generations of Christians. The first generation of Christians needed by miracle what they could not acquire by development, namely, the ability to witness to Christ in multiple tongues, so they could multiply in numbers and advance from the beachhead which they now occupied to establish themselves fully in a hostile world.

You are asked to examine this historic incident in terms of its significant words and their consequent meaning to the present generation of Christians.

I. "PENTECOST" (verse 1) "And when the day of Pentecost was fully come, they were all with one accord in one place."

This was the time when the phenomenon of speech occurred. It was on the fiftieth day after the resurrection, and was given the name Pentecost after a Jewish feast. It was also called the Feast of Weeks because it fell seven weeks plus one day after the Passover, thus making a week of weeks. It was likewise the fiftieth day after the first harvested sheaf of the barley harvest. At that time the first sheaf was brought into the temple and waved before the Lord and was the promise of the gathering of the rest of the harvest. In a similar manner Christ was the firstfruits of the resurrection and the promise that all who sleep in Him will be gathered up in resurrection glory.

On the morning of this fiftieth day the disciples were gathered as they had been for the prior ten days. It was the continuation of their prayer meeting. It tells us that "they were all with one accord in one place." The *"one accord"* was their united spirit in obedience to the command of Christ to wait for the Holy Spirit. The *"one place"* was the upper room rather than the temple, which is commonly thought to be the place of the Spirit's manifestation.

What is the continuing significance of Pentecost? Is there a pentecostal experience in the sense of multiple tongues? Does this pentecostal experience remain as a valid experience to be sought by present day Christians? Pentecost was something as historical as the incarnation, the crucifixion, the resurrection and the ascension of Jesus. As such it can no more be repeated than these experiences can be repeated. It accomplished a once-for-all purpose as did these other experiences; for Jesus is not born anew every Christmas or crucified anew every Good Friday.

Pentecost was the fulfillment of a promise in one of the upper room discourses of Jesus as well as being related to the Prophet Joel's prediction. Christ promised His disciples the gift of the Holy Spirit. That promise was fulfilled at Pentecost. It can never be repeated again any more than Christ can die, be raised from the dead, or ascend into heaven again.

No one rightfully tarries for the gift of the Holy Spirit today; no one rightfully waits for the fulfillment of Jesus' promise. The reason for this is that the gift has been given and the promise has been fulfilled and what has been accomplished cannot be repeated. The Holy Spirit is now the possession of every child of God through regeneration. What is available as a continuing experience is the blessing of the Holy Spirit through the believer's faith and obedience.

II. "WIND" — "FIRE" (verses 2, 3) "And suddenly there came a sound from heaven as of a rushing mighty wind, and it filled all the house where they were sitting. And there appeared unto them cloven tongues like as of fire, and it sat upon each of them."

The Holy Spirit manifested Himself in both sound and sight. In sound He came as "a rushing mighty wind." In sight He came as "cloven tongues like as of fire."

1. The Wind. This was the manifestation of power. Wind is one of the most irresistible forces of the natural world. The Holy Spirit is such a force in the spiritural world.

The Holy Spirit's manifestation was not limited to the disciples at Pentecost. It is involved in three other redemptive experiences.

First, Incarnation. "And the angel answered and said unto her, The Holy Ghost shall come upon thee, and the power of the Highest shall overshadow thee: therefore also that holy thing which shall be born of thee shall be called the Son of God" (Luke 1:35). Incarnation was achieved by the Holy Spirit coming upon Mary.

Second, Regeneration. "The wind bloweth where it listeth, and thou hearest the sound thereof, but canst not tell whence it cometh, and whither it goeth; so is every one that is born of the Spirit" (John 3:8). (Here the word for spirit and wind are the same — "pneuma.")

Third, Inspiration. "All scripture is given by inspiration of God, and is profitable for doctrine, for reproof, for correction, for instruction in righteousness" (II Tim. 3:16). Inspiration means to "in-breathe."

In this pentecostal experience it was the breath of God that was involved (as at the creation when God "breathed into the nostrils of man and he became a living soul").

2. The Fire. This was the manifestation of *purification* and *cleansing.* John had spoken of a baptism of fire (Matt. 3:11). This was that baptism. There was this spiritual baptism of fire and the physical baptism of water.

The text says, "And there appeared unto them cloven tongues like as of fire and it sat upon each of them" (verse 3). The marginal rendering is "tongues distributed among them." The Revised Standard Version reads, "there appeared to them tongues as of fire, distributed and resting on each of them." Phillips translation says, "tongues of flame, which separated off and settled above the head of each one of them." It is apparent that the word "cloven" refers to the dividing of the tongues among the disciples so each received the same effect of the manifestation, rather than any dividing in the tongues themselves like cloven hooves. In this fashion the disciples all participated in the manifestation of the Holy Spirit.

This two-fold manifestation of the Holy Spirit as wind and

fire marks the beginning of a new relationship between God and man. It is, in effect, the ratification and confirmation of redemption. It is the beginning of the new spiritual life of the church and of the believer. The believer is now sealed with the Holy Spirit and his salvation confirmed and ratified (Eph. 1:13).

A transformation now takes place in these first Christians. They become new men and women. All fear of men is gone. Peter is no longer immobilized by the fears that once caused him to deny his Lord. The lips of the disciples are no longer sealed and silent, but become filled with their witness to Christ. Here are one hundred and twenty bold, fearless, power-full disciples who will soon "turn the world upside down."

This marks the new relationship of the Holy Spirit to man. In the Old Testament the Holy Spirit manifestation was from the *outside* in. In the New Testament the Holy Spirit manifestation is from the *inside* out. Before Pentecost the experience of the Holy Spirit was *transient* and *exceptional*. Now the experience of the Holy Spirit is *permanent* and *regular*.

III. "FILLED" (verse 4) "And they were all filled with the Holy Ghost. . . ."

This does not mean to be made full of the Holy Spirit in the sense of a bottle being made full of water or a basket being made full of grain or a room being made full of incense. It means full in the sense of occupancy, authority and control. These pentecostal disciples not only had the Holy Spirit but the Holy Spirit had them. He was in control of their lives for sanctification and service. This is the fulness of the Holy Spirit.

The result of being filled was not only in the inward transformation of their spiritual natures, but in the outward manifestation of their service and ministry.

IV. "OTHER TONGUES" (verse 4) " . . . And began to speak with other tongues, as the Spirit gave them utterance."

The effect of being "filled" was the ability to speak with "other tongues." In Old Testament times the special consequence of being filled with the Holy Spirit was in many instances the ability to prophesy. This New Testament manifestation was not prophecy, in the sense of foretelling future events, but rather prophecy in the sense of forth-telling events immediately present and current. This was, in effect, inspired oratory or what we would know as preaching.

But the peculiar nature of this pentecostal preaching was not only in *what* was said, such as the crucifixion and resurrection of Jesus; but in *how* it was said—"with other tongues." These other tongues were not merely a form of ecstatic speech which came out of a trance-like experience of catalepsy, which put utterance beyond the control of the speaker. There is this kind of speaking in tongues but it was not this which happened at Pentecost.

There appear to be two aspects of speaking with tongues in the early church. One was the *Pentecostal aspect* of using different languages to proclaim the message of salvation. "They were all filled with the Holy Spirit and began to speak in different languages as the Spirit gave them power to proclaim His message" (Acts 2:4 — Phillips). The other aspect was the *Corinthian aspect*, or the use of ecstatic speech in which the speaker had lost the conscious control of his faculties.

Look at the first aspect at Pentecost, or the use of different languages. Here is an event which climaxes redemption. It is specifically given as an ability to proclaim redemption as a saving message to the people at Jerusalem which included Jews of the Diaspora and the Jews who lived at Jerusalem.

This was their preparation to become witnesses. In terms of numbers they were so overwhelmed by both pagans and Jews they could not hope to survive. The normal acquisition of speech necessary to multiply their numbers would give them no hope of survival. It was for this reason that we have the miracle of Pentecost in the multiplicity of tongues. Its similarity to inspiration which resulted in the written word is found in the fact that both the spoken word of the Pentecost Christians and the written word of the New Testament came by the breath or wind of God.

Those who were in Jerusalem at this feast-time verified this linguistic phenomenon, for they said, "How does it happen that every single one of us can hear the particular language he has known from a child?" (verse 8—Phillips). And again, "Yet we can all hear these men speaking of the magnificence of God in our native language" (verse 11 — Phillips).

The use of ecstatic speech was another and dissimilar experience. Speaking in tongues continued for a considerable time in the church. We know of its continuance for at least twenty or twenty-five years. There are at least two more instances in Acts where the use of this gift is recorded, Acts 10:46 and Acts 19:6. But its chief manifestation, after Pentecost, was in the Corinthian Church where it became a very disturbing and divisive factor. In fact, its use was prostituted and abused, and resulted in such gross and vulgar disorders in the church that it required the writing of Paul's First Epistle to the Corinthians.

Speaking in tongues in Corinth was largely ecstatic with the speaker's faculties beyond the control of his intelligence or his conscious effort. It could not be understood by others except through an interpreter. This was unlike the pentecostal version, where the speaker spoke with his intelligence and in control of his faculties and was understood directly without the use of an interpreter.

Although Paul says he "spoke with tongues more than they all" (at Corinth that is) he ranked this gift, not as the first but as the last of the apostolic gifts (I Cor. 12:10). He did this for the following reason.

First, it did not edify others.

Second, it tended to cause disorder in the church.

Third, it opened the door for abuse, confusion, perversion and counterfeiting. For these reasons another gift, "discerning of spirits," was necessary to determine the difference between the true and the false, the genuine and the counterfeit gifts and experiences in the young churches. Furthermore, as the new life of the church, which began at Pentecost, became mature and normal, speaking in tongues, whether as language or as ecstacy, gradually dropped off and died away (Rackham).

IV. "DWELLING" (verses 5-11)

Jerusalem was crowded with Jews of the dispersion (Diaspora) who had come to celebrate the Feast of Weeks (Pentecost), because only here at the temple could they attend special services and festivities prescribed for the observance of this feast. With these Jews there were many proselytes of Jewry.

Assuming that the Holy Spirit came upon the disciples while they were in the upper room, they must have come down into the street speaking with tongues and attracted the notice of these pilgrims who followed them to the temple area where Peter later addressed them; for by this time there were assembled in excess of three thousand people.

An impressive roll-call of the people of the Diaspora who were present in Jerusalem at the Feast of Weeks appears in verses 9-11: "Parthians, and Medes, and Elamites, and the dwellers in Mesopotamia, and in Judaea, and Cappadocia, in Pontus, and Asia, Phrygia, and Pamphylia, in Egypt, and in the parts of Libya about Cyrene, and strangers of Rome, Jews and proselytes, Cretes and Arabians, we do hear them speak in our tongues the wonderful works of God." "This range of language . . . suggests that Luke thought of the coming of the Holy Spirit more particularly as a preparation for the world-wide proclamation of the Gospel" (Bruce).

The effect of the phenomenon upon the assembled people was two-fold:

1. "And they were all amazed, and were in doubt, saying one to another, What meaneth this?" (verse 12).

What amazed them was that they heard in their own indigenous languages, these tongues of the Diaspora, the proclamation of the mighty acts of God from the lips of the disciples. Here was a miracle which was the opposite of Babel. Instead of the confusion of tongues which divided men into ethnic classifications, there was the division of tongues which united men into a common company of believers.

2. ". . . These men are filled with new wine" (verse 13).

They concluded that the disciples were intoxicated. They concluded that these men had imbibed too freely of new (sweet) wine which was very intoxicating. There is an interesting connection between the false assumption that these men were intoxicated and the human search for self-transcendence. Self-transcendence means to go beyond the limits of experience. It means to surpass or exceed the ordinary experiences of life. Salvation, when rightly understood, is a legitimate and proper experience of self-transcendence. It enables the saved person to live better than he knows how and to transcend or exceed the average level of life. Jesus said, "I am come that ye might have life and that ye might have it more abundantly." It is self-transcendence when one can live a more abundant life.

In an article by Aldous Huxley, under the title "Drugs that Shape Men's Minds,"* he gives the philosophical view of man's effort to achieve self-transcendence. Man, says Dr. Huxley, does it by intoxication through the use of mind-changers such as alcohol and narcotics. The use of tranquilizers is another, though milder form of this effort. In one year alone American doctors wrote forty million prescriptions for tranquilizers. Behind the search for self-transcendence through use of tranquilizers is the idea that if you cannot control your temper let a tranquilizer do it for you; if you cannot manage your tensions let a tranquilizer do it for you. This is an effort to achieve self-control by the physiological use of chemicals.

Dr. Huxley believes that just around the corner there is a drug capable of making people feel happy in situations where they would be distressed. Thus a dictator could reconcile an entire population to a state of affairs to which no self-respecting person would be reconciled. It is also Dr. Huxley's view that the famous revival of religion "about which so many people have been talking for so long, will not come about as the result of evangelistic mass meetings. . . . It will come about as the result of biochemical discoveries that will make it possible for large numbers of men and women to achieve a radical self-transcendence and a deeper understanding of the nature of

---

*Saturday Evening Post.

things." Once again man is trying to achieve by psychological and physiological means what God has provided by spiritual and moral means.

Paul expresses this same idea in a detailed personal experience in the seventh chapter of Romans and concludes, "O wretched man that I am! who shall deliver me from the body of this death? I thank God through Jesus Christ our Lord. So then with the mind I myself serve the law of God; but with the flesh the law of sin. There is therefore now no condemnation to them which are in Christ Jesus, who walk not after the flesh, but after the Spirit. For the law of the Spirit of life in Christ Jesus hath made me free from the law of sin and death. For what the law could not do, in that it was weak through the flesh, God sending his own Son in the likeness of sinful flesh, and for sin, condemned sin in the flesh" (Rom. 7:24-8:3). Here is self-transcendence. It is the ultimate of the human search for self-control, personal peace, happiness, achievement, destiny and everything in the human desire.

Pentecost was the beginning of this self-transcendence. The disciples experienced it in their use of other languages. They experienced it later in their use of ecstatic languages at Corinth. They experienced it in the transformation of their lives from fearful, weak, visionless disciples to fearless, bold, courageous men and women who later turned the world upside down.

There are two things which summarize this pentecostal experience. First, am I a Christian? If not, the first thing on the agenda of business with God is to get right with God. Second, if I am a Christian what is the state of my life? Have I achieved this self-transcendence in which I am living better than I know how? Have I achieved temper control and all the other emotional controls? Normality in the Christian life is a life of self-transcendence in which one rises above the normal levels to express the power and nature of Jesus Christ.

6

THIS IS THAT

or

THE EXPLANATION OF PENTECOST
Acts 2:14-21

When Peter spoke at Pentecost to explain the phenomenon of tongues on fire, he preached the first Christian sermon and identified this miracle of languages with a great prophetic utterance. He said, "this is that which was spoken by the prophet Joel." The place of his preaching was the temple in Jerusalem. The occasion was the outpouring of the Holy Spirit. The reason was the wonderment of the assembly of people gathered at the temple who had witnessed the miracle of languages as the one hundred and twenty flowed out into the streets from their upper room prayer meeting.

We have already had many "firsts" including the first suicide, the first business meeting, the first prayer meeting, the first manifestation of the Holy Spirit, the first preaching of the gospel through the witness of the disciples and now the first Christian sermon. The result of these firsts, particularly the manifestation of the Holy Spirit in speaking with tongues, is described in verses 12 and 13, "And they were all amazed, and were in doubt, saying one to another, What meaneth this? Others mocking said, These men are full of new wine." As a result Peter preaches the first sermon in the history of the church.

There are three important parts to this sermon:

1st — The Explanation of Pentecost (verses 14-21)
2nd — The Reason for Pentecost (verses 22-36)
3rd — The Results of Pentecost (verses 37-47)

I. THE EXPLANATION OF PENTECOST (verses 14-21)

The first sermon was biblical and expository in nature. It was based upon scripture for Peter appeals very confidently to the Old Testament.

This was not a sermon whose attempt was to palliate the people; neither was it a so-called "peace of mind" sermon. Its contents reveal such words as crucifixion, resurrection, repentance, salvation and baptism. These are definitely Christian in nature and biblical in form, although the New Testament had not yet been written.

Peter explained that what happened to the one hundred and twenty disciples was a spiritual phenomenon. It was not a form of social corruption like drunkenness, as the bystanders had thought. They supposed them to be the victims of their own excesses and were intoxicated. It was hardly this, said Peter, for it was only nine o'clock in the morning. Then he appeals to scripture, which ought to be the basis for all appeal. He refers to the prophet Joel who had said, "And it shall come to pass in the last days, saith God, I will pour out of my spirit upon all flesh: and your sons and your daughters shall prophesy, and your young men shall see visions, and your old men shall dream dreams: And on my servants and on my handmaidens I will pour out in those days of my Spirit; and they shall prophesy: And I will shew wonders in heaven above, and signs in the earth beneath; blood, and fire, and vapour of smoke; The sun shall be turned into darkness, and the moon into blood, before that great and notable day of the Lord come: And it shall come to pass, *that* whosoever shall call on the name of the Lord shall be saved" (verses 17-21).

Fortunately we can understand Joel's prophecy in the light of its history, that is, in the light of what happened at Pentecost. What happened was the coming of the Holy Spirit upon men. These men were one hundred and twenty disciples of Jesus who, in effect, comprised the sum total of the then existing church. They were not only the first church but they stood for the church of all ages because the basic fact of Pentecost was the *continuing experience of the Holy Spirit*. He did not come only upon the one hundred and twenty as such. He came upon the church. It was a corporate filling as well as an individual filling. In other words, the Holy Spirit is here *now* because He came *then.*

Joel had prophesied a certain effect, ". . . your sons and your daughters shall prophesy, and your young men shall see visions, and your old men shall dream dreams: And on my servants and on my handmaidens I will pour out in those days of my Spirit; and they shall prophesy" (verses 17, 18).

Peter is explaining a New Testament experience in the light of an Old Testament prophecy. The New Testament experience was the coming of the Holy Spirit so that men would prophesy. This is not prophecy in the sense of being predictive but being witnesses. Jesus had promised that when the Holy Spirit came He would make the disciples witnesses.

The Old Testament language of the prophecy uses the words dreams and visions. This was the way God communicated His mind to men in the Old Testament. It is explained in Numbers 12:6-8, "And he said, Hear now my words: If there be a prophet among you, I the Lord will make myself known unto him in a vision, and will speak unto him in a dream. My servant Moses is not so, who is faithful in all mine house."

In the Old Testament only individual men received the Holy Spirit whereas now everyone receives the Holy Spirit. "I will pour out my Spirit upon all flesh" (verse 17). In the Old Testament only a few men were prophets. In the New Testament everyone was intended to be a prophet and speak for God. In the Old Testament prophecy was to foretell the future as well as witness. In the New Testament prophecy is witnessing to the mighty acts of God which were wrought in Christ for our salvation (Acts 2:11).

When you have summarized Peter's explanation of Joel's prophecy in the light of the history of Pentecost it says this:

1. The Holy Spirit is a Continuing Experience. Paul later writes to the Corinthians to say, "For by one Spirit are we all baptized into one body" (I Cor. 12-13). This baptism is an

accomplished fact. It is a continuing experience. Its effect continues for the present day church.

While the fact is automatic the experience is not necessarily so. It is conditioned upon each believer's spiritual surrender to the Holy Spirit. The baptism of the Holy Spirit occurs at the time of conversion when the believer is born into the Kingdom of God and made a member of the Body of Christ. Because of this baptism the believer does not need to seek the Holy Spirit, for He is already present; He is already in his possession. What must follow is each believer's spiritual conditioning so he can receive the benefits of the resident Holy Spirit. This spiritual conditioning is accomplished through prayer, faith, fellowship, consecration and personal surrender to God.

2. Everyone Receives the Holy Spirit. By everyone we mean, of course, every believer, for within the Body of Christ the Holy Spirit is a universal fact. To realize this is to recognize a blessed fact. Here is a spiritual truth that could revolutionize the life of the Christian. This means that the potential of power, greatness, victory, strength and all the anticipations of Christian fulness already exist in us. This was in fulfillment of Joel's prophecy who said this experience was to be for "all flesh."

3. The Purpose of the Coming of the Holy Spirit is to Make Us Witnesses. Peter has already explained the New Testament witness in the terms and imagery of the Old Testament prophet. The difference is that the New Testament witness is subject to the indwelling Holy Spirit and not to dreams and visions. These belong to the Old Testament manifestation. Today the believer's strength comes from his intimate relation to the Holy Spirit as the indwelling manifestation of God. The purpose of the Holy Spirit is to establish communion with God, fellowship with believers, illumination of God's Word and the communication of the gospel which is the message of salvation. In other words, everyone is going to be a prophet to speak, not in ambiguous prophetic terms from the mystical preparation of dreams and visions, but in the simple terms of the message of salvation inspired by the Holy Spirit.

Joel spoke not only of dreams and visions but of wonders and signs (verses 19, 20). The fulfillment of this aspect of Joel's prediction is two-fold. There is its *secondary fulfillment* in the preceding events which transpired seven weeks before at the crucifixion, when the sun was darkened and the full paschal moon appeared blood-red in consequence of the sun's darkness. Then there is its *primary fulfillment* which will be in the events immediately related to the second coming of Christ. At this time the darkening of the sun in no sense means that the sun itself will be affected any more than the turning of the moon into blood means that the moon itself will be affected. (One preacher suggests that the Russians will send a rocket to the moon that will spray a blood-red powder all over it and change its color). The bloodied moon will probably occur from the clouds of dust and debris that arise from the earth in its judgment period and which, by the principle of refracted light, gives the moon a blood-red appearance.

Joel speaks of these things happening in "the last days." This is a time which the apostle understood as being between the first and second advent of Christ. Here is a prime example of prophecy. It is both fulfilled in its secondary sense and unfulfilled in its primary sense. Joel did not see the time-gap between the primary and secondary phases. The secondary phase related to events associated with the first advent while the primary phase related to events associated with the second advent.

There is nothing more important in the knowledge of the modern Christian than to understand the meaning of the coming of the Holy Spirit. His coming has been ritualized by some and made utterly meaningless and of no effect. It has been prostituted by others and turned into an emotional orgy. It has been theorized by others and made a captive to theological terms and phrases. But if we ever understand its simple yet profound experience in the life of the individual believer, it would completely revolutionize the Christian and the church. Think of what would happen if we acted on the fact of every Christian being a personal witness of his experience of salvation and the communication of the message of salvation to others.

The understanding of the meaning of the Holy Spirit is the key to personal excellence as Christians, to the meaning of our existence in life and to the evangelization of the world.

If this should ever materialize in the church it would be the solution of all our present fears: our fears of a moral collapse of the world, our fears of communism, our fears of the lessening influence of the church in modern society. It would suddenly transform a lethargic church into a mighty giant of power and influence which would in turn transform contemporary society.

If we do not understand the meaning of the Holy Spirit in terms of a continuing experience in the church and individual witnessing by the Christian in the church, it makes no difference how much property we hold or how many buildings we build or how much equipment we provide for the use of our church workers. We are doomed to formality and mediocrity without the Holy Spirit.

This also is the number one objective for the Christian. To understand the meaning of the continuing experience of the Holy Spirit in the life of the believer is to understand the key to Christian progress. Nothing is available to us in spiritual experience apart from the historic provisions of God through the Holy Spirit at Pentecost. Apart from these provisions and our spiritual attention to them we are doomed to spiritual impotence.

The greatest need of the church today is Christian action and Christian action is Christians acting as witnesses. It is not Christians worshipping, studying or fraternizing or even engaging in social service, as important as these are. It is witnessing; for society's transformation rests in the person of Christ to whom we are to bear witness.

How shall one say it so that it will become the number one goal and objective of every Christian? How shall one put it so that we will rise up as one person and address ourselves to this, the greatest purpose of the existence of the church?

First of all, we must recognize our place in the Body of Christ. We are members of His body by virtue of the Holy Spirit. We must recognize it.

Second, we must realize the Holy Spirit has come and is present; and in full realization of this fact we must abandon ourselves and yield our lives to the dominion of the indwelling Holy Spirit.

Third, we must consider the urgency of this action, because no one has a right to live and die as a Christian until he has reproduced himself in another Christian.

Fourth, we must not confuse the work of the church with church work. We may do church work valiantly and faithfully by attending committee meetings, working on organizational projects; but we have not done the work of the church until and unless we have witnessed to others for Christ and reproduced ourselves spiritually in those persons.

7

THE DIVINE BREAK-THROUGH

or

THE REASON FOR PENTECOST*

Acts 2:22-36

The subject matter in hand is a continuation of Peter's great sermon on the day of Pentecost. There are three parts to this sermon. First, The Explanation of Pentecost (2:14-21); second, the Reason for Pentecost (2:22-36); and third, The Results of Pentecost (2:37-47). We are now involved with the second part from verses 22-36.

What we are witnessing in the transpiration of these events is a transition from Judaism to Christianity; from what was exclusively Jewish to a universal emphasis which includes the Gentiles. It is what we can properly call the divine break-through, for God is breaking through the barriers of race and manifesting Himself in grace to all people.

In the course of creative and redemptive history there have been three such break-throughs. There was the creative break-through when by creation man was made in the divine image. There was the redemptive break-through when by incarnation God was man in the human image. There was the pentecostal break-through when the Holy Spirit came into the redeemed life and revealed God to man.

This break-through at Pentecost is something to be experienced individually. It is utterly impossible for the individual to comprehend the gospel and be saved unless there is the break-

---

*Second part of Peter's sermon at Pentecost.

through of the Spirit of God upon the consciousness of man. "But as it is written, Eye hath not seen, nor ear heard, neither have entered into the heart of man, the things which God hath prepared for them that love him. But God hath revealed them unto us by his Spirit: for the Spirit searcheth all things, yea, the deep things of God. For what man knoweth the things of a man, save the spirit of man which is in him? even so the things of God knoweth no man, but the Spirit of God. Now we have received, not the spirit of the world, but the spirit which is of God; that we might know the things that are freely given to us of God. Which things also we speak, not in the words which man's wisdom teacheth, but which the Holy Ghost teacheth; comparing spiritual things with spiritual. But the natural man receiveth not the things of the Spirit of God: for they are foolishness unto him: neither can he know them, because they are spiritually discerned" (I Cor. 2:9-14).

Spiritual education is many times a futile and fruitless experience because people hear and receive only what their prejudices and dispositions permit them. Only when there is the breakthrough by the Spirit of God can there be any effective penetration of light or comprehension of truth.

Any pastor who is in a church for any considerable time has opportunity to observe this spiritual immobility in his people. Some never make a trace of spiritual progress although exposed year after year to the truth. There is no spiritual apprehension or comprehension. There is no character transformation. They are controlled by the same prejudices, ruled by the same personality defects and in general show no difference in disposition, personality, character, mannerisms, habits and service than if they had never heard God's Word.

The intent of contact with the truth of God's Word is change through the Holy Spirit's application of truth to life. "But we all, with open face beholding as in a glass the glory of the Lord, are changed into the same image from glory to glory, even as by the Spirit of the Lord" (II Cor. 3:18).

Peter has just interpreted the coming of the Holy Spirit in

the light of Joel's prophecy in which he reminds them of the continuing place of the Holy Spirit in the church's experience to the intent that everyone should be a prophet, or in New Testament language, a witness. It is this which constitutes one of the chief reasons for the coming of the Holy Spirit. But a very important thing appears at the close of Peter's explanation of the phenomenon of the Spirit's coming to the church. If each believer is to be a witness, to whom is he to do this witnessing? Hitherto the Jews had considered their religion an exclusive possession. It would also develop in the first phases of the church that certain teachers, called Judaizers, would attempt to put Christian converts into an exclusively Jewish world. Peter now says something basic to our understanding of the gospel and the function of the church. It is in verse 21: "And it shall come to pass, that whosoever shall call on the name of the Lord shall be saved."

Before Pentecost salvation was something national. It was to be through the nation of Israel. The transition is now from national to individual for the word here is, "whosoever shall call upon the name of the Lord shall be saved." The promise is to individuals as individuals through an individual relationship with God. There were to be no intermediaries. It was the individual sinner coming directly to an individual Savior. There were no intermediary sacrifices, altars, ceremonies, veils, saints or priests for there is now "one mediator between God and man, the man Christ Jesus."

The question of election and predestination intrudes itself at this point. How many sinners are going to be saved? Who has God elected to salvation? Are these elect a predetermined number of people with all the rest predetermined to be lost? Obviously the people who are to be saved are not a certain predetermined number of people but a "whosoever" who will come, for these are promised salvation. Election and predestination are set forth in terms of response. Salvation is not arbitrary from God's standpoint but from man's. God has not predetermined;

but we determine. God has predestined all who believe to be saved.

In verse 21 it is man's call upon God for salvation, while in verse 39 it is God's call to man to salvation. All men may call upon God because God's call is to all men.

The question of election and predestination is resolved only when we determine from God's Word whether the death of Christ provided a limited atonement for the elect, or a universal atonement for all. By a limited atonement we mean that when Christ died He died only for the elect whose number was predetermined by an arbitrary act of God beforehand. This kind of atonement forgets God's love for a whole world that is wholly lost; and it forgets that the gospel is universally intended for the whole world that is wholly lost. By a universal atonement is meant that Christ died for the whole world and that anyone in the world may believe and be saved.

"Twelve shipwrecked men were laboring in heavy seas in an overloaded boat, when one of the seaman, in order to lighten the boat, deliberately sprang overboard. The rest were saved. For which of the eleven did the sailor give his life? If Christ died for all, He died for each; for no one more than another, and no one omitted. The sun shines for nineteen hundred millions of mankind; but I know that it shines for me, and would tomorrow morning if not another soul survived on the globe. So Christ loved me and gave Himself for me."*

Christ's death saved no one but it made the salvation of everyone possible.

There are various schools of thought about the extent and purpose of salvation. These include the Lutheran view that election is God's determination from eternity to provide an objective salvation for universal man. There is the Arminian view that election is God's determination from eternity to save certain individuals upon the ground of their foreseen faith. There is the Calvinistic view that election is God's determination from eternity to choose certain out of the number of sinful men

---

*Arthur T. Pierson.

to be the recipients of His grace so as to be made voluntary partakers of Christ's salvation.

Somehow there has to be, for practical purposes, a reconciliation of all these conflicting views so we can see that, while all men are sinners and while salvation is of divine initiation, God has to make some willing to be saved and impart faith to these so they can voluntarily and of their own free will choose the salvation offered them in Christ. We must reject the idea of divine sovereignty, arbitrarily choosing some to be saved and some to be lost.

We must accept the order of the divine decrees as follows:

1st. The decree to create.
2nd. The decree to permit the Fall.
3rd. The decree to provide a salvation in Christ sufficient for the needs of all men.
4th. The decree to secure the actual acceptance of this salvation on the part of some, i.e., the decree of election.

Perhaps we can resolve it in this way. God has elected *all men* to be saved in the sense that "whosoever will may come." God has elected *some men* to be saved in the sense that they among all men have responded or will respond to God's call. The elect are those who validate God's choice of them by their choice of Him. The lost are those who invalidate God's choice of them by their rejection of Him.

God is sovereign in His offer of salvation while man is sovereign in his choice of salvation. Whenever a person exercises the sovereignty of his will and chooses to accept God's provision of salvation in Christ, he is of "the elect," for God has promised that "whosoever shall call on the name of the Lord shall be saved."

It is at this point that the apostle undertakes to give the second point of his great sermon on the day of Pentecost.

THE REASON FOR PENTECOST (verses 22-36)

Peter was speaking solely to Jews and Gentile proselytes. He is undertaking to prove the claims of Jesus as Messiah. He does so from the Old Testament scripture and the events of Pentecost, because Pentecost and its related preceding events, proves Jesus to be the Messiah.

Who was the Holy Spirit who came at Pentecost? He had been promised by Jesus to be the comforter, one like unto Himself. Who then was Jesus? Peter's answer is given in verse 22, "Ye men of Israel, hear these words; Jesus of Nazareth, a man approved of God among you by miracles and wonders and signs, which God did by him in the midst of you, as ye yourselves also know." These were fresh in the minds of all in Jerusalem and were the credentials by which Jesus established His claims to be the Son of God.

What happened to Jesus? Peter says in verse 23 that He was "crucified and slain." And while this was done by the very generation of Jews to whom Peter was talking, these men were unconsciously fulfilling God's purpose for it was done "by the determinate counsel and foreknowledge of God." You see, Christianity and salvation are not improvisations. They are not historical coincidences. God did not do something extemporaneously to meet an emergency. This was His plan and purpose and he used the natural hatred, rebellion and sin of man to carry it out. But although man carried out his evil intentions in the context of the divine plan, God reversed what man did in the slaying of Jesus and raised Him from the dead.

Furthermore, all this had been forseen and forewritten by David, speaking as a prophet. He spoke of the coming divine Messiah being raised from the dead and this Messiah was none other than Jesus of Nazareth. And then, having been raised from the dead, God further exalted the Messiah by raising Him to His own right hand. When He was raised to God's right hand it was the place of authority, power and coming glory for it would be "until I make thy foes thy footstool."

To climax the proof of Jesus' messiahship, God has given the Holy Spirit. "He hath shed forth this, which ye now see and hear" (verse 33).

All these indisputable facts point to one conclusion, "Therefore let all the house of Israel know assuredly, that God hath made that same Jesus, whom ye have crucified, both Lord and Christ" (verse 36).

These are solemn considerations. To every Jew there is indisputable proof that Jesus of Nazareth is their Messiah. To every sinner there is the way of salvation made plain. To every Christian there is background for Pentecost, and the reason for the coming of the Holy Spirit. To every church member there is reason to examine one's faith and determine whether it is a valid commitment to God and to divine realities; or whether it is only a vacant profession of religious faith that has no relation to divine life and power.

To summarize the reasons for Pentecost: First, it was to implement divine election. Second, it was to make every believer a witness. Third, it was the climactic proof that Jesus was God and the long-promised Messiah of the Old Testament. Fourth, it constitutes the greatest reason why a modern Christian's faith should be a commitment of life to witness to this One who is indeed "both Lord and Christ."

8

CONTINUED STORY

or

THE RESULTS OF PENTECOST*

Acts 2:37-47

This records results which are continuing today. There are twenty-eight chapters in the Book of Acts. That is, there are twenty-eight chapters of record, for here is a continued story. It is still being written in deed if not in recorded word. The Book of Acts is the only unfinished book in the Bible. What was intended to be written by its author, Dr. Luke, was finished; but what was intended to be enacted by the Holy Spirit is still going on in the life of the church and the experience of believers. The thrilling thing about this fact is that you and I can be writers and enactors of this continued story.

A few years ago a great teacher of preachers, Halford E. Luccock urged a group of ministers to get busy and write the twenty-ninth chapter of Acts. He challenged them to get on with the story. So far, much of what we say is purely academic. It is in words, theories, theology and ideas. But Acts is a book of action. It is deeds and not words; and if today we are to get on with the story it has to be done with action. We have to do things, not simply say things. For instance, if we are going to be writers of this continuing story we can only do so in terms of a witness; one who is controlled by and possessed of the Holy Spirit. What will it take to jar us loose from our complacency? If we read this story rightly, it will be the very things that these earliest writers experienced—persecution, hardship and suffering.

---

*Third part of Peter's sermon at Pentecost

At this point we must bear in mind an important thing. This is God's universe no matter how many sputniks and explorer satellites orbit the earth. This is Christ's church for whom He gave Himself. This is your life and you must use it to advantage as a professed believer in and follower of Jesus Christ. You are a person under orders, obligation and direction. You must either renounce your profession or you must fulfill your purpose and your purpose is to continue the story.

What is being recorded at this point in the Book of Acts is—.

THE RESULTS OF PENTECOST (verses 37-47)

The results are in terms of a number of things including the immediate personal effects recorded in verses 37-39. "Now when they heard this, they were pricked in their heart, and said unto Peter and to the rest of the apostles, Men and brethren, what shall we do? Then Peter said unto them, Repent, and be baptized every one of you in the name of Jesus Christ for the remission of sins, and ye shall receive the gift of the Holy Ghost. For the promise is unto you, and to your children, and to all that are afar off, even as many as the Lord our God shall call."

Their response to Pentecost was, "What shall we do?" Here you have the action verb "do." Yes, there are things that must be done, but they are not the things that are often suggested to be done. What Peter suggested they do had nothing to do with adding to the work of redemption already accomplished by Christ. It was a finished salvation. They could do nothing to make it better or make themselves better to receive it. It was final, complete and finished.

But there were things they could and must do to make that finished salvation effective to them.

First, they must repent. This meant a change of heart and a right-about-face. It must be said here that anything that anyone does to fulfill the conditions upon which salvation is received depends solely on the sincere intent of the recipient. No profession of faith, no baptism or church membership is valid or genuine unless it is based upon a change of heart. It does not make any difference how much holy water, incantation, incense or religious phrases are employed in ceremonies attending initiation into a church body of whatever name or branch. No one has a valid experience with God apart from a changed heart and life.

This fact is emphasized when we remember that the people to whom Peter was preaching were religious Jews. While religious they were at the same time unsaved. They were not profligates, heathen or pagans. They were the children of the covenants given to Abraham and David. They had come to Jerusalem because of their religious devotions. But these religious people had to repent, an act which consisted of their acknowledgment of Jesus as Messiah.

Second, they must be baptized. This was not an unfamiliar rite. John the Baptist had been baptizing since before the public ministry of Jesus. He had inaugurated Jesus' ministry by baptizing Him in the river Jordan. But there was something new and different about baptism now. It was to be "in the name of Jesus Christ." That is, it was identified as Christian baptism. It was a public confession of faith in Christ. This confession included His deity and His salvation.

But there was something else that was different about baptism. It would result in receiving "the gift of the Holy Spirit." On man's side it meant confession of sins. On God's side it meant bestowing upon the confessor the gift of the Spirit. John's water baptism of repentance is now Jesus' Spirit baptism of confession. But the Spirit baptism in no sense does away with the water baptism. "The baptism of the Spirit which it was our Lord's prerogative to bestow was, strictly speaking, something that took place once for all on the day of Pentecost . . . and constituted them the new people of God; baptism in water continued to be the external sign by which individuals who believed the gospel message, repented of their sins, and acknowledged Jesus as Lord, were publicly incorporated into the spirit-baptized fellowship of the new people of God."*

If you were to read the last part of verse 38, "ye shall receive

---

* Bruce, pg. 76, 77.

the gift of the Holy Ghost," apart from the rest of the verse which speaks of repentance, baptism and remission of sins, you would make a serious mistake in spiritual chronology because receiving the gift of the Spirit is not subsequent to or following salvation; but something coincidental with and accompanying salvation.

What is recorded in this second chapter of Acts of what Peter preached in his Pentecost sermon is not to be considered all the things he preached about on that day for it says in verse forty, "And with many other words did he testify and exhort." Then he appends this significant warning, "Save yourselves from this untoward (perverted) generation." In other words, beware of your contemporary environment and the gravitational pull of an unregenerate society upon you. Every generation of Christians must do likewise. It must save itself from an intractable generation.

Peter gives us herewith the first picture ever recorded of the first church.

1. It Consisted of Believers Who First Believed and Then Were Baptized (verse 41)

This is what is called believer's baptism. It would be better to deviate on the amount of water used in baptism, i.e., the mode, than to abandon the principle that only understanding believers are to be baptized. The order here is "they that gladly received his word" or believed, were then baptized. They were not baptized in anticipation of future believing. Believing was a conscious and accomplished fact.

The first recorded additions to the church were about three thousand people. These were added to the one hundred and twenty who comprised the original body of Spirit and water baptized Christians.

2. It Consisted of Baptized Believers Who Sustained Their Faith and Life In the New Community by Specific Means.

First, they continued steadfastly in the apostles' doctrine (verse 42). This constituted the authority of the church. It was the authority of doctrine or revelation; not a hierarchy of apostles.

It was the authority of truth; not men. The apostles were present to instruct; not to police.

The subject of the apostle's teaching was the things concerning Christ: His messiahship, death and resurrection; the relation of the Old Testament to these New Testament events; the meaning of Pentecost. This teaching was later expanded to include the teaching content of the expanding New Testament books inspired by the Holy Spirit.

Second, they were joined in Christian fellowship (verse 42). This bound them in oneness of heart and purpose. It gave them something to belong to and something to be responsible to. This constitutes one of the prime responsibilities of the continuing church, to provide fellowship for Christians. We cannot walk alone, live alone or stand alone.

In a recent denominational survey to determine why people attend church the following reasons were given:

1. Fellowship.
2. The attractiveness of the church building.
3. Christian education program.
4. Musical program.
5. Denominational loyalty.

Apparently the need of fellowship is an innate desire transcending all other attractions.

Third, they observed the Lord's supper (verse 42). The "breaking of bread" is the observance of the Lord's supper. At this time it was observed in a house-to-house fellowship of believers. No indication is given how often this observance was held, whether weekly or quarterly or annually. It was clear, however, that it was done on the first day of the week.

In the Jewish way of speaking, to break bread is the same as to make a meal; and the meal here seems to have been one of those which was called the "love-feast." Such of the heathen as were converted could not partake of meats offered to idols and these were the main support of the poor in the heathen cities. The Christians seem, very early, to have commenced this custom of giving love-feasts. They were made on the first day of the week, for the benefit of the poorer Christians. It was toward the end of these feasts, or immediately after them, that they celebrated the Lord's supper.

Fourth, they were reverent and full of fear (verse 43). This means a deep sense of awe. This undoubtedly came because of their nearness to the events of the crucifixion, resurrection and Pentecost; and also because of the newness of what they were experiencing. It came because of "the many wonders and signs done by the apostles" in fulfillment of Joel's prophecy.

Fifth, they shared all things commonly (verses 44, 45). This is presumed by many to teach communism. While the disciples shared things commonly it was not a socialistic experiment. While they had all things together it was a far cry from Marxist communism. It was because of the sheer necessity of survival. They had been dispossessed of their property and had lost their employment as a means of livelihood and needed to pool their resources for survival.

There was no thought here of distributing property on a permanent basis for economic reasons. It was a temporary expedient that completely disappeared when the church expanded numerically and geographically. It was for the time being, but as faith matured and the church settled into more normal living the need for communal living disappeared. Furthermore, this community of goods and services was on a voluntary basis called the "haburah," a central feature of which was the communal meal which was eaten from house to house.*

Sixth, they attended the temple daily in a body (one accord) for public worship. Here they observed, not the Jewish ritual of sacrifices now made obsolete by the rending of the temple veil, but the teaching of the apostles. They met together on Solomon's porch, a place familiar to them because Jesus had used it on occasion.

Here, then, you have the entrance of this new society called the church and the conditions under which the faith and life

---

*Bruce.

of this society of Christians were sustained and preserved. The conditions are the same today for it is the same faith and the same church.

What effect did this have upon the contemporaries of these events? It is said in the last statement of this chapter, "the Lord added to the church daily such as should be saved (were finding salvation)." This means that the Holy Spirit guided these people, mostly Jews and proselytes, into the way of salvation.

What happened to the people who were thus saved? They sustained their faith by the means which have already been suggested and became witnesses to Christ as powerful exponents of the new way of life.

Here is born a new meaning and respect for the church. It gives pause for modern people to consider their relation to it. If they are in it what have they done to meet its conditions? Are they sustaining their faith and life in vigor and vitality? Are they witnesses unto Him?

The church is a continued story. What are we doing to write the continuing chapters?

9

SUCH AS I HAVE

Acts 3:1-11

Pentecost is over and the tremendous excitement in the city has temporarily subsided. Then one day, not long afterward, Peter and John went up to the temple at the hour of prayer, being three o'clock in the afternoon. There they saw a congenital cripple whom friends had brought and put down at the Gate Beautiful. As Peter and John passed they were strongly attracted to the man and stopped to look at him and appraise his plight. Whereupon the crippled confidently expected to receive a gift of alms. But Peter said, "Silver and gold have I none; but such as I have give I unto thee."

The key to this incident is not the cripple's helplessness; nor even the subsequent miracle which, by the way, is the first miracle of the church age. The key lies in the phrase of Peter, "such as I have." He and the rest of the apostles and disciples were in possession of a new power; the power of God.

Something wonderful was about to happen. The infant church was beginning to flex its muscles and feel the power of a new experience. New and great things were in the air. There was once an old farmer who was so convinced that nothing important could ever happen in his village that he hitched up his team and drove to a neighboring town to see an eclipse of the moon. Yes, something important had already happened in the coming of the Holy Spirit and the infant church was in possession of something more valuable and powerful than silver and gold.

The church, however, was not about to embark upon a gigantic social service program to relieve the economic distress of Jerusalem; or heal all the sick through city-wide healing campaigns. It was not about to engage in a great legislative crusade to change the laws in favor of the masses. It had something better than new laws; a new life.

This did not mean that the church was in the business of creating miracle-spectaculars. One can well imagine how tempting this would have been. But the disciples did not use their new power for miraculous purposes. In fact, if you examine the Book of Acts carefully, you will notice the diminishing number of miracles which were performed by the apostles. There are only sixteen recorded miracles in the rest of the book and after that only four cases of sickness dealt with in the epistles.

The new power, while possessed of a certain definite purpose in confirmatory miracles, which were the credentials of the new church, was to be employed as a spiritual force. It is in this spiritual realm that the church exerts its greatest influence and not as a performer of miracles. It is in this sense that the church ought to major in being the church, "constantly reminding men and women in all walks of life of God's grace and God's glory, but leaving international affairs, for better or worse, to the statesman. If statesmen fail it will be because the church previously failed to lead men to an appreciation of what it means to be children of God, to love God with all one's heart, mind, soul and strength, and one's neighbor as himself."*

"It is easier," said Charles L. Allen, "to crusade than it is to repent. It is easier to write letters to congress than it is to pray. It is easier to clean up the slums than it is to clean up one's heart. It is easier to talk about the redemption of society than the saving of one's soul."

It is an obvious fact that most Christians pray for power in their lives because they want spectacular Christianity rather than spiritual Christianity.

The character and tempo of this new power is established at the very outset of the Book of Acts by Jesus. He said, "But ye shall receive power, after that the Holy Ghost is come upon you:

*John H. Alexander, First Congregational Church, Wauwatosa, Wis.

and ye shall be witnesses unto me both in Jerusalem, and in all Judaea, and in Samaria, and unto the uttermost part of the earth" (Acts 1:8). The new power was not for economics, politics, peace of mind or healing, but for witnessing.

Instead of a few people possessing miraculous gifts, every Christian would possess one gift—the gift of a witness. Let us be sure we exercise it and not employ our time trying to do the spectacular.

At this point the infant church had no colleges, seminaries, church buildings, books, libraries, hospitals, clinics or political prestige. Yet even in the absence of these things they were embarked upon a course of events that would shortly turn the world upside down. And why would this be? Because Peter could say to the crippled alms-seeker, "such as I have."

The infant church was identified by the following things:

I. A BODY OF PEOPLE

This body of people included the original one hundred and twenty who tarried at Jerusalem among whom were Mary, the mother of Jesus, the brothers and sisters of Jesus, the original eleven apostles, plus Mathias; and now to these had been added the three thousand converts of Pentecost. These constituted the body which made up the church.

There are people who are professing Christians who say they do not believe in belonging to churches. But where would the church be today if the one hundred and twenty and the three thousand had taken this attitude at the beginning of this age? Why don't these people say they do not believe in citizenship and take the next plane for Lower Slobbovia and plant themselves in a comfortable snowdrift? Why don't they say they do not believe in families and head for the nearest hobo jungle? Why don't they say they do not believe in being a human being and resign from the human race? We cannot escape the implications of Christianity and hold ourselves aloof from the church and expect to fulfill our destiny as a child of God.

The reason most of these people do not join the church is

because of a basic desire to do as they please and not be subject to the discipline imposed by church membership. A missionary, so the story goes, was building his station out in the bush under the close scrutiny of the local natives who gathered around to watch his every move. They were fascinated with his tools, materials and procedures and, like children, gave vent to their amazement. They were particularly intrigued with a small, round, shiny, ticking object he took out of his pocket at intervals for a brief inspection. Finally one asked him what it was. That's my watch," he answered. "It tells me when to get up in the morning, when to eat, when to begin my day's work, what time to quit working, and so forth." "Oh!" the native exclaimed, "why don't you throw it away and do as you please?"

II. A Message

This is what we call the church's ethic or the sum total of what it has to say to the Jewish and pagan world which constitutes its responsibility. Up to this point the message consisted of the messiahship of Jesus, His deity and supreme Lordship, His crucifixion and resurrection, the relevancy of the Old Testament prophecies to the immediate events of Pentecost, the coming of God into their midst in the person of the Holy Spirit, the necessity of repentance and turning to a new life, the acceptance of Jesus Christ as Lord and the requirement of baptism as a means of entrance into the church.

These items constituted the mighty ethic which, when preached in the dynamic of the Holy Spirit, shook the Roman Empire to its foundations, reduced Judaism to obsolescence, put paganism to rout, cleared the heavens of all its false gods and made flaming evangelists of fisherman, tradesmen, soldiers, courtiers and peasants.

III. A Method

The infant church was without organization at this point. It had no headquarters office, no embossed letterheads, no Bibles, no tracts, no radio or TV stations, no committees, no printing presses and no list of prospects. It had nothing but a message and a method. The message has already been reviewed; the method was simple, "ye shall be witnesses unto me."

A witness is a person who has been involved in an event which he reports having seen, heard and experienced. This method accounts for the genius of Christianity. It accounts for its miraculous conquest of pagans within a few generations. Its absence today is the one thing which stands in the way of the church's conquest of the Twentieth Century world. In its place we have a professional Christianity; we have reduced it to promotional schemes by paid publicists; we have limited it to the responsibility of a few people who cannot possibly accomplish the objective of reaching this generation with the Christian ethic. We have witnessed, to the shame of the church, the bloodless conquest by communism of millions of people by the very method by which we should be winning the world.

The average church congregation will listen to sermons and agree in principle to what is being said and then go home and do nothing about it. That is why communism is winning the world; why crime is on the ascendency; why a moral collapse dooms our civilization. We have the method but indolent, self-satisfied, impotent Christians are not implementing it with their witnessing.

IV. A POWER

This fact was apparent by what happened at the Gate Beautiful in the temple when Peter healed the crippled man. He disclaimed any credit for what had taken place and said it was all due to the Messiah whom the Jews had rejected. This power was the power of the Holy Spirit released at Pentecost. It was personal power released into the regenerated personalities of believers. It was power for action; not for contemplation, personal satisfaction or personal enjoyment. It was power for accomplishment. When Peter preached at Pentecost it resulted in three thousand converts. When Peter beheld the crippled man it resulted in a miraculous healing. When the collective disciples of the new Christian community were dispersed across Asia they made a conquest of the Roman Empire.

With this power surging through his being, Peter could say to the unfortunate alms-seeker, "Arise and walk." Thomas Aquinas called upon Pope Innocent IV when the latter was counting a large sum of money. "You see, Thomas," said the Pope, "the church can no longer say, 'Silver and gold have I none.' " "Truly, holy father," said Thomas, "and neither can she now say, 'Arise and walk.' "* We may well ponder the aptness of this incident in the modern church.

This power does something more for men than give temporary relief to the distressed; it enables them to function as redeemed, reconstructed personalities, filled with the presence of God.

V. Two Ordinances

The infant church was without an elaborate ceremonial arrangement. It had a message and a method to propagate that message; plus a dynamic to proceed with its mission to the world. It presented this message in the framework of two visible acts of worship—baptism and the Lord's Supper. We define these as ordinances or visible representations of the death and resurrection of Jesus. The ordinance of baptism was the simple and meaningful act of immersion in water as demonstrated by John on the person of Jesus. It had not become a rite for infants, as later developed; nor vitiated as a ceremony of initiation into the church. It was an act of confession by believers who confessed an adult faith in Jesus as Savior and Lord.

As for the Lord's Supper there was nothing mystical or mysterious associated with it. Not until the theologians tampered with it, and not until the church turned a worship for the spiritual man into a worship for the natural man did it become corrupted by meaningless words and usages.

The Lord's Supper is an act of remembrance in which two

---

* Bruce

things are involved: bread and wine. One represents Jesus' body and the other represents Jesus' blood. These two things were involved in the crucifixion and their memorial use at the Lord's table would unite believers into an indissoluble fellowship in every land among every race of people.

VI. A PURPOSE

The purpose of the church had actually been given to it before it became the church. It is found in the great commission of Jesus, "Go ye into all the world, and preach the gospel to every creature." Its purpose corporately and individually was and is to vocalize and publicize the message of the gospel. Its purpose was and is to bear witness to Jesus Christ, God's answer to the human dilemma. That purpose gives every Christian a reason for living.

It is important to have a reason for living. It gives life dignity and importance. To belong to and labor in the church of the living God means to belong to and labor in the only institution that has perpetual continuity. Here the investment of life, talent and substance is of eternal consequence. "Therefore, my beloved brethren, be ye stedfast, unmovable, always abounding in the work of the Lord, forasmuch as ye know that your labour is not in vain in the Lord" (I Cor. 15:58).

10

THE POWER OF FAITH

Acts 3:12-26

In the consideration of what constitutes the greatest power there are many measuring rods. But none of these can measure the power that was received at Pentecost and displayed by Peter when he healed the paralytic who sat at the Gate Beautiful seeking alms.

The circumstances are quickly recalled and it is seen that Peter identifies the source of this healing power with a name. He said, "And his name through faith in his name hath made this man strong. . ." (verse 16). Henceforth among this new society, soon to be given the name Christian, the name of Jesus was synonymous with power, stability, righteousness and survival.

We recall, at this point, that this handful of disciples was at a critical juncture. They faced the sheer necessity of survival. They had hardly begun to exist before they had to fight to survive.

We are at one of the many critical junctures of modern times in world affairs and as Christians we ought to be aware of it, even though we would neither propose nor support many of the nostrums and remedies that are being offered for the world's survival. We must believe, if we are in the church, that the world and the church are two different societies. The church must forever remain apart from the world if it is going to do its best work in the world.

One modern writer has said, "I do not believe the greatest threat to our future is from bombs or guided missiles. I don't think our civilization will die that way. I think it will die when we no longer care—when the spiritual forces that make us wish to be right and noble die in the hearts of men. Arnold Toynbee has pointed out that nineteen of twenty-one notable civilizations have died from within and not by conquest from without. There were no bands playing and no flags waving when these civilizations decayed; it happened slowly, in the quiet and the dark when no one was aware. . . .

"If America is to grow great, we must stop gagging at the word "spiritual." Our task is to re-discover and re-assert our faith in the spiritual, non-utilitarian values on which American life has really rested from its beginning."*

Since we are part of the human scene in the last half of the Twentieth Century we are the people who must face these critical situations and apply such remedies and engage in such action as will be effective.

Let us go back to the beginning of the church and see what these early Christians did; for what they did is what we must do.

I. They Survived By the Power of Faith

This is what Peter possessed and demonstrated in the healing of the paralytic. But this does not mean that we must heal all the paralytics in the world in order to make it a better world. Sickness is a part of the original wrong that afflicts all men and not until that original wrong is dealt with in redemption's ultimate purpose in the return of Christ, will sickness be finally and fully dealt with. In the meantime we have access to the power of faith in meeting the current problems of life, including sickness. Along with faith we are grateful for hygiene, and antibiotics and the knowledge of the laws of God and such a possibility as faith-health.

The power of faith lies patiently, even if dormant, in the life of every Christian. It must be used or else it is useless.

During one of the battles in the Cuban campaign, Colonel Theodore Roosevelt approached Clara Barton for some needed supplies. Miss Barton was working with the Red Cross unit,

---

*Lawrence M. Gould.

which at that time was not too well known and understood. The Colonel offered to buy the supplies but was told that she could not sell him anything, nor would she do it for anybody on the face of the earth. "Well," he said, "how can I get what I need?" Her answer was, "By asking for it."

II. THEY SURVIVED BY A NEW LIFE

These Christians were transformed people. They did not live by national categories such as Jews or Romans, but as Christians. It was through their new lives that they possessed both the purpose and strength of survival.

III. THEY SURVIVED BY BELIEF IN TRUTH

We cannot survive unless we believe something. This something is not anything. It is that which by its nature has the power of survival. The truth of Christianity has this power; but it must not be vitiated by men's doubts. We have been robbed of the positive convictions of faith in our national life. We no longer believe in the things that are sure and certain. Our faith is ephemeral and transitory.

These Christians believed in a faith which could be defined by words. The words they used are found in this incident, as well as others that follow. They are such words as repent, be converted, faith, forgiveness, salvation and prayer.

A well-meaning but badly mistaken minister recently suggested that Biblical words are outmoded and should be changed. He said, "It is a waste of good breath to tell a large section of our modern-day city population to repent, to believe or to depend on God's love. They haven't the slightest idea what you are talking about." But these words are really not outmoded since the spiritual problems they deal with are not outmoded. As long as there is such an experience as sin there is fitness in using the word repent. It is not the words that need to be changed so much as the men who use them.

IV. THEY SURVIVED BY GOD BEING IN THEIR MIDST

These people believed in and experienced the presence of a personal God. This, in fact, was the meaning they found in Pentecost. As Christmas and the incarnation means *God with us;* as Calvary and the crucifixion meant *God for us;* so Pentecost and the coming of the Holy Spirit means *God in us.* Here was the presence of God to be practiced in daily life. It was this experience that enabled them to survive the critical situations during the founding days of the church.

V. THEY SURVIVED BY STRENGTH WHICH CAME OUT OF HARDSHIP

There is no doubt that these early Christians paid a great price for their faith. This was not a price exacted by a bargaining God that they might achieve salvation by works. Salvation is totally of grace without any consideration of works. It was the price which principle demands of us. They were living by the principles of a new faith, and it was inevitable that these should come in conflict with current religious and political ideologies.

It is to be doubted if anything is worth while unless we have to pay a price for it. Even a free lunch is not free, for someone has to pay for it.

"There were two ships that sailed for America in the early Seventeenth Century—one, the Mayflower, and the other a smaller ship, that brought passengers to Vera Cruz. They had expected to sail about the same time and keep each other in sight, but for some reason it did not turn out that way. One went to the 'stern and rock-bound coast' in New England, where the fates decreed that the elements would be unkind to them. After clearing the timber from the land, they then had to dig the rocks out of the soil before they could till it. The Indians harassed them continually, and life was indeed hard, but under this stress they developed into a folk whose descendents are among the highest type of people in the nation today. The ones who came to Vera Cruz had a different life. They found a country where watermelons grew the whole year round, and fruit grew on trees without cultivation. Fishing was easy, and all kinds of meat were quickly supplied. If one grew hungry, all he had to do was to go to the nearest grove of bananas and eat his fill. They did not need well-built houses to protect them from the elements—all they actually needed was a protecting roof. They intermingled with Indians and intermarried. Life was easy. The result of this ease was that few men of large calibre developed where bananas grew so effortlessly."

But how can people be concerned with worldly problems when they have so many personal problems? Sharing the confidences of many people, a minister comes to know the troubles of many hearts in spite of the facade of serene faces. Trouble is no respecter of persons and all of us must face it in some form. The world situation is but a multiplication of the individual situation. We have trouble without because we have trouble within. We have trouble abroad because we have trouble at home. After all, the problems of the world are an individual matter. We must all learn to live with our troubles. If we do not we will be sucked into a vortex of despair and hopelessness. Jesus said, "In the world ye shall have tribulation: but be of good cheer; I have overcome the world."

These early Christians lived, survived, won and made a revolutionary contribution to their times in the same manner that the individual Christian today must live, survive and make his contribution. It is expressed in Colossians 2:6, "As ye have therefore received Christ Jesus the Lord, so walk ye in him."

But suppose we do not survive? Is it really important that we survive at all in the character that civilization has moulded us? We think not. The final form of life, as the Christian knows it, is neither of this world or of this body. It is of another world and of a new body both of which are associated with redemption.

There is the poignant story of young John Gunther, son of the famous author of the same name. While the parents faced the impending death of their child and when it was all over, they asked themselves the seemingly inevitable question, "Why?" It then became apparent to them that "there are other criteria for measuring a life as well as its duration."

What are some of these criteria for measuring life in a Christian?

1. Faithfulness

This is perhaps the greatest of all. It takes care of the problem of disparity in many life situations. All have not the same talents and abilities, or the same opportunities; but all have the same capacity for faithfulness.

2. Love

To live by and with love is to live for the highest goals of life. Here is something that transcends every other reason for living. Here is something that makes life livable and conspicuous.

3. Service

To accomplish something is to give purpose to life. To be able to leave behind you a contribution to life is to make life worthwhile. This is achieved by service.

4. Faith

We end where we began, with the power of a new life. Faith is the means by which we may achieve and accomplish. Faith is life's modus operandi.

11

NO OTHER NAME

Acts 4:1-12

As we pick up the threads of the story of the church in the Book of Acts we arrive at another significant moment when Peter, the spokesman for the new community of Christians, signifies, for the first time, that salvation and the name of Jesus are synonymous.

The occasion for this signification was the healing of the impotent alms-seeker at the Gate Beautiful in the temple. It had caused a great stir and no little wonder and much questioning. It disturbed the religious leaders whose impotency was revealed in the immobility of their religion to be a practical help to their generation. So the best thing they could think of was to incarcerate the offending Peter and John who were thrown into prison, and thus removed from immediate contact with the agitated populace of Jerusalem.

The grievance of the religious leaders did not hinge so much on the fact that a crippled man stood once more on strong legs, as that it was done through power associated with a despised name—Jesus. But what was even worse, it was associated with a certain event in the life of Jesus—His resurrection. This was the crux of their disturbance for in crucifying Jesus they did it to silence His ministry and destroy His influence upon the people. Now it was being declared that He was no longer dead, but alive. He was alive with a power to do miracles. If this was true it doomed these religious people to obsolescence. They had to do something about it and their only answer was prison for the protagonists of the despised Jesus.

Reducing all these things to a few words you end up with the words: Jews, resurrection, name and salvation. With these words we see the mission of the church and the purpose of Christianity in the world. No one would be right in saying that the purpose of Christianity is to heal the cripples. Peter and John could have healed all the cripples in Jerusalem and not have fulfilled the mission of the church. They went on from this event to do the business of Christianity which was to preach the name of the resurrected Christ and secure the salvation of men.

What is the mission of the church? If we declared a moratorium on church work long enough to consider the work of the church and brought to a halt the ecclesiastical machinery and stopped our religious pretensions, we would make a startling and strategic discovery about the purpose of Christianity and the place of the church in modern society.

The church is a unique institution which lives in two worlds. It is first of all a *divine institution* composed of people who are in fellowship with God. In the next place it is a *human institution* which is involved with the affairs of this world. It must never allow its involvement with the affairs of this world such as social service and foreign policy, to obscure its divine mission. But this is what has happened today for now we find the official church bodies of America so involved in the foreign policy of our government that they are advising our government concerning its various duties. Foreign policy is not the business of the church for when the Kingdom of God comes it will not come by the promotion of foreign policy, disarmament, hygiene or foreign aid. It will come by promoting God's foreign policy. And what is God's foreign policy? Jesus proclaimed it on the Mount of Olives. "But go ye into all the world and preach the gospel to every creature."

The dynamics of Christianity represented in the Holy Spirit is worked out, not in foreign aid or foreign policy, but in the church when it proclaims the name of Jesus for salvation, for "neither is there salvation in any other: for there is none other name under heaven given among men, whereby we must be saved." Therefore the church has a special mission in today's world: it is to proclaim salvation through the name of Jesus, the resurrected, living Son of God.

The essence and significance of this proclamation of salvation lies in the fact that Jesus Christ has solved the problem of human sin which has caused the division among nations, disease and poverty among men; and provides through that solution the basis of brotherhood and the means of a new life.

What the specifics of this remedy for the ills of the world? They are two: the resurrection of Jesus and faith in the name of Jesus.

I. THE RESURRECTION OF JESUS

Easter is not an island separated from the rest of the year by three hundred and sixty-four days. It belongs to every day of the year. In fact, fifty-two days of the year we proclaim the truth of the resurrection by worshipping a risen Christ every Sunday. The resurrection meant that Christ was alive, not dead like every other religious leader. It meant that He had a new life, something unlike that possessed by any other person. In fact, this new life was God's life who said, through Jesus, "And I give unto them eternal life and they shall never perish." It meant that this life was released by Jesus through His resurrection and was available to every man on the basis of faith.

Now the question is, how does a person get this new life? This leads us to the second specific of the remedy for the ills of the world.

II. THE NAME OF JESUS

One does not possess the resurrected life of Jesus by being born of physical parents; we must be born again. We must share in a new birth, which Jesus described to Nicodemus as a birth from above.

This new life is not the result of creation. It is the result of salvation and this salvation does not come naturally. It comes supernaturally. It comes through an encounter with God by the name of Jesus. This salvation is not found in religion *per se*. Religion as we know it obscures rather than reveals salvation. Salvation is a revealed thing; revealed in the life and personality of Jesus, and when we know Him we can experience salvation. The church has obscured salvation by offering a lot of secondary things like forms, ceremonies, symbols and a host of sacerdotal and extraneous matters.

It is not any religion one wishes to choose that will save. This is one of the commonest fallacies which men make. They say, just believe anything, because all religions are commonly alike and all will effectively work. It is not so, for "there is none other name. . . ."

It is not any church that saves. In fact, the church does not save at all. Once more, salvation is a personal encounter with God through the ministry of the church. But just like a thirsty man, it is the water that quenches and not the pipe or the pump that brought it. Salvation is a Christ-related experience.

If we are to wholly and completely believe the Christian message we must believe that salvation is exclusive to Christianity. It is not a question of being a Buddhist or a Baptist, a Catholic or a Protestant. It is a question of identity with Jesus Christ. This identity is expressed at the very beginning of the Christian era when Peter said, "Neither is there salvation in any other. . . ."

Remember it is either/or. It is either salvation through His name or damnation without His name for "there is none other name." Why is the emphasis upon the name of Jesus? It is not the use of His name as some shibboleth, magic phrase or charm. It is His name as the revelation of God to mankind. Jesus Christ became the Son of man that we might become the sons of God.

You will remember that this is Peter's polemic before the Sanhedrin to which he had been summoned on the morning after the miracle of the healing of the paralytic. And when the members of this council had been seated Peter and John were brought from the temple lock-up and asked by what authority they presumed to act as they did. It was this setting in this council of Jewish rulers that gave significance to what Peter said when he identified the source of the miracle-power with the name of Jesus of Nazareth, whom they had crucified.

Peter pinpointed the crux of the matter when he said that this Jesus of Nazareth is the same "stone which was set at naught of you builders, which is become the head of the corner." The Jews had considered themselves to be the builders of God's Kingdom and the cornerstone of this building was the Messiah. Now they were being accused of having crucified the Messiah and rejecting the stone which was the key to the whole Kingdom structure. They had perpetrated a national catastrophe! They had witnessed the coming of God's anointed and refusing to believe, they had crucified Him. This, said Peter, was their crime. But Peter also said it can be our crime too, because here is God's salvation and we can reject it by rejecting Jesus Christ. And if we do we reject the only source of salvation there is, for "there is none other name. . . ."

A name, did Peter say? Yes, a name, the name of Jesus Christ of Nazareth. Peter used that name to cause a crippled man to walk. He said, "Silver and gold have I none; but such as I have give I unto thee: in the name of Jesus Christ of Nazareth rise up and walk."

The reason this name represented the power of healing and a new life was two-fold. When He was born He was given two names: first, Jesus, "because He shall save His people from their sins." This is the name of the Savior. Second, "Immanuel, God with us." This is the name of deity. These two factors give power and authority to the use of the name of Jesus.

A name less than His name is a name impotent to save; for salvation is only possible by the One who was both Savior and God. His is the name at which every knee will bow and every tongue confess that Christ is Lord.

A woman missionary in Africa was taking a trip by bicycle to visit an out-station. She took her bicycle boy with her. On the way her cycle developed trouble and she asked him to fix it.

While he was doing so she walked on ahead and coming to a rise of ground in the jungle path she was confronted with a lion looking straight at her. The sensible thing in this kind of predicament is to look right back at the lion and reveal no fear. Soon another lion, then two lionesses, appeared. In this posture of staring down the lions, her bicycle boy came up the path and she motioned him to be quiet. He came up very quietly and she whispered, without taking her eyes off the lions, "This is dangerous. Are you ready to meet God?" The boy did not say, "You know my relation to the missionaries on the compound." He said confidently, "Yes, I have peace with God. My soul is saved. I know whom I have believed." He faced reality with the facts of faith and confidence in the name of Jesus.

12

CHRISTIANITY FACING NEW CHALLENGES
Acts 4:13-31

Two Christian laymen had been called to answer for their actions before the supreme court of the Jewish nation. Their actions had been the miraculous healing of a crippled beggar. So ably did these laymen sustain their position before these distinguished religious leaders that they evoked praise and comment from them. It was noted that they were "unlearned and ignorant men." They had not been trained in the technical learning of the rabbinical schools. Moreover they were "ignorant" which means they had no professional status. But the word for ignorant actually means idiot: not in the sense in which we commonly use it but of a commoner, layman or unskilled or unclassified person.

Beside the successful defense of their position and actions two other things impressed the members of the Sanhedrin.

First, these men had been companions of Jesus. This troubled them more than anything else because they had consented to the execution of Jesus at Roman hands for the specific purpose of getting rid of a trouble maker who threatened their religious citadel. Now they were confronted with the same problem in another form; Jesus was succeeded by men who were doing the same things He had done and were commanding the attention of the people. But their dilemma now was that these men had broken no law in curing the cripple.

Second, a notable and bonafide miracle had been performed. The facts of the healing of the paralytic were incontrovertible. It had been witnessed by many and furthermore the healed man stood before the Sanhedrin in strength and vigor. Just as Jesus had supported His teaching by miracles of power to prove the divine nature of His mission, so His disciples were doing the same. It was a very serious situation.

To these two things that impressed the members of the Sanhedrin we should add a third, even more impressive than the two—the resurrection of Jesus. The resurrection was the apostles' central affirmation. They never failed to speak of it. And there was no way the Jews could disprove it, for the body of Jesus had vanished so completely that no one could produce it and without the body of Jesus to disprove the claims of resurrection the Jewish position was hopeless and the Christian cause secure.

Under these circumstances the judges imposed a ban on the disciples, commanding them not to speak at all in the name of Jesus.

Here was the first test of principle and strength between the Christians and the law. Whether it was the law of the Jews or the Romans was of little importance. It was the first test. If the law could be made to hold, the Christian cause was dead. But if these unlearned and ignorant men were indeed supported by the divine power of a living Christ the legal restrictions would be of no consequence. And it was soon proved that they were of no consequence for Peter and John spoke eloquently, bravely and courageously when they said, "Whether it be right in the sight of God to hearken unto you more than unto God, judge ye. For we cannot but speak the things which we have seen and heard" (verses 19, 20).

One of the reformers upon being told "All the world is against you," replied, "Then I am against all the world."

On John Knox's tomb was inscribed, "Here lies the man who never feared the face of clay."

Here is the first crisis of the church. It surmounted it and survived it. The church is in a new crisis today. Christianity faces the most formidable foes of its career in the modern civilization which it was instrumental in shaping and forming. It faces a competition of forces never equaled in its history. One of these forces is communism which seeks to challenge the very foundation and existence of Christianity. It has recently founded the first university of atheism, while Red China has attempted the liquidation of the church by massive mass murders.

Islam is also a force to be reckoned with for it is stronger than ever before and reinforced by the immense wealth of the oil-rich Arabian countries, all of which are fanatically Moslem. Secularism and humanism are twin forces in our own hemisphere which face the church in force. The political activities of sacerdotal systems also threaten. The very civilization which Christianity laid on the foundations of the Graeco-Roman world is in the agony of what could be its death throes.

Are we Christians who sit smugly behind our creeds and traditions, who monotonously repeat our rituals, ready to face up to the crisis and the challenge that faces the church today? Are we even aware that there is a crisis and that Christianity faces competition and challenge to end its very existence?

What is to be our answer to this challenge? It is being answered by religious stategists with the concept of an ecumenical church as if the reconciliation of the divisions within the church were the solution. But this is futile for unless the quality of Christianity is improved the quantity is useless. The answer to the threats of communism, Islam, secularism, humanism and atheism lies in the quality of individual Christians.

What mattered most to these two untrained laymen before their judges was their personal commitment to God as witnesses of Christ and the gospel. And if there could be a revival of that spirit and that quality of Christianity the cause of Christ would be secure in the world. It was the answer to the church's crisis once; it can be the answer again.

It is not suggested that there is danger of the demise of the Christian church for this is the most unlikely eventuality in all the world. It is so for two reasons: First, where it is founded. Jesus said, "Upon this rock . . . and the gates of hell shall not prevail against it." Second, how it has survived. It has lived in spite of its enemies and the mistakes of its friends; and it is not about to give up to the threats of any force or combination of forces which threaten it today.

When I think of the modern crisis of the church and its possible implications to one as an individual Christian, I am fortified by the assurance that the fate of the individual Christian is not tied to the fate of the church. My salvation is a personal matter between God and myself and its security or satisfaction does not fluctuate with the state of the church.

How different this concept of salvation is for a Roman Catholic whose salvation is not immediately related to Christ as a personal Savior but intermediately through the church so that the fate of the church determines the fate of the individual.

There is no intermediate church, priest, altar or ceremony between me and God and I can say, "I know whom I have believed, and am persuaded that he is able to keep that which I have committed unto him against that day."

Another source of security and strength for these proscribed and indicted Christians lay in the fact that they had a place of spiritual and communal refuge to which to retreat. It is recorded in verse 23 that "being let go, they went to their own company and reported all that the chief priests and elders had said unto them." It undoubtedly meant that they returned to the upper room which was the common rendezvous of the disciples and gave them a running account of what happened.

It immediately evoked a flood of praise to God; and the disciples, steeped in the literature of the Old Testament, turned to the opening words of the second psalm. They had found proof in their own experience of the fulfillment of this Messianic prophecy. They had entered into a personal relationship with Him. What they had found individually they hoped Israel would find nationally.

Every person needs what these disciples had — a company of their own kind as a place of refuge from the threats, deceits and perils of the world. The continuing church is that company and that refuge today. Here values are preserved, strength is renewed, courage is restored, faith is revitalized.

How long do you think these two disciples would have been able to sustain their position in a hostile world without retreating to this refuge? Not very long. And we can be sure that the absentees that are so numerous in the company of God's people assembled in worship will not be able to sustain their position in today's world. They need the comfort of the communal strength of assembled Christians who have been given the injunction — "forsake not the assembling of yourselves together as the manner of some is."

What happens when Christians return "to their own company"?

1. They Strengthen the Impact of Their Witness to the World.

The joy that poured out of their souls as a result of the victory their leaders achieved became strength for their own witness. They went forth from this gathering of their own company "to renewed faithfulness to their own witness."

2. They Found New Reasons for the Support of Their Own Faith.

Their own faith was greatly strengthened. Their faith was supported by the Word of God as found in the Old Testament. In any assembly of God's people where God's Word is expounded and the souls of sincere believers exposed, it means a strengthening of faith.

3. They were Helped to Do the Right Thing and Not the Expedient Thing.

There was no thought of expediency upon the part of Peter and John as they stood before the court. They must do what was right. This they declared and it paid off.

Interviewed recently at Lambeth Palace, his official residence, Dr. Geoffrey Fisher, the Archbishop of Canterbury, reaffirmed his long-standing support of the United Nations. "Politicians and statesmen are concerned primarily with whether a thing works. My responsibility is to try to interpret —as nearly as I can — whether a thing is pleasing in the eyes of God. That temporarily it may or may not 'work' very well, for me has to be secondary."

4. They were Emboldened in Their Own Actions and Became More Vocal (verses 29, 30). "And now, Lord, behold their

threatenings: and grant unto thy servants, that with all boldness they may speak thy word, by stretching forth thine hand to heal; and that signs and wonders may be done by the name of thy holy child Jesus."

5. They Received God's Answer By a New Manifestation of God's Power (verse 31). First, there was a physical manifestation as at Pentecost (verse 30). "The place was shaken." Second, there was a fresh filling of the Holy Spirit. Three fillings of the Holy Spirit are recorded up to this point in Acts — once at Pentecost (2:4), once when Peter stood before the Sanhedrin (4:8), and once at this point in the upper room after Peter and John returned to the waiting disciples (4:31).

Jesus said, "And whatsoever ye shall ask in my name, that will I do, that the Father may be glorified in the Son" (John 14:13). How little power we experience in our daily lives, simply because we spend so little time alone with the Lord! In New York City recently, a massive new organ was to be dedicated in a certain church. Everyone had come out to hear a guest musician play the familiar songs of the sanctuary on the huge console. The service began, and as the organist pressed his fingers to the keys, he was horrified to find that not one single musical note would come forth. He pressed the start button, but still nothing happened. Then the custodian, sensing that the electricity had not been turned on, wrote a hasty note and handed it to the organist, telling him that after the invocation, the generator would be on and he could proceed with the service. The note read: "After the prayer, the power will be on." What great words of wisdom this man wrote without realizing the depth of this meaning. For, in our own lives, if we want power with men, and a testimony that rings true and clear, we must find that time of personal power with God in prayer. The secret which Jesus followed was to depart into the secret place and there meet with His Heavenly Father. How we need to cultivate the daily habit of communion with God, bringing to Him those things which burden us. "After the prayer, the power will be on!"

13

THEM THAT BELIEVED

Acts 4:32 — 5-11

Imbedded in the continuing account of the events surrounding
the beginning and establishment of the church is a phrase which
reveals an important characteristic of the people who made up
the first generation of Christians. The phrase is, "And the
multitude of them that believed" (Acts 4:32).

To begin with they were not an inconsiderable number. They
are described as a multitude, and while the word does not mean
a vast number we are already able to account for over eight
thousand people. These people are now given a name which is
to characterize them as long as the church exists. It is the name,
"believers." This means that they must believe something to
belong to the new society which God is bringing into existence.

It has already been established that these early Christians
believed three things which centered in the person of Jesus Christ.
They believed His divine Messiahship, His crucifixion for sins
and His resurrection from the dead. These three things constituted the basis of faith demanded of the believers before they
could be members of this new society. Here is the crux of the
Christian faith and any deviation from these three things changes
the true and real nature of Christianity. We shall see that
gradually Jesus Christ is substituted by an ecclesiastical structure
and the nature of Christianity, so far as its popular conception is
concerned, is changed. It becomes faith in an institution,
tradition, ritual, instead of faith in Jesus Christ.

One of the things that characterized this infant church was its
solidarity and unanimity. It says, "They were of one heart and

one soul" (verse 32). The specific manner in which this unanimity was manifested was in a very mundane, material and practical way because "they had all things in common." That is, they shared their possessions such as houses, food and clothing. The result of this sharing is described in verses 34 and 35: "Neither was there any among them that lacked . . . distribution was made unto every man according as he had need."

Does this indicate an incipient communism? Certainly not. This experience was not even remotely related to communism or socialism, as we know it, for the following reasons:

1. Communism is by force; this was voluntary. These people were not compelled to sell their property and make it available to others. Freedom to act according to one's convictions is the basis of all Christian enterprises. No one is forced to give, and no one is forced to receive.

2. Communism is materialistic; this had a spiritual purpose. This communal sharing was not employed merely to satisfy the physical and material needs of the people. Its higher purpose was to sustain the new community so that it could act in the capacity of a witness for God.

3. Communism is socialistic; this was based on individual merit and need. People did not give away what they had in an indiscriminate manner. They gave to a need and this need was based on merit. The merit in this situation was the loss these people had suffered when they became believers and experienced dispossession and disinheritance of their property.

This was a form of Christian communalism and not communism. Like many things in the early days of the church it was temporary and expedient, due to local conditions. When the believers consolidated their position they abandoned this practice of voluntary sharing as something no longer necessary.

Look at this idea of voluntarism. It is the basis and heart of Christian action. Things were done because of the free will of individuals who had been responsive to the stimulation of the Holy Spirit. Voluntarism is not to be mistaken for individualism. A lot of people who act on the basis of individualism think they are acting voluntarily. They glory in their independence. They do things differently than other people. They do not conform to the actions of the group. If the church decides on a course of action, they dissent and say they will not be forced to do anything. This is not true Christian action by the stretch of anyone's imagination. It is anarchy, individualism and selfishness. It never glorifies God, helps an individual or adds to the success of the church.

To demonstrate the state of unanimity in the early church Luke gives two examples in connection with the practice of Christian communalism. One concerns Barnabas, a Cypriote Jew. Out of a genuine spirit-filled attitude of love, Barnabas sold his estate and brought the money as a love-gift to the common treasury for use among the needy. The other example concerns Ananias and Sapphira who acted from a totally opposite motive. They succumbed to the sin of deceit and wanted to gain a reputation for generosity: to be known as large givers; to be well thought of by their fellow Christians. And while they might have succeeded in deceiving the people they did not deceive God and their ill-conceived scheme came to a tragic end in the swift judgment of death for both of them.

If many of the methods which the early Christians employed were temporary to meet immediate conditions, it is apparent that the remedy God used to judge Ananias and Sapphira was also temporary. We have no other evidence of the summary act of God in bringing death upon other acts of sin. This does face us, however, with the solemnity, seriousness and sacredness of a Christian's relationship to the church. Some of this should reflect itself in our intentions and purposes when we unite with the church.

Returning now to the main thesis of this message, we recall that these believers centered their faith in the person of Christ, rather than the institution of the church. During the intervening centuries an imperceptible and subtle change has taken place in many instances. We have substituted the church for Christ, religion for redemption and ritual for fellowship with God. Anyone who reads church history knows that the great historical turning point in this attitude came when Constantine espoused the Christian faith and established a church-state relationship. In any such relationship citizens of the state are automatically members of the church and their relationship is a religious relationship to the church rather than a personal relationship to Christ.

It is assumed in this kind of a church relationship that if one subscribes and is submissive to the church and observes its orders, sacraments and rituals that salvation is an accomplished fact. But this poses a vital question. Which church saves? You see, the church is divided into many communions whereas Christ is one. There is the Roman Catholic Church, the Protestant churches, the Eastern churches, and many other kinds like Mormons and Jehovah's Witnesses. To which of these churches are you going to attach yourself to be sure of salvation?

Because of the Reformation we have divided ourselves into Catholics and Protestants and asssume that either in or out of these categories we are saved or lost, Christian or non-Christian. But this is not true. These are not God's categories; they are man's. Christianity is not a package labeled Catholic or Protestant. Christianity is not a piece of ecclesiastical ground fenced in by denominational walls. It is a personal relationship to Jesus Christ. When a person stands before God he does not stand there with any of these labels on him. He is accepted there solely because of his relationship to Jesus Christ, who is "the way, the truth and the life; no man cometh unto the Father, but by me."

The church as we know it in many phases is a collection of ecclesiastical accretions until in some of its manifestations it is not even a reasonable facsimile of the church found in the Book of Acts. This is chiefly because of its substitution of institutions and innovations for Christ.

It will forever remain as one of the greatest assurances of the faith of a Protestant Christian, that his faith is completely contained in the New Testament. There are no additions to it from paganism and no carry-overs from Judaism. It is not Christ and a thousand other things which churchmen have invented. It is not salvation by faith and works, but salvation by faith alone in the atoning sacrifice of Jesus Christ. One of the devil's greatest deceits is in the field of religion. Here are to be found the tares of deceit which are to grow in all their deceptive forms until the final discernment of the harvest.

One can make no mistake if he takes his stand with Jesus Christ and the New Testament. But he can make a tragic mistake if he leaves the simplicities of a faith in Him for the multitudinous involvements with ramified religion.

When we look at the organized church in its final Laodicean phase it fails both God and man. If one's faith is institutional then it will fail.

There is a very startling verse at the end of Paul's second letter to the Corinthians. It says, "Examine yourselves, whether ye be in the faith; prove your own selves. Know ye not your own selves, how that Jesus Christ is in you, except ye be reprobates?" (II Cor. 13:5). Dare we examine ourselves? Dare we permit the Holy Spirit to give us conviction or confidence? Conviction because He has come to reveal our lost, undone and hell-deserving, sinful condition. Confidence because "His Spirit beareth witness with our spirit that we are the children of God."

14

WORKS OF WONDER

Acts 5:12-16

The breath-taking events which surround the beginning of the church continue with a fast and fascinating tempo. There is great joy and exultation among the Christians for the victories which have been won and the manner in which they have been able to sustain themselves in the fast changing scene of events since the resurrection and Pentecost. The Romans stand aghast at the ability of this small (eight thousand one hundred and twenty) company of Christians to face their adversaries with such boldness and confidence. A receding and decadent Judaism is overwhelmed by the vitality and power demonstrated by the followers of Jesus, who were attracting the universal notice of the people by their works of wonder as well as everyday fortitude. All of this is described by a single superlative adjective, the word "great." It is used four times in the context of these verses to note the immense success, growth and experience of the burgeoning church as it establishes itself in the world.

The record speaks of great power in 4.33; great grace in 4:33; great fear in 5:11; great persecution in 8:1.

Great power was the manner in which the Christians witnessed to the gospel. Great grace was the sustaining element of their lives as they faced each day's events. Great fear was in the spirit of reverence and awe which pervaded the Christian colony as they noted the judgment of God upon infidelity. Great persecution was the inevitable concomitant of their espousal of Messiah's cause, and their powerful witness to the saving power of the gospel. This was exactly what Jesus had promised if they followed Him (John 16:1-4). Now they were living it and facing it with courage and distinction. These were indeed "great" days for the church. It would be good for us if they returned once more, so that we would find the glory and joy that goes with this kind of greatness.

If we are not to make grave mistakes in both church polity and individual expectation, it should be remembered that we are in a transition period in the area of time and events covered by the Book of Acts. The transition is from Judaism to Christianity; from the dominion of the law to grace; from the era of the Old Testament to the New Testament. God does not deal with men on the same basis in these opposing periods. Likewise the period of transition from one era to another is temporary and not permanent. Because of this transition many of the things that take place are of a temporary nature and are not to be considered precedents, policies or promises to be expected and realized in the continuing experience of the church age that follows the transition period.

Some of these temporary and transitional things which we note here are worshipping daily in the temple; communal sharing of possessions; physical accompaniment to prayer, such as the building being shaken; sudden death for deceit in financial matters; opening of prison doors by angels to release Christians who were imprisoned for their witness; and speaking with other tongues. This latter was a transitional gift and experience which every evidence of the record shows as disappearing. It continued among the Corinthians as an abuse of something given for another purpose. It appears as a diminishing experience as the church comes of age.

The same is true of the "signs and wonders" (5:12) wrought by the apostles, which at this point are seen in the form of many healings. They appear to be temporary and transitional and for a specific purpose which applies to the time of the establishment of the church.

The reason for healings today would not be the same as during this early day of the church's transition. Then they were evidential, whereas today they would be providential. Then they were general, whereas today they would be selective. Then they were institutional, whereas today they would be individual.

These miracles, or, as they are called here, "signs and wonders," were the direct answer to the apostles' prayers, for it is recorded in 4:29 and 30 that they had prayed for these things. The reason for their prayers was to establish the validity and divinity of their witness to salvation. This is the key to the understanding of these miracles of healing. It was their relation to the salvation of the individual. In other words, healing was not performed simply to relieve people of their physical sicknesses, but to demonstrate a divine power to relieve people of their spiritual ills. When Jesus was tempted of the devil to perform miracles for the sake of appearing miraculous He declined, saying that man should not tempt God. Wanting to perform miracles is tempting God and seeking to have God act unworthy of Himself.

The miracles of healing that resulted from the previous prayers of the apostles were their credentials as the agents and ambassadors of God and proclaimers of the gospel of salvation. The primary and permanent mission of the church was to preach Christ and Him crucified as the Savior. The temporary and passing credential of that mission was found in these works of wonder.

Notice how specific incidents of these things are linked with the mission of the church and the salvation of the individual. "Then Peter said, Silver and gold have I none; but such as I have give I thee: In the name of Jesus Christ of Nazareth rise up and walk" (Acts 3:6). This is the miracle of the cripple who was healed by God through the faith of Peter and John at the Gate Beautiful in the temple. But what has this miracle to do with salvation? Follow the incident and you will see. When the people saw what had taken place they "were filled with wonder and amazement." Taking advantage of this amazement Peter explained the significance of the miracle in relation to the crucifixion and resurrection of Jesus, the Messiah. And then he called upon them to "repent and be converted that your sins may be blotted out." Peter and John associated this healing with the necessity of personal salvation through "the name" of Jesus (4:12). The effect was that "many of them which heard the word believed: and the number of the men was about five thousand."

What has happened in the long years since this event, and the specific necessity of salvation residing in a personal relationship to Christ, has been the subtle and growing substitution of the church and its creeds, rituals and sacraments for a personal encounter with Jesus Christ. Salvation has become institutional rather than individual.

These works of wonder are described in the language of the record: "And by the hands of the apostles were many signs and wonders wrought among the people; and they were all with one accord in Solomon's porch" (Acts 5:12). These were "signs and wonders" performed by all the apostles and were identified as healings of the sick (verses 15, 16). Again these miracles were associated with the salvation of the individual. See verse 14: "And believers were the more added to the Lord, multitudes both of men and women."

In three instances where the salvation of the Jews takes place, as the result of the performance of miracles, it is described as the process of "adding." In 2:41 it says they were "added unto them." But the words "unto them" are omitted from the latest translations, indicating that they are not in the original text but were added by translators in order to make a better reading. In 2:47 it says they were "added to the church." Once more you have a case where some words are not in the original text. In this case the words, "to the church," are omitted from the best manuscripts so you actually have this reading: "and the Lord added such as should be saved." Again in 5:14 it says that believers were "added to the Lord." Here is the central and basic idea of salvation. It does not result from believers added "to them," the people; or being added "to the church," an institution. It results solely from believers being added "to the Lord." They are not names written on church records but "names written in heaven."

Believing in "the name of the Lord" and being added "to the Lord" is the central fact of salvation in the New Testament. Apart from this fact people may have religious experiences but not saving and redemptive experiences. To this extent the church may become a peril and a deception by a false emphasis upon adhering to it as a substitute to adhering to Jesus Christ.

The church has become big religious business. It is a vast and extensive institution. It is divided into many categories. It is vocal with many voices. It has many things for people to do. But the simple condition is to "believe on the name of the Lord and thou shalt be saved." Jesus called the Jews from a decadent Judaism to faith in Himself. It is foolish to exchange one religious system for another. Salvation is no longer through a nation as was true of the Jews; nor is it on an institutional basis as is so often true today. It is on a personal basis by being "added unto the Lord."

Before we leave this incident relating to the miracles of healing performed by the apostles, our attention should be called to a very important observation which relates to modern attempts at healing the sick. It is found in the words "every one" in verse 16. It refers to the kind and extent of these healings. Every one of the sick was healed no matter what the nature of his illness might have been. They not only healed the organically sick but the demoniacally possessed. Here was both ordinary and extraordinary sickness. And every one was healed. Regardless of the printed claims of today's healers, this is not being duplicated today. But in apostolic healings there were no exceptions and no failures. This leads us to observe that the purpose of healings today is not the same as at the beginning of the church. Then they were credentials for the apostles which resulted in the salvation experience of multitudes of people. Today they are providential and selective experiences to fulfill the mysteries of the divine will of God.

That these universally successful healings were temporary and peculiar to the beginning of the church might also be indicated in the unusual manners in which they sometimes occurred. Here it was by Peter's shadow passing over the sick person. Before it was by the hem of Jesus' garment. Later it was by the use of handkerchiefs. But none of these are valid healing methods today.

Again the record speaks of other works of wonder: "But the angel of the Lord by night opened the prison doors, and brought them forth. . ." (Acts 5:19). Because of the sensation caused by the apostles' miracles of healing, the officers of the Sanhedrin had them remanded to the temple prison. It does not say who of the apostles were thus jailed, but perhaps it means all who participated in the incident. But they were not there very long, nor hindered at all in their ministry of witness, because that night "the angel of the Lord" opened the prison doors and carefully charged the servants of God to return to the temple and speak "all the words of life."

Here again a miracle is identified with the redemption of man. In this case it was not a healing, but a miracle of physical deliverance from prison. But their mission was clear, go and speak "all the words of life." The significance of this miracle developed later when the authorities and the people found out about the sensational deliverance of these proclaimers of the new message. It gave authority and credential to all they had to say to the people.

It is a good thing to go back to the headwaters of this stream of new life, which is the church, and see what God meant when He sent Christians on their mission to this world. It is Satan's strategy to vitiate the waters and substitute the secondary for the primary and give men a counterfeit religion. This has been his strategy from the beginning when he caused Cain to offer a counterfeit sacrifice. This is what he has been doing ever since.

Since we have visited these early scenes and re-lived these first events we must remember the primary necessity of life—the salvation of the individual. To bring this message of salvation to man is the mission of the church.

15

THE NEW WAY OF LIFE
Acts 5:17-42

What was developing in the events recorded in this portion of Acts was a new way of life. It was not, we must emphasize, the evolution of Judaism or an improvement of paganism, but something new and different. This life was new in its concept for it began in a personal redemptive experience later to be described by the Apostle Paul in these words, "Therefore if any man be in Christ, he is a new creature: old things are passed away; behold, all things are become new" (II Cor. 5:17).

This life was new in its conduct for it was to be lived on the basis of Jesus' teaching, a part of which is found in His Sermon on the Mount, which contains a totally new set of ideals for life. The further basis for the conduct of this new life was to be the yet-to-be principles of the New Testament letters of Paul and other apostles.

This newness of life was in keeping with the whole concept of Christianity for it was not to be another form of religion. It was to be something new which God would do for the world.

Christianity was given to correct a basic defect in human nature, sin. It was given to set a new standard and new trend in human behavior so that these early Christians would be able to conquer the pagan world by out-living it rather than out-fighting it. It was in this spirit that the church actually conquered much of the world before the end of the Third Century. This sets Christianity apart from all religions for it does not pattern itself after the best judgments and traditions of men. It is, instead, a new life which offers man what cannot be found in any other direction. Because of this we see an entirely new set of experiences being enacted in Acts beginning with Pentecost.

There are here seven new things.

1. A NEW SOCIETY. "And great fear came upon all the church, and upon as many as heard these things" (Acts 5:11).

This new society is the church. This is the first time the word church occurs in the original text (see 2:47 where the word church is omitted from the best manuscripts). *Ecclesia* had originally meant any meeting of people summoned or "called out" from their homes by the sound of a trumpet or otherwise. In this sense it is applied to Christians who were called out of the existing social, racial and national categories to compose a new society. The church was to be made up of a new and different people who were to gather together to hear the new word of the gospel and follow its new instructions.

Most of these "called out" people at this time were Jews whom Peter and Paul would speak of as "peculiar" people. These were not peculiar in the sense of being strange, odd or fanatical; but peculiar in the sense of origin and purpose. They were actually God's "purchased" people, and on this basis they were "called out" from the general society of people. Here is the essential nature of the church. It does not consist of the people of the state or community or family who inherit a religious tradition. Neither does it consist of a people who are trying to be good, or who are working at the problem of salvation. This new society consists of those whom God has saved by His grace, and has called into this new relationship to Himself and called the "ecclesia."

What does the New Testament actually mean when it speaks of "the church" or, as in some cases, "the churches" (Gal. 1:2)? Is the church the local body of believers as it was at Jerusalem, Rome, Corinth, Ephesus, and so forth, or is it the vast assembly of people gathered in many churches? It is both. It is the local body of believers who possess all the powers, rights, privileges and prerogatives of God's redeemed children. But it is also the totality of believers everywhere.

Let no one suppose that the New Testament church has any kinship with the monstrous and monolithic structure which grew out of the Dark Ages after Constantine espoused Christianity as the state religion of Rome. This body, in its vast and extended monopoly is not of itself the church, although it indubitably contains many who are in the church in its New Testament sense. II. A NEW DELIVERANCE. "But the angel of the Lord by night opened the prison doors, and brought them forth" (Acts 5:19).

This is another of the "firsts" recorded in Acts. It is the first deliverance of Christians by force from the power and authority of the law. It was to serve as an example of divine power and was to call attention to the importance and significance of this new society in the pagan and Jewish world.

The nature of this deliverance was both unique and important. It was "the angel of the Lord" who did the delivering. This is, what the original text indicates, the equivalent of the angel of the Lord, or Jehovah of the Old Testament. Thus, you do not have an impersonal event, as sometimes is read into the text, but the personal deliverance of the apostles by the Lord. This angel was in human form who spoke to the delivered apostles and charged them to speak and "tell the people all about this new life."

This deliverance by "the angel of the Lord" was not an isolated occurrence so that some mistake could be made regarding the unique nature of the deliverance. Similar appearances of "the angel of the Lord" occur five times in Acts alone, — once in this instance; then to Stephen who speaks to the angel; then to Philip who is guided by the angel; then to Peter who is liberated by the angel; finally to Herod who is smitten with death by the angel. III. A NEW AUTHORITY. "Then Peter and the other apostles answered and said, We ought to obey God rather than men" (Acts 5:29).

Here was a new authority to govern the lives and conduct of the members of this new society. These Christian Jews had been member of a theocratic nation, which God had repudiated in the captivities, and which had passed through successive stages of rule by judges, priests, kings and prophets. At this particular time it was the Sanhedrin and the law. This was to be no more, for God was establishing a new economy of grace through the personal relationship of men within the framework of the ecclesia.

Here the apostles are challenged by outside legal authority and even though it is the religious authority of the Jews, it was another conflict between the church and the state. Jesus had said, "My Kingdom is not of this world." He had also said, "Render unto Caesar the things that are Caesar's and unto God the things that are God's." Peter recognizes divine government as being supreme. At the same time it would not be an attempt to bring the church into the business of running the government. These are distinct and separate realms of authority. The reason for this is plain. This new society was composed of new people, distinct and separate from the state. Their origin was different for they were the product of regeneration. Their very name indicated this for they were a "called out" people. Hence they were to remain apart from the state while still living within the framework of its social, political and economic laws.

In a church-state relationship citizenship in the state provides membership in the church, provided you pass through the initiating rites of the church. But God's word distinguishes between citizens of earth and citizens of heaven. One results from the first birth and the other from the second birth.

The church in its New Testament sense consists of a society of regenerated and twice-born people who are responsive to different authority, motives and ideals than those of the state.

IV. A NEW VOCATION. "Go, stand and speak in the temple to the people all the words of this life" (Acts 5:20).

Religion was not to be a private matter. It was not for personal consumption alone. It was something for export. Remember this, "We import the teaching of Christianity and export the experience of Christianity."

Christianity is now to become a missionary faith. It was not something to be confined to the Jews or left to remain among the converts. You never read of a single missionary in the Old Testament. These do not appear until this point and a bit later on the great exponent of missions, the Apostle Paul, undertakes three great missionary journeys and establishes churches all over Asia Minor.

Each Christian is obligated to promote, promulgate, propagate and extend his faith. This was not to be done merely by propaganda, but by propagation through reproduction. The early life of the church reveals how this was to be done, through the rapid multiplication of Christians. When peace, plenty and protection came to the church through the evil of church-state union, the force of propagation ceased and the church grew by Constantine's soldiers rounding up the peasants by the thousands and driving them into the rivers where his priests forcibly baptized them. Later on all sorts of ecclesiastical devices were used, such as family relationship, national citizenship and religious works.

Christians today are a generation of religious auditors who come to audit a sermon and file it away in unconsciousness and indifference. When a Christian hears a sermon, that, in all likelihood, is the end of it. But when a communist attends a meeting of his party, he is expected to carry out what he hears. He is checked to see if he carries out his instructions and is disciplined if he does not.

V. A NEW MESSAGE. "The God of our fathers raised up Jesus, whom ye slew and hanged on a tree. Him hath God exalted with his right hand to be a Prince and a Saviour, for to give repentance to Israel, and forgiveness of sins. And we are his witnesses of these things: and so is also the Holy Ghost, whom God hath given to them that obey him" (Acts 5:30-32).

These new workers had to have tools and materials to work with. The materials were the souls and minds of men. The tools were the message which they inherited from the teachings of Jesus and the events surrounding Pentecost. These men did not invent, construct, devise or even edit this message. It was God-given. Paul would later say to the Christians at Thessalonica, " . . . when ye received the word of God which ye heard of us, ye received it not as the word of men, but as it is in truth, the word of God. . ." (I Thess. 2:13).

The new message of the new society, like its experience, centered largely in the person of Jesus Christ. Christian experience is the experience of Jesus Christ. The Christian message is the message of Jesus Christ. Paul would soon write to the ecclesia at Corinth and say, "For I determined not to know anything among you, save Jesus Christ and Him crucified" (I Cor. 2:2). This is the heart of the message which the New Testament amplifies into an evangel and this is "the power of God unto salvation to everyone that believeth."

As we have observed before, so now again, we see the subtle and gradual effect of the years, resulting in vast ecclesiastical organizations; we observe the substitution of the church and its rituals for the personal, saving relationship of Jesus Christ.

This new message was three-fold:

1. The Crucifixion and Resurrection of Jesus (verse 30).

Here is renewed emphasis upon the central fact of redemption. It lay in the sacrifice of Christ. Here, in Peter's language, it was a stinging and stunning rebuke to the Jews. In spite of Jewish intention, God vindicated Messiah who is here associated with "the God of our fathers." This was no incidental or peripheral matter. It went to the heart of history and revealed the slain Jesus as the Messiah whom God sent for the remission of sins.

2. The Exaltation of Jesus (verse 31).

Jesus' exaltation is summarized with the significant titles, Prince and Savior. These linked Him with a mission and destiny that far ·exceeded a mere tribal or national existence. It was something that affected the whole world.

3. The Gift of the Holy Spirit (verse 32).

The Holy Spirit is given to them that obey Him. What obedience is this? It is the obedience of a will surrendered to the Savior and committed to live for Him. This refers to the experience of redemption and the baptism of the Holy Spirit, at which time the believer receives the gift of the Spirit.

The reaction of the members of the Sanhedrin to this summary of the new message was one of indignation and reprisal. It was proposed that these Christians be put to death. But in their midst sat a distinguished scholar and leader, Gamaliel. He cautioned patience and consideration, and when he summed up his advice it was one of waiting and seeing. It was the policy of opportunism. Instead of coming out with forthright support for the new message and justification of the Messiah, Gamaliel, wishing to save his place and prestige, advised caution. Gamaliel prevailed and after the traditional flogging of the apostles, they were released to return to the temple and their witnessing, which consisted of teaching and evangelizing (verse 42).

VI. A NEW NAME. "And they departed from the presence of the council, rejoicing that they were counted worthy to suffer shame for his name" (Acts 5:41).

Here is a significant development in the new community. For the first time Christians suffer for the name of Christ. Before they had suffered because of their acts of preaching and deeds of wonder. Now their suffering is associated with "the name."

The actual attachment of the name "Christian" upon the members of this new society was a later development at Antioch, but it began in these circumstances at Jerusalem when the apostles were persecuted for their association with the Messiah.

All of this adds up to —

VII. A NEW WAY OF LIFE

Christianity became identified with a characteristic expression. It was called "the way" (Acts 22:4). Thus "the name" and "the way" were identifying marks of the new movement which was shaking the world to its foundations. Men believed on "the name" and walked in "the way." This was the entrance into and the experience of Christianity. It was something unique and exclusive. It was not a name like other names or a way like other ways. None were just as good as these. This was it. Here was the ultimate and the absolute.

16

THE CHURCH AT WORK

Acts 6:1-8

The church girds itself for work.

We have seen the waiting church in the one hundred and twenty disciples who tarried in Jerusalem for the advent of the Holy Spirit. We have beheld the worshipping church in the increased number of disciples who gathered in the temple portico for daily worship and in the various disciples' homes for prayer. Now we are about to see the working church as it prepares itself to work through organizational structure. It is to be noted that to be able to work requires waiting and worshipping; but it also requires organization.

The first evidence of organizational structure in the church is in Chapter One where the first church election is recorded at which the eleven apostles chose a twelfth apostle. This election was participated in only by the eleven and not by any of the disciples. This now changes and the choice of the next order of Christian servants is made by the disciples themselves. But it should be noticed that the need for these new officers and the decision to hold the democratic election was made by the twelve apostles. They then proceeded to call the church together, set forth the qualifications for the officers and then confirmed their election. The apostles finally ordained those whom the disciples had chosen.

This is the beginning of the democratic process in the church. The apostles might easily have maintained a tight knit, hard core hierarchical system. In this manner we have moved out of the theocratic system into a democratic system in the management of spiritual affairs. The theocratic system was under the Jewish order and the democratic system is under the new Christian order. There were and are strengths and weaknesses in both, depending upon the human element involved in both; but there is no justification whatever for the subsequent development of the hierarchical system which came later on during the Dark Ages. This has created a monstrous religious monopoly resting in a few which has no reasonable nor scriptural resemblance to the original composition of the church as we are presently seeing take shape in the events of the Book of Acts.

Let us recapitulate the situation as it has developed. We began with the Olivet command of Jesus to the disciples to "Go into all the world and preach the Gospel to every creature." This command to "go" was followed by another to "tarry." It involved one hundred and twenty disciples (including the eleven, Mary the bereaved mother of Jesus, our Lord's brethren and others) to wait for an enduement of power by the Holy Spirit as their preparation for their world-mission of evangelism. When this occurred at Pentecost it resulted in an immediate addition of three thousand to the original one hundred and twenty. Then, one day when Peter and John visited the temple, they were accosted by a cripple who begged alms of them and seeing his opportunity Peter said, "Silver and gold have I none but such as I have give I thee; in the name of Jesus Christ of Nazareth rise up and walk." The miracle of this man's healing was identified with "the name." This name was to be involved forever in the great social, religious and political events which would transpire from this point onward. In fact, Christianity was to be identified with this "name" and was to be known as "the way." After this healing took place with the resultant preaching of Christ, crucified and risen, a great excitement broke out among the citizens of Jerusalem, resulting in the imprisonment of Peter and John. With so many people adhering to the new faith a great many changes and uprootings were taking place. It caused hardship, economic reprisal, loss of employment and so forth. In order to meet the economic emergency Christians pooled their resources and shared commonly.

At this point in the record it appears that a considerable interval of time elapsed between what is recorded in Chapter Five and what is recorded in Chapter Six. It seems that it had become the custom to have a daily distribution of food, especially to widows. It also seems that there had now come into the church a large number of Greek or Hellenistic converts to the Christian faith. (Up to this time the converts were largely from the Jews). With this influx of converts a social problem developed. It centered in the care of the widows. It appears that the Hellenists complained that the Hebrew Christian widows were being given preferential treatment.

It was out of a social crisis of this nature that the need for the next order of Christian workers developed. Because of this need the election of the first deacons took place. It should be pointed out that these men were not at this time called deacons. The noun "deacon" is not used in this account and is not found at all in Acts. But it does use the verb "diakoneo" which means to wait on, serve, or minister. This would seem to indicate a ministry more particularly than an office, an obligation more than an honor. The fact that the name of the office does not appear at the time of the inception of the office shows that more stress was laid upon its duties rather than its titles. Our danger is to lay more stress upon its titles than its duties. Later on the title came into common usage as we observe in Phil. 1:1 and I Tim. 3.

At first the duties of deacons were divided between a ministry to the apostles and a ministry to the people. They were to relieve the apostles of all distraction from their duties of prayer and ministering God's Word. They were also to look after the temporal needs of those whose faith had put them in need.

Somewhere during the years we have lost this idea and incentive of service. This is not only true of deacons, but it is true of Christians in general. We do not want to serve as teachers and workers in the Sunday school, and so we are constantly faced with a personnel shortage. We do not want to serve in the Vacation Bible School, and so our mission to boys and girls is limited. We do not want to serve in visitation, and so our outreach into the community is limited. We do not want to serve as witnesses, and so we watch communists outgain Christians in the conquest of the world. We do not want to serve—period, and so the greatest, most necessary work in the world languishes and we become spiritually opulent, obese and flabby.

Perhaps the idea of service and courtesy can be linked together in the story of a man riding in a crowded bus. He gave his seat to a woman and she was so overcome by his act that she fainted. When she came to and saw he was still there she thanked him for his thoughtfulness and he fainted. Perhaps if volunteers for service came forward without pleading and pressure there would be some fainting out of surprise.

At the beginning these deacons had three simple but important qualifications:

1. An Honorable Reputation. This was important, not only at the beginning of the church when the prestige of Christians counted for so much, but it is just as important now. An honorable reputation is a "must" for Christian service.

2. A Sound Judgment. These men were administrators. They must divide and decide. They must admonish and counsel. They must have good, sound judgment. In our opinion, knowing what faces deacons, this is more important than their ability to pray in public.

3. Full of the Holy Spirit. This stems from the Pentecostal experience but it might indicate that not all were so filled. It might also point up the fact that many disciples were added since Pentecost and these too must have the spiritual qualification of the indwelling Holy Spirit. But whatever it meant it apparently did not mean that some special gift of the Holy Spirit was to accompany their placement in this office.

Still another stipulation was made which must have been temporary and not arbitrary or binding in the future. It related to the number of deacons which was to be seven. It was by this number that they were known for they were called "the seven" in distinction to "the twelve." Thus there were seven deacons and twelve apostles. The deacons were elected by the disciples and the apostles were called by the Lord Jesus in person and in the flesh. And because of the special nature of the calling and qualifications of the apostles, such as being witnesses to the resurrection, it was a diminishing office which lasts only with this first generation of apostles. But the office of deacons and later presbyters goes on throughout the continuing church age.

The result was the choosing of "the seven" by democratic process and there is listed the names of these seven men who were chosen at this church election. These men are as follows: ". . . Stephen, a man full of faith and of the Holy Ghost, and Philip, and Prochorus, and Nicanor, and Timon, and Parmenas, and Nicolas, a proselyte of Antioch" (Acts 6:5).

What seems remarkable is that they were all Greeks, that is, Hellenists. This could mean that they were Jewish converts with Greek names, or pure Hellenists or, as in the case of the seventh man, a Greek proselyte to the Jewish faith who had now become a Christian. Of these seven two were to become men of distinction in the church. Stephen was to become the great defender of the faith, even with his life as the first martyr. Philip was to become the great extender of the faith, through his evangelistic ministry. The rest? Well, they are just names, unheard of again in scripture, and like most of us without fame or outstanding accomplishment. But this does not mean that they, or we, need be without distinction for fame is not the greatest thing to be achieved. The greatest distinction is faithfulness.

Since Stephen and Philip stand out from the rest of the seven, could it not be because of their personal faithfulness in two things? First, the defense and preservation of the faith. Second, the proclamation and extension of the faith. This could also reveal that while the office of deacon was originally created to meet a social crisis, it was continued to meet the spiritual crises that the church later faced and would meet through the defense and extension of the faith by these same deacons.

When the people or "the multitude of the disciples," had made their choice of "the seven" by the democratic process of an election, the seven deacons were then presented to "the twelve" for their approbation or confirmation, who then proceeded to ordain them by prayer and the imposition of hands.

There is a tendency of church historians to read too much into this ordination, as if the imposition of hands by the apostles conveyed a special gift of the Holy Spirit. They had already been chosen because they were full of the Holy Spirit, and how much fuller can full be than full? Their ordination served to emphasize the importance of their office and of the qualifications of that office and the need for dependance upon God for the fulfillment of its duties and obligations.

This is the story of the church girding itself for work, for if the choice of "the seven" means anything it means service, work and action. This election in the church and any subsequent election of anyone to any office is not the end — it is the beginning. It is the beginning of service.

The search for identity goes on among all of us. We want to feel that we have arrived at a place of usefulness. There is no place where this can be more true than when one sets out to do God's will through the instrumentality of the church.

17

HOW LONG IS A FULL LIFE?
Acts 6:8 — 7:53

Six years of time have passed between Pentecost and the martyrdom of Stephen. During these six years a great many things have transpired including the gradual formulation of the Christian message; the establishment of the Christian church and its growth into "a multitude of the disciples"; the election of the first officers.

The story of Christianity is the story of people. It is not a glorified list of precepts and principles isolated from life and experience, but rather life and experience based upon precepts and principles. This chapter of the story of Christianity could be titled, "How Long Is a Full Life?" This is the story of Stephen, who suddenly appears on the scene as the first of a list of names of men who were elected by the disciples as the first deacons of the Church at Jerusalem. The reason this title fits the story of Stephen is because Stephen's career is very brief. It is cut short almost as soon as it is begun, and what is to be accomplished has to be done in a very brief span of time.

Life is not a matter of years. Some have lived long lives in terms of years, but it could never be said of them that they lived full lives. Life is actually a matter of accomplishment, achievement, influence and fruitfulness.

The science of geriatrics is aiding us to live long lives by reducing the mortality rate at birth and producing disease killing drugs. While it can add years to life it is unable to add life to years. This is the function of Christianity, and this is among the lessons to be learned by the life and death of Stephen.

In order to proceed in an orderly manner, let us first say that what you have in this text is the account of Stephen's work, trial, defense, martyrdom and the over-all results.

I. STEPHEN'S HISTORY

It is always interesting to know something about a man's history. In Stephen's case we must say that there is very little known about his personal history and there is nothing known about him beyond what we find here.

Stephen was a Hellenist. This means that he was a Greek-speaking Jew, who had come to Jerusalem from some other part of the empire. Proof of this is in the fact that when he came to Jerusalem he attended a certain synagogue. It was the synagogue where the Libertines, Cyrenians and Alexandrians worshipped. These were foreign Jews who had formed a congregation of their own, and because Stephen was a Hellenist, it was natural and proper that he too should gravitate to this particular place.

We notice that although Stephen was a follower of "the way" and a believer in "the name," and thus a Christian and also a deacon, and thus an official in the Christian Church in Jerusalem, he is found in a Jewish synagogue. But he was far from compromising his faith or trying to be on both sides at the same time. While it appears that these Christians still continued worshipping in the temple after they became Christians, and commonly frequented the synagogues, it was not a compromise of their faith. Stephen went to this Hellenist synagogue to debate with these foreign speaking Jews about the Christian faith.

Stephen worked through the regular and accepted channels of the current religious organizations at Jerusalem. What Stephen did was to march right into the midst of Hellenist Judaism and debate the case for the new Christian sect. And what better thing could he have done than to have gone into this synagogue and proclaimed the word of Christ. But the purist would have condemned him for not totally, completely and unequivocally separating himself from the synagogue of which, no doubt, he was even now a member.

Compromise does not come because we do our service in an organizational framework that may hold in it people who do not believe exactly as we do, but rather when we depart from the faith either by dilution or denial.

It has always, and never with any exception, been the history of church movements that when people have separated from the main stream of a church body because of doctrinal defection, that in course of time those who have thus separated are themselves faced with doctrinal defection in their separated ranks; and then their only remedy is another separation. So separation is an endless chain that really never settles any doctrinal dispute.

It is significant that Jesus did not separate from the synagogue, the apostles did not separate, Stephen did not separate and neither did the Apostle Paul. And there is not a single precedent, nor a single directive, to indicate that this is the remedy for doctrinal defection. And when later Paul wrote to the Church at Corinth and said, "Wherefore come out from among them and be ye separate . . . " he was talking about Christians coming out from paganism and not Christians separating from Christians.

II. STEPHEN'S CHARACTER

Stephen faced the supreme test of his life when he had to defend his faith with his life. In the last analysis this was a test of character.

He is described as a man full of four things:

1. Full of the Holy Spirit (6:5). This fullness of the Holy Spirit was the direct result of Pentecost, even though Stephen was not one of the original one hundred and twenty who experienced Pentecost. This is so because every subsequent member of the Body of Christ is baptized with the Holy Spirit upon his admission to that body. Whether the believer's experience bears out that filling or not is entirely dependent upon that believer's yielded life to the Holy Spirit's possession.

2. Full of Faith (6:5). This was faith both as an item of belief in the things commonly believed by the disciples, and as a force and power in life.

3. Full of Power (6:8). This was displayed in "the wonders and miracles" which Stephen wrought among the common people; and which brought again into focus the divine nature of the Christian community which was being established in the world.

4. Full of Wisdom (6:3). There is no evidence that this was other than native wisdom with which Stephen was endowed; plus the fact that Stephen, unlike the Twelve, was a man of learning. It is undoubtedly true that Stephen's native wisdom was sanctified by the Holy Spirit and used by Him.

The result of this quadruple fullness was the overwhelming force of his disputations in the Hellenistic synagogue. This was revealed in the fact that these Hellenized Jews "were not able to resist the wisdom and the spirit by which he spake." So if you cannot resist wisdom, logic and truth the thing to do is to resort to force and coercion. The history of Christianity has been this very thing. And let it be remembered that while Christians have suffered much at the hands of pagans, the cause of Christ has suffered more at the hands of a pseudo-Christianity which has come to power in a vast ecclesiastical system which sustains itself by these very elements of force and coercion. Only the unjust live by the use of force, fear, coercion, threat, reprisal, brainwashing and persecution. Wherever you find that kind of a system parading as Christian, you know it is false because its weapons are not the weapons of true Christianity which are not carnal; for Paul said to the Corinthians, "For though we walk in the flesh, we do not war after the flesh: (For the weapons of our warfare are not carnal, but mighty through God to the pulling down of strong holds;)" (II Cor. 10:3, 4).

III. STEPHEN'S LIFE

Stephen's life is largely the story of his death for he is remembered as the first Christian martyr.

1. His Defense of the Faith. The important thing about Stephen's defense of the faith is not that it is the longest speech in the Book of Acts (or the New Testament for that matter);

but that it is here as a fact of Stephen's faith and Christianity's foundation. Stephen spoke up and spoke out. Speaking as witnesses to the faith and defenders of the faith, was the outstanding characteristic of the first generation of Christians. It is not of our generation.

It would be quite impossible to consider, in this brief time, all the items of Stephen's defense; but this can be summed up in a single sentence: Christianity is God's way to a new life based upon His sovereign revelation in both history and scripture.

You will notice that the first word Stephen used, after his salutation to the Sanhedrin, is "God." He speaks of "The God of glory," and links this God with Jewish history in Abraham. Here is a fact essential to Christianity. The starting point of salvation is not man's search for God, but God's search for man. This search for God is documented from the very beginning of the Jewish Scriptures; and now has its full and complete revelation in the New Testament and the birth, death and resurrection of Jesus Christ as Savior and Lord.

2. His Life and Death. Stephen's life and death mark the transition of Christianity from its Jewish beginnings to embrace Gentiles. This is the turning point of the Book of Acts. It swings outward to face the whole Gentile world and remains no longer an appeal to Jews alone. What Stephen is declaring to be true is that Christianity is the fulfillment of prophecy and the ultimate and final goal of Hebrew history. Now that it has come it belongs to Gentile as well as Jew, and so Paul would later write to Rome and say, "I am not ashamed . . . to the Jew first and also to the Greek."

Anyone who, for propaganda reasons, still maintains that the gospel is to "the Jew first" has forgotten that there is now no preferred national position for salvation. This happened when Stephen pointed out in his defense that the church no longer remained exclusively Jewish. Paul, at the close of Acts, said, "Be it known therefore unto you, that the salvation of God is sent unto the Gentiles, and that they will hear it" (Acts 28:28).

3. Stephen's Short Life. The test of any life is what it

accomplishes; not what it consumes or how long it lives. We do not know how old Stephen was but we assume he was young. At any rate, we know that no matter what his life span was, his service span was very short, and in that short time his heroic act of defending the faith achieved a major result. It resulted in turning Christianity from the provincialism of Judaism to the revolutionary aspects of a world-wide faith.

Just how long is a full life? Length of life so far as its Christian values are concerned depends upon several qualities.

1st. It depends upon faith. This is a fact demonstrated by the people whose record is found in the eleventh chapter of Hebrews. Their faith gave their lives significance, breadth, depth and length.

2nd. It depends upon spirituality. Anything associated with the fleshly aspect of life is definitely dated to this world. It begins and ends with this world. But what is related to the spirit lengthens life into expanding proportions.

3rd. It depends upon eternal life. What difference does the shortening of life on earth make when one is destined to live forever? It is not the years here that count, but what we do with those years.

4th. It depends upon service. One cannot make a significant contribution in a life span apart from service.

5th. It depends upon witness. He who multiplies himself through his witness is doing what Stephen did. And this act of witness is the surest way to escape anonymity, oblivion and failure.

How long is a full life? It is as long as the faith that saves you. It is as long as the service that occupies you. It is as long as the witness that multiplies you. It is as long as the eternity that extends you.

The fullness of Stephen's life is revealed in the way he died, as well as the way he lived. He died with the stones and rocks of an angry mob raining upon his body, crushing and mangling it beyond recognition. But in dying he lives again. In dying he vindicated his own faith for those stones did not end Stephen's life; they only transferred his sphere of influence from this to the other world. And in making the transition Stephen was vindicated by a vision vouchsafed to him in his dying moments. He saw the Son of God at the Father's right hand. This was the first appearance of Jesus in His divine and exalted glory after the ascension. It confirmed the experience of the three disciples on the Mount of Transfiguration. It anticipated the redeeming experience of Paul on the Road to Damascus. It was climaxed by the apocalyptic experience of John who beheld the glory of the Son of God in the concluding event of the ages.

18

THE CHRISTIAN LOOKS AT DEATH

Acts 7:54-60

The sequence of the story of Life in Action in Acts brings us to the death of Stephen. Apart from the deaths of Ananias and Sapphira, which were certainly not under any normal circumstances, the death of Stephen is the first recorded death in Acts and therefore another one of the "firsts" and something of great significance to us. We are not to suppose that in these six or more years of the church's existence there were not any other deaths. There undoubtedly were many but this is the first one that is recorded. It is for this reason that we take a look at death.

Although Stephen's death is a death of violence in which he suffered the first martyrdom, and to that extent unusual in itself; it gives us occasion to look at the whole problem of death as we face it from time to time in the death of our friends and loved ones, and as we must face it in our own experience.

Has Christianity an answer to the problem of death?

Christianity tells us about something behind us in the record of the redemptive events of the Bible. It tells us about something among us, in the ability of its precepts and power to meet daily life as an experience. It also tells us about something beyond us in the realm of events including death and what follows as to process and place.

Life is like a story with a beginning and ending. "That woman gets more out of a mystery novel than anyone I know," said the library clerk. "How come?" "Well, she starts the story in the middle, so she not only wonders how it came out, but how it began."

How does the story turn out? That is always enticing and fascinating, and we are all intrigued to know how it comes out. When it is fiction it is of little consequence, but when it is the life story it is of the greatest importance. While you and I have life and can do something about it, let there be the greatest concern and attention to its conclusion.

We who live in this century do not expect that the end of the story for us will be what it was for Stephen — violence. He paid for his faith with his life, in an era of persecution. He died with the rocks raining upon his body to batter it and mangle it into a mass of bruises and breaks. In all probability ours will not be such a death as his, although the end of this age may come more quickly than we suppose, and if that happens the return of violence may come again. Let us not forget Europe and the violence of the recent years of the last war.

What does the Christian see when he looks at death? He sees two things — a process and a place.

I. THE PROCESS

From a physiological standpoint death is the ending of life, through the breakdown of the living cells of the body. Given a means to sustain the cells we could have the means of physical immortality. As scientists now understand it there is no reason, from the standpoint of the composition of the body, why there should be death at all. This throws us back upon the revelation of scripture where death is introduced as a spiritual condition which ultimately brings death physically, spiritually and eternally.

The Bible uses a number of different expressions to describe the process of death. In the case of Stephen the expression is that he "fell asleep." This is the same expression that Paul uses in I Corinthians 15 where you have his great chapter on the resurrection of the body. Those who are to experience the resurrection are those who have "fallen asleep." Thus the process of death is the process of sleep. What is sleep? A period of suspended animation in which the individual has lost consciousness, but in which life itself is not ended or concluded. It is momentarily suspended, while the body is in a state of repose. It is also a time of regeneration when the body is recharging itself with energy. But in all these things it is not the final state. Sleep is temporary. There is the expectation of awakening when life goes on refreshed, regenerated and revitalized. If you take all these things suggested in sleep you have the symbolism or similitude of death, as the Bible presents it.

Another expression is "depart." This is found in Philippians 1:23 where Paul is speaking of his own personal desire. " . . . having a desire to depart. . . . " In this case, departure is not simply an exit or a leave-taking or a simple going away. It is a nautical term implying the lifting of an anchor and the sailing of a vessel. But in its departure it is going on a scheduled voyage, with a definite sailing course in mind that brings it ultimately into another port so that departing implies an arriving. This is what death is for the Christian. He departs, not into nothingness or to nowhere. He departs as does a sea vessel, to leave one port with the scheduled intention of going to another port. The vessel that passes out of sight for some on one shore comes into sight for others on another shore. There are those who shout "Bon Voyage" and "Goodby." There are others who shout "Welcome" and "Home at last." This is death for the Christian.

Another expression is, "absent." It is found in II Corinthians 5:8 where Paul says, " . . . to be absent from the body, and to be present with the Lord." It speaks, as you notice, of absence "from the body." There is a leave-taking when the body is laid aside and left behind. Life is not left in the body, but the processes of dissolution take hold of it and reduce it to its original anonymous and impersonal elements. The person who inhabited it, and lived in it, and made it his vehicle of expression, goes on to live a larger, fuller and better life in another bodily manifestation called a spiritual body. Paul expresses it to the Philippian Christians in this way: "Who shall change our vile body, that it may be fashioned like unto his glorious body . . . " (Phil. 3.21).

Another expression is, "put off this tabernacle." This is Peter's expression in II Peter 1:14. A tabernacle is a tent. A tent is a temporary dwelling place for those who are living under emergency conditions or else are on a journey. It is something the sojourner lays aside and leaves; and in the case of a Christian the tabernacle is his body which is put aside. The body is left to dissolve. The person who leaves it goes on to live under more permanent circumstances. Paul has an expression quite similar to this for he speaks of it in this way: "For we know that if our earthly house of this tabernacle were dissolved, we have a building of God, an house not made with hands, eternal in the heavens" (II Cor. 5:1).

In the process of death something happens to the body which is two-fold. First, it is cast off and laid aside to experience dissolution. Second, it is held within the embrace of death against a day of resurrection when it is to experience another change. This change will be resurrection. It will be a resurrection patterned after and pledged by that of our Lord, and is described in I Corinthians 15:42-44; 51-54.

There is a story told of a workman of the great chemist Faraday. One day he knocked a little silver cup into a jar of acid. It disappeared by being eaten up by the acid, and could not be found. The question came up whether it could ever be recovered. One said he could find it; another said it was held in solution and there was no possibility of restoring it. The great chemist came in and put some chemicals into the jar, and in a moment every particle of silver was precipitated at the bottom. He lifted it out a shapeless mass, sent it to a silversmith, and the cup was restored. If Faraday could precipitate that silver and recover his cup, God can restore our sleeping and scattered dust.

But the process of death which both dissolves and resurrects the body does something with the spiritual or immaterial part of man. This involves his consciousness and personality. This part of man is released by death to the presence of Christ, and following the resurrection, to an expanded and extended life in its eternal and heavenly phase.

This brings up the question, "What happens to time in eternity?" There will be no such thing as time in eternity. Time accounts for the change and the decay that takes place while we are in this present phase of life.

It appears, from recently acquired scientific knowledge, that aging stops when one gets out of this time-related earth and its orbital space. If Einstein's theory of time is true, man could cover immense distances in space without aging nearly as fast as his counterpart on earth. "According to Einstein's theory of relativity, time is a dimension and affected in the same way as length or width or depth. Time and the other dimensions, according to Einstein, would contract as a space ship approached the speed of light, one-hundred eighty-six thousand miles a second." Time would literally "slow down" for the person traveling in space at extremely high, but by no means improbable, speeds. As a result, a person traveling, for instance, at two-thirds the speed of light, would find upon his return from a trip to the star Sirius, brightest in the heavens, that the journey had taken him five or six years less than his eighteen year absence as recorded on earth. The savings in time would be even more significant if the destination was Arcturus, a star that is thirty light years from earth. If the voyager traveled at speeds approaching that of light, the trip would take only ten years because of time contraction, while sixty years would have gone by on earth. This is the basis for the contention that a man could possibly travel in space and return to earth only to find most of his contemporaries dead, or at least greatly aged in comparison to himself.

Here is something approaching the meaning of eternal life.

II. The Place

Death for the Christian involves a place as well as a process. It could not be less than this for if the process changes us, then there must be a place in which to experience the blessings and benefits of the change.

Death as a place is described in the Bible under a number of figures.

Death is described in terms of a "new heavens and new earth." This is found in II Peter 3:13, "Nevertheless we, according to his promise, look for new heavens and a new earth, wherein dwelleth righteousness." Here is man's new and eternal environment, which is the end of the redemptive process involving three new things; a new man, a new body and a new world.

Death is described in terms of "a city." It is the city "whose builder and maker is God." It is the city described in the 21st and 22nd chapters of Revelation.

Death is described in terms of a "house." Jesus spoke of it in this language in John 14, "In my Father's house are many mansions. . . . " There is nothing more definite, more familiar and more common to an earth dweller than "home." This is what heaven will be to us. A Frenchman, Jean-Paul Sartre, says death is "a long day's journey into nothingness." But we prefer to believe Jesus who came from heaven and went back there and said it was like home. Dvorak speaks of it in his immortal song, "Going Home"; and the negro spiritual, "Swing Low Sweet Chariot," reflects the same spirit when it says, "coming for to carry me home." This was the spirit of Tennyson's "Crossing the Bar" when he said —

> "But such a tide as moving seems asleep,
>   Too full for sound or foam,
> When that which drew from out the boundless deep
>   Turns again home."

What are we going to do when we get "home"? Some people would like to sleep for a few thousand years because they are so tired. Some would like to listen to heaven's Hi-Fi and celestial stereophonic music. Some are anxious to know what we are going to eat and what the fruit of the Tree of Life tastes like. But it is to be doubted that anyone wants to go to work.

At the funeral of a friend who had taught school for years, the minister had many fine things to say about her character, ending on the theme that she is probably carrying on her work in heaven. The teacher sitting next to me leaned over and snorted into my ear, "Good heavens, don't we ever get to quit?"

These are some of the things the Christian sees when he takes a look at death. Somewhere in life must come the concern of a great question, "Am I a Christian?" Always there must be the prayer of pilgrimage, "Lord, I'm nearing home. Help me to be homelike." And constantly there must be the remembrance of faithfulness in life's labor, "Therefore my beloved brethren, be ye steadfast, unmoveable, always abounding in the work of the Lord" (I Cor. 15:58).

19

THE EXPULSIVE POWER
OF A GREAT COMPUSION
Acts 8:1-14

By the time we have arrived at the sixth year of the church's existence, we have seen it grow from one hundred and twenty disciples to an indeterminate group of people, consisting of upwards of eight thousand plus others who are not identified numerically. But a crisis has arisen, for opposition has solidified against this Christian sect. There have been imprisonments, legal threats, and commands to desist preaching in the name of Jesus. Now we have the incident involving Stephen. He was killed. He paid for his faith with his life. Is this to be the pattern of reward for becoming a Christian?

It appears to be a basic lesson in Stephen's case that progress is impossible without sacrifice. It took Stephen's life to open the door to the Gentiles. It took Stephen's life to expand the church from its Jerusalem center to all of Asia Minor and the world; for it was upon this event that persecution came to Jerusalem and the disciples were scattered abroad. This was the beginning of the rapid expansion of the church, but it began with the death of Stephen, establishing the church-long precedent that "the blood of the martyrs is the seed of the church."

Out of this fact of martyrdom grew a great fallacy. As the church grew and martyrs increased, it became common to equate salvation with martyrdom and to put salvation on a pay-as-you-go basis, so that works instead of faith became the basis of salvation. Let us remember this distinction. The cost of salvation is God's, while the cost of discipleship is ours. Stephen's salvation was not established by his martyrdom; that was the cost of his discipleship. He was saved solely and only by reason of his faith in Jesus Christ.

Our chief interest now is to discover the reason for the rapid advance of the Christian community, which up to approximately six years had increased in excess of eight thousand one hundred and twenty Christians. The increase of the Christian community, it has been established, was given a tremendous acceleration by the death of Stephen and the resultant "great persecution" against the other Christians at Jerusalem, so that they were "scattered abroad . . . and went everywhere preaching the word." This means one thing — communication. The church was able to grow with such great acceleration because the message was so rapidly communicated. How was it communicated? It was communicated by the common disciple, who took the message and carried it to places and people where it had not been known before. This was the reason for the great strides and advances in the first centuries of the church.

Growth was accelerated by persecution for when persecution ceased, after the first three hundred years, the church fell into the lap of luxury through a church-state union, and in its corruption lost its zeal and spirituality, and lapsed into the kind of progress that comes from organizational machinery rather than from organic life and vigor. From that time on the temptation was to do church work rather than the work of the church. It was also a fact that the church became occupied with organizational activity rather than being occupied with the Lord of the church. "Few things are more pathetic than the sight of one who has become so busy with the Lord's work that he has neglected the Lord himself." *

What is the work of the church? Review for a moment the organizational structure which had thus far developed in the church. You had the over-all body of "the disciples." Then within this over-all body you had, from the very beginning, a

* J. W. Chapman

group known as "the twelve." These were the apostles. Then you had a group known as "the seven" who comprised the first deacons. Divided between these two groups were the spiritual and material responsibilities of the church. Both the apostles and the deacons, however, were engaged in a common activity. They witnessed to the gospel in synogogues, in the temple, in home services and in market places.

Now a change takes place and it is a profound and important change. When the great persecution broke out against the Christians in Jerusalem, it resulted in the disciples, that is, those belonging to the over-all body of believers or the common Christians, being scattered throughout Judea and Samaria. Then the text adds, "except the apostles." The disciples fled from Jerusalem, but the apostles remained behind to hold the main base of operation intact.

The function of the apostles was not the function of a hierarchy. To begin with, there was no new body of truth to define or defend for the New Testament did not come into existence as a recognized canon of scripture until the Fourth Century. There was no existing body of tradition to act as precedent for their actions. The apostles were chosen because of their immediate association with Jesus, particularly His death and resurrection. And in the light of these events, and Jesus' authorizations and commands, they were to guide the burgeoning church and keep it on an even keel.

The function of the deacons had already been established. Beyond their specific function to relieve the apostles of social responsibilities, so they could give themselves to prayer and the ministry of the Word, two of the deacons distinguished themselves as evangelists. One was Stephen and the other was Philip. Stephen became the defender of the faith at the Jerusalem center. Philip became the evangelist-at-large, preaching in many cities of Asia Minor.

But now the great change comes and the common rank-and-file disciple becomes the purveyor, the communicator and the evangelist. It is he who goes "everywhere." And when he goes everywhere it is to preach the Word. This was one of the strategic moments of the church. It established a precedent to which the church must return if it, humanly speaking, is to survive as a force in the world. At least it must return to this precedent if it is to meet the tremendous challenge of our modern world. It was at the apogee of the Roman Empire, when it threatened to engulf and control the destinies of the world for generations to come, that the church was born and that the disciples fanned out to infiltrate every part of the empire and turn Romans into Christians.

We have reached another such moment. But the threat is the threat of communism occasioned by the scientific technology of our age which is opening a new age to the primitive peoples of the world. These people, so lately living as savages, are unable to cope with the spiritual and moral problems with which they are so suddenly faced and communism is threatening to engulf them.

Industrial corporations in Europe and the United States are spending millions of dollars in a crash effort to win control of the vast pools of raw materials and the vast markets of people being challenged by our technological revolution. Communism is engaged in an all-out effort to win these same markets and control these same pools of raw materials. They are flooding Asia and Africa with literature. Their agents are infiltrating these countries which have so lately been released from colonialism. The present prospect of this two-pronged invasion of Asia and Africa is that they may engulf the schools, hospitals, mission stations and institutions established by the Livingstones, Carys, Taylors, Judsons and their successors. The reason for this dire prospect is that while the communists are proceeding at revolutionary pace, and while commercial interests are developing crash programs, the church is moving at a feeble pace. While communists are running we are walking.

The church has allowed itself to be maneuvered into an untenable position as the result of years of ecclesiastical encrustation. It has lost its "first love." It has lost its doctrinal purity.

It has inherited forms that bind it into immobility. It has acquired attitudes of professionalism that limit its accomplishments both as to space and time. Billy Graham is authority for the statement that "the communists have become the greatest missionaries and evangelists in history, having reached the whole world in forty years."

Statistics of church finances released by the National Council of Churches for 1957 reveal the pace at which the church moves to fulfill its responsibilities to this generation. Thirty-seven million church members belonging to fifty-two Protestant church bodies, gave a total of eighty-four million dollars to foreign missions. This means very little until you look at it on a per capita basis. On this basis we discover that the per capita giving to foreign missions was two dollars and forty-five cents. Let these figures speak for themselves, but let us look at our predicament. Sheer survival as nations is at stake. The engulfment of the world by communism is the threat. The winning of our generation to Christ is our obligation. But it will never be done the way we are going at it. We have to return to the pattern of communication originally established at the beginning of the church age, which accounted for its conquest of the Roman world, and caused its rapid growth and great influence.

This pattern involves three things:

1. The Individual Disciple.

Here you have the New Testament concept of the priesthood of the believers. The old priesthood was now completely obsolete. It was abolished and discarded, and in its place stood the individual disciple with free and ready access to God.

2. The Individual Disciple Goes on a Mission.

It says here that he "went everywhere." Where is everywhere? The primary meaning is Jerusalem, Judea and Samaria, but the ultimate meaning is the uttermost parts of the earth. Here is the beginning of the carrying out of the Great Commission of Jesus, who sent His disciples on a world wide mission. God's instrument in this mission was the individual disciple. It was not to be confined to a few apostles or professionals. His mission was one of propagation and not merely propaganda. They had life to distribute to the world and life is communicated by propagation.

3. The Individual Disciple is on a Mission Preaching the Gospel.

This preaching is described here as the preaching of the Word. They did not actually have a written word. There was no established message or body of truth up to this time. What you actually have is the preaching of Christ, the declaration of the mighty acts of God in the crucifixion and resurrection.

Christianity is essentially a new way of life and throughout these early ages it was constantly described as "the way." And a saving faith was described as believing in "the name." So now "preaching the word" is a recital of the great events surrounding the Messiah and a calling upon men to repent and be saved.

This reveals the missionary nature of Christianity. It is essentially a missionary faith and in this sense unlike Judaism. It is to go out and present the ultimate, the ultimate in truth and the ultimate in life. It is to give men a new hope for this world and the next. It has heaven to talk about as well as earth. It has something to be saved to as well as from. It is God's authoritative message for this age. It is something finished and final. It is the *summum bonum* of truth.

But the message is of little consequence without the method for unless it is communicated to all the world by each generation reaching its own members, it cannot accomplish its purpose.

The church today is faced with these two things—the message and the method. Where are the men?

20

THE FIRST MISSIONARY

Acts 8:5-13

This portion of Acts records another of the many "firsts" to occur in the establishment of the church. Here is found the first missionary, and the first missionary effort of the church, when Philip undertook to go to Samaria and preach Christ.

There unfolds from this initial missionary enterprise one of the greatest achievements in the annals of human enterprise; for stemming from Philip's missionary journey to Samaria is the great missionary movement of the church, which has accounted for the winning of countless multitudes to become followers of Jesus Christ. As other great movements, it had a humble, simple and insignificant beginning. There was no fanfare, no publicity and no commotion. It states simply that "Philip went down to the city of Samaria and preached Christ unto them." Here is a completely spontaneous action. It was not ordered by some apostolic hierarchy, under whose direction Philip went on a preaching mission. Instead it was produced by two factors: first, the general persecution of Christians which scattered the disciples everywhere; second, the leadership and direction of the Holy Spirit.

Perhaps what should be said about this incident can be brought out by a series of questions.

I. WHO WAS THE FIRST MISSIONARY?

He was Philip. Philip, as you will recall, was one of the seven deacons chosen to be almoners, or ministers of relief, because of the recurrent crises of persecution which produced need among the disciples. However, his duties as a dispenser of relief were subservient to a higher service, the spiritual. And he became a witness to and a preacher of Christ.

One of the things that anyone must notice about Philip is the fact that he had no training for his missionary work. This was not unusual because there were no training facilities in existence. We do not know the length of time involved in the period between Philip's election to the diaconate and his missionary journey to Samaria, but we assume it was very brief. In this brief time there was neither facility nor opportunity to be trained for his service. Are we then to assume that this is a precedent to be followed by the church in every age? Not at all.

In the first place, we are not to assume that Philip was unequipped, even though he was untrained. We recall the fact that he was chosen "full of faith and of the Holy Ghost." Furthermore, in the election instructions which the disciples received from the apostles they were told to "look ye out among you seven men of honest report, full of the Holy Ghost and wisdom." Thus you have the equipment of the Holy Spirit, faith and wisdom.

More than this, you will also remember that when the Holy Spirit was given at Pentecost His coming was in terms of certain gifts. Those gifts are detailed in I Corinthians 12. And we are to assume that since the nine gifts of the Spirit were available since Pentecost, which had occurred six years prior to Philip's going to Samaria as a missionary, he had the advantage of these gifts. So in this sense he was not an unequipped man.

The purpose of the gifts of the Holy Spirit was to fill the vacuum that would occur between the establishment of the church and the ultimate maturity of the church when missionaries, evangelists and pastors would have the advantage of time for preparation. Perhaps the most important factor was that, while at the beginning the Holy Spirit had to work immediately and directly in the believer, later on it would be intermediately and indirectly through the written Word, which at this time had not even begun to be written. This was not to be a fact for another twenty or twenty-four years when the first portion of the New Testament would come into being under the pen of a man who, at this time, was not even a Christian.

II. WHERE DID THE FIRST MISSIONARY GO?

He went to Samaria and more specifically, "the city of Samaria," which we identify as old Samaria, or the capital which had been rebuilt by Herod the Great and called Sebaste.

But why Samaria? It was alien territory. It was inhabited by mongrel Jews who hated the Jews and would certainly hate the new Christian sect, and did. But since this action of Philip was in obedience to the leadership of the Holy Spirit it was no doubt in fulfillment of the initial missionary pattern given by Jesus when He said, "But ye shall receive power, after that the Holy Ghost is come upon you: and ye shall be witnesses unto me both in Jerusalem, and in all Judaea, and in Samaria, and unto the uttermost part of the earth" (Acts 1:8). After six years the witness had been given in Jerusalem and without a doubt it was being given in Judea, and now under the sovereign leadership of the Holy Spirit, it was to be given in Samaria.

No doubt the argument against missions, so often heard today, that there are enough heathen at home so why go to foreign countries, was originated in Jerusalem at the time Philip undertook his mission to Samaria. It is not a question of how many heathen may be at home but a question of mission. We have a mission to the whole world, and Samaria is one of the concentric circles to be reached in the missionary operation of the church. There can be no doubt that when the church is sensitive to the leadership of the Holy Spirit it will go to Judea, to Samaria, and to the uttermost part of the earth.

III. WHY DID THE FIRST MISSIONARY GO?

The answer is "to preach Christ." We ought not to try to oversimplify the answer by stopping with the simple statement given here that Philip went to Samaria "to preach Christ." You cannot reduce it to that simple a statement and say that preaching

Christ is just preaching Christ. It ultimately involves a whole range of preaching and teaching that includes theology as well. But what is intended to be conveyed here is the fact that the theme of the preaching mission of Philip, when he went to Samaria, was Christ. It was exactly what Paul meant when some years later he would write to the church at Corinth and remind them of the manner of his preaching when he first visited that city. This is what he wrote in I Corinthians 2:1 and 2: "And I, brethren, when I came to you, came not with excellency of speech or of wisdom, declaring unto you the testimony of God. For I determined not to know any thing among you, save Jesus Christ, and him crucified." After all, the fact of salvation is associated with the person of Christ. It involves a personal encounter with the Savior which requires an act of personal faith in Him.

IV. What Was the First Missionary's Message?

Preaching Christ was his theme, but his message consisted of something more. In verse 12 it says, "But when they believed Philip preaching the things concerning the kingdom of God, and the name of Jesus Christ . . . ." So here you have two things that were found in the first missionary's message, the kingdom of God and the name of Christ. This is the first time the kingdom of God is mentioned since the first chapter of Acts; but it does not mean that it is the first time it was used as the subject of preaching. It is linked here with the name of the Messiah because the Samaritans clung to the law. Philip proclaimed the fulfillment of the law in a new kingdom, dominated by the name of the Messiah, who had already come and was crucified, resurrected and ascended to the right hand of God. Here you have the proclamation of a full and complete gospel which dealt with the racial, national and provincial needs of the Samaritans. It also dealt with the personal needs of the Samaritans and all others to whom this message would be brought.

V. What Were the Credentials of the First Missionary?

Since this was a new faith and a new message and since there had been no time for the establishment of a body of people who could vouch for the authenticity of its many messengers, Philip had need of credentials. How did these people know the message was authentic? The same way Jesus' hearers knew His message was authentic. This is the record: "And the people with one accord gave heed unto those things which Philip spake, hearing and seeing the miracles which he did. For unclean spirits, crying with loud voice, came out of many that were possessed with them: and many taken with palsies, and that were lame, were healed" (Acts 8:6, 7). His message was authenticated by miracles. This was not unusual. It was true of Jesus' ministry and it was true of the apostles', and in this case of a deacon. This dispels the idea propounded by ecclesiastical opportunists that the power to work miracles was in their exclusive possession. But this was not the case as we see from Philip's experience. In Philip's case it was the credential of his mission and the authority for his message. Are we to expect miracles to continue everytime a missionary presents his message? That this is not to be the case is proved by the facts of missions. How many times does one have to present his credentials? When we send an ambassador to the Court of St. James in England he goes with written credentials. These are presented with fanfare and ceremony. But the ambassador does not have to present these credentials everytime he speaks or everytime he appears in public. He presents them once for the whole course of his ambassadorial career. And once at the beginning of the church, over a period of its early years, the credentials of the gospel were presented to authenticate the message. What was done then does not need to be repeated now.

VI. What Did the First Missionary Do with His Converts?

It says, " . . . when they believed . . . they were baptized, both men and women." When Peter preached the first Christian sermon on the Day of Pentecost he concluded by saying, "Repent and be baptized everyone of you in the name of Jesus Christ . . . " (Acts 2:38). Then it said, "Then they that gladly received his word were baptized . . . " (Acts 2:41). So you have the instruction and the response and not until you get to this point in Samaria, six years later, does it speak again of baptism. But we must assume that during all those six years all who believed were baptized. These who were now baptized were Samaritans, and belonged to a new segment of people. This points to the universality of the instruction. What this baptism consisted of is to be for later consideration, but why these Samaritans were baptized is plain. It followed their faith, therefore it is what is called believer's baptism. This is the only kind of baptism the Bible knows anything about. You will search it in vain for any justification of any other kind of baptism than believer's baptism. The Samaritans were baptized, and immediately became subjects of the kingdom of God and members of the body of Christ, and part of a distinct and separate community of people in the world.

VII. WHAT WERE THE RESULTS OF THE MISSION OF THE FIRST MISSIONARY?

The results are recorded as being "great joy in that city." The rejoicing was not confined to isolated individuals or even to a considerable company of people, but to the whole city. It was the occasion for a civic celebration in which the whole city participated.

We have seen some magnificent city celebrations upon important occasions. New York City has its ticker tape parades to honor celebrities. And everyone of us have participated in celebrations of one sort or another, but here is the spontaneous and exuberant outbreaking of rejoicing for reasons different than we have ever known in our civic celebrations. Here was a city celebrating its deliverance from sin, rejoicing in forgiveness, recording its membership in the body of Christ and the kingdom of God. What a celebration! Here was a city delirious in its happiness because it had come to know the Lord.

This is the normal effect of finding the Lord. It results in great joy and this is for numerous reasons:

1. Because something has happened to the past. The record of sin is blotted out. Forgiveness has been given and there is freedom from the sense of guilt.

2. Because something has happened to the present. Freedom from guilt produces the release of emotions for their highest expression. It results in a new sense of freedom and exhilaration. The person thus affected has become, by the grace of God, a new creature. In this experience old things have passed away and all things have become new.

3. Because something has happened to the future. The future is now secure. It is no longer a thing of danger and dread. Heaven is in the future. This means the Father's house. This means home and contentment.

All of these things compounded into one glorious experience of salvation multiplied by as many people as were in the city of Samaria meant "great joy."

21

THE RELATION OF THE HOLY SPIRIT
TO THE BELIEVER
Acts 8:14-25

With the coming of the Holy Spirit into the experience of the one hundred and twenty disciples on the Day of Pentecost, we find a new element in the affairs of God among men. In fact, the nature of the Holy Spirit's coming meant God at work among men. In consequence of this you have these acts of the Holy Spirit which are being described for us in this so-called Acts of the Apostles.

At this particular juncture, in the procession of events in the early church, Philip had gone to Samaria and preached Christ, declaring the things concerning the kingdom of God. In consequence many were baptized and became identified with the new community called the church. When news of this extensive revival at Samaria reached Jerusalem, the apostles were not only greatly encouraged over the results but concerned about conserving the results; and in order to do this they sent Peter and John to investigate. As a result of their coming to Samaria the new believers received the Holy Spirit. Here was an unusual thing for it did not follow the formula set down by Peter on the Day of Pentecost when he said to the people, "Repent and be baptized everyone of you in the name of Jesus Christ for the remission of sins, and ye shall receive the gift of the Holy Ghost" (Acts 2:38). When Peter and John came to Samaria they prayed for the believers, laying hands upon them; and they received the Holy Spirit.

Why did they not receive the Holy Spirit immediately as Peter said they would in the formula of Acts 2:38? Why was this delayed action necessary? Why did Peter and John have to lay hands on them? Is this the establishment of a precedent, so that in ages to come the gift of the Holy Spirit is to be a subsequent bestowment at the hands of ecclesiasts? Peter's formula at Pentecost must be viewed as the normal procedure. First, faith; second, repentance; third, receiving the Holy Spirit, with this chronological order accomplished simultaneously. Later on Paul would write to the Corinthians and say, "For by one spirit are we all baptized into one body" (I Cor. 12:13). This was a spiritual baptism and it was accomplished at the time of the believer's regeneration. This would be the normal experience of all believers.

In the Book of Acts we are dealing with transitional experiences. These experiences created conditions and manifestations that are not normal. They would not be the normal pattern, such as speaking in tongues, signs, wonders and miracles.

There are four comings, or outpourings, or initial manifestations of the Holy Spirit recorded in Acts.

Pentecost - Acts 2:1-4. Here the Holy Spirit came upon the one hundred and twenty assembled in the upper room. These people began immediately to speak in tongues as witnesses to Christ. The effect was to bring conviction on the multitude of pilgrims and residents in Jerusalem who inquired of Peter, "What shall we do?" And in response he gave the formula of repentance, baptism and receiving the Holy Spirit.

Samaria - Acts 8:15-17. Here Philip preached the kingdom of God. As a result, the people believed and were baptized; but they did not receive the Holy Spirit until Peter and John came down from Jerusalem, prayed for them and laid their hands upon them. There was no physical manifestation such as speaking in tongues.

Caesarea - Acts 10:44-48. Here Philip had carried the first word of the gospel, and later Peter preached Christ; and as he did the Holy Spirit fell upon them and they spoke with tongues and were later baptized.

Ephesus - Acts 19:1-6. Here Apollos, a Jewish convert to the Christian faith, preached to the Ephesians. Unlike the preachers in the other instances, Peter and Philip, Apollos was not fully instructed. But when later Paul went to Ephesus he preached to them and asked, "Have ye received the Holy Ghost since ye believed?" they replied (they were Gentiles unacquainted with the facts of Pentecost) that they had not even heard that there was a Holy Spirit. Whereupon Paul instructed them and they believed, were baptized, and Paul laid hands upon them and they received the Holy Spirit and spoke with tongues.

Here you have the four instances of the coming of the Holy Spirit and in each instance there is a variance with the Pentecostal formula of Peter in Acts 2:38 which was: repent, be baptized and receive the Holy Spirit.

At Samaria they believed and were baptized; but the Holy Spirit was delayed until two apostles came down from Jerusalem, prayed for them, laid hands upon them and they received the Holy Spirit without speaking in tongues.

At Caesarea, while Peter was preaching, the Holy Spirit fell upon them, they spoke with tongues and were baptized afterward.

At Ephesus they had Apollos' teaching without instruction concerning the Holy Spirit. Then when Paul came he filled them in doctrinally. They were then baptized, Paul laid his hands upon them, the Holy Spirit came and they spoke with tongues.

Which of these four outpourings or comings of the Holy Spirit is to be adopted as the normal pattern of experience for the modern church? None of them. We are not going back to Pentecost to tarry for the Holy Spirit because He has already come. We are not going to Samaria to believe, be baptized and then wait for some apostle to lay hands on us for a delayed reception, because the Holy Spirit is not conferred by the laying on of hands in some rite of confirmation. We are not going to Caesarea and expect that everytime the Word of God is preached there will be the manifestation of the Holy Spirit coming, after which we are baptized. And we are not going back to Ephesus to listen to eloquent Apollos who had not been fully instructed; nor have to wait until Paul comes to tell us what Apollos did not know. We know, and the order is not what it was for the Gentiles at Ephesus because we have the full orbed teaching of the completed New Testament for our instruction.

This brings us to the crux of this whole matter. Here are four diverse experiences of the Holy Spirit, whereas in the completed New Testament we have the full and complete teaching of the Holy Spirit. We must not make the tragic spiritual mistake of "teaching the experience of the apostles but rather experience the teaching of the apostles." The experience of the apostles is in transitional Acts. The teaching of the apostles is in the settled and completed epistles that follow Acts. If we go back to the experience of the apostles in Acts we find four diverse and different experiences. Which one are we going to choose? Why were they different? We do not know; we only know that the circumstances were different and the manifestations different. We know that the original one hundred and twenty at Pentecost were Jews who had been in the immediate company of Jesus. We know that the three thousand at Pentecost were apparently Jews and Jewish proselytes. We know that the Samaritans were neither pure Jews nor pure Gentiles. They believed Moses and looked for a messiah. The Caesareans were Gentiles as were also the Ephesians, so you have a diversity of national background and circumstances. It was apostles whom God used to bring the Holy Spirit to the Samaritans, Caesareans and Ephesians; but the pattern is broken when you look at the experiences of Paul, for here a humble disciple by the name of Ananias is used to give the Holy Spirit.

Where are you going to find the pattern for your experience? Well, where would you start to find what you are to believe in the way of Christian truth in the Book of Acts? Teaching is not complete at one given moment. It is progressive and does not become complete until you have the complete New Testament. What then is the teaching of the complete New Testament concerning the experience of the Holy Spirit? It is seven-fold.

1. The Gift of the Holy Spirit (Acts 2:1-4).

This is what happened at Pentecost. It is as final as what happened at Bethlehem, when God gave Jesus to be the Savior. It is as final as what happened at Calvary, when the Savior "offered one sacrifice for sins for ever." It is as final as what happened in the resurrection, when Jesus Christ was raised from the dead to manifest eternal life. Pentecost is no more repeated in the experience of the church than the virgin birth, the crucifixion or the resurrection. Pentecost is historical and not personal. People no longer tarry for the coming of the Holy Spirit. People no longer experience the Pentecostal gift of speaking in tongues. They may experience tongues but it is not Pentecostal. It may be Corinthian or it may be something else because it is not Pentecostal; for if it was they would immediately preach Christ in the languages of men. There are gifts of the Holy Spirit to be experienced but the gift of the Holy Spirit has been given as a once-for-all historical fact.

2. The Baptism of the Holy Spirit (I Cor. 12:13).

This is not a water baptism, but a spiritual baptism into the body of Christ. It occurs at the time of regeneration when the believer receives the Holy Spirit. It does not occur at a time subsequent to salvation after agonizing searching or praying. Its effect is the witness of the Holy Spirit to our spirit that we are God's children and brings the assurance of salvation.

3. The Sealing of the Holy Spirit (Eph. 1:13).

This is simultaneous with the baptism of the Holy Spirit and is actually our marking with the Holy Spirit which determines His possession of us. We now belong to God. We are His eternal possession. This is an act comparable to putting a brand upon cattle or burning an owner's mark on a log. When that log with many others reaches the mill area it is sorted out and placed with others of a similar mark belonging to a certain owner. We are God's and are so marked by the Holy Spirit.

4. The Earnest of the Holy Spirit (Eph. 1:14).

This is also simultaneous with the baptism and the sealing of the Holy Spirit, because the Holy Spirit is given as God's earnest money, or pledge-penny, as a down payment to ensure to completion the redemptive transaction. Here the coming of the Holy Spirit is the guarantee of what is to come. He is God's promise that "He who hath begun a good work in you will perform it until the day of Jesus Christ."

5. The Filling of the Holy Spirit (Eph. 5:18).

This is not simultaneous with anything but continuous with the fulfillment of certain spiritual conditions. These conditions are faith, surrender, consecration and prayer. While it is true that every believer is full of the Holy Spirit no believer experiences that fulness except under the fulfillment of these spiritual conditions. We may have all there is to have of the Holy Spirit, but not until the Holy Spirit has all there is of us do we have the complete manifestation of the Holy Spirit.

6. The Anointing of the Holy Spirit.

This is neither simultaneous nor continuous, but occasional and is the Holy Spirit's act of preparation for special service. It was done even for Jesus who was anointed to "preach the gospel to the poor" (Luke 4:18).

7. The Indwelling of the Holy Spirit.

This is continuous and permanent (I Cor. 3:16). The indwelling of the Holy Spirit is His presence within the believer as a result of the believer's presence in the body of Christ. There is a difference between the indwelling and the infilling of the Holy Spirit. The indwelling is continuous, whereas the infilling may be intermittent. The indwelling depends on our position in Christ, whereas the infilling depends on our condition in Christ. The indwelling is like the gift, baptism, sealing and earnest of the Holy Spirit, all related to our unchangeable position; whereas the filling is like the anointing, related to our changeable condition.

In these seven things you have the New Testament's summarized teaching concerning the Holy Spirit. These seven things stand in contrast to the diverse and different experiences of the early Christians, who lived in the transitional age of the early church and whose experiences we noted at Pentecost, Samaria, Caesarea and Ephesus. Do not make the mistake of going back to historical experiences to teach the diverse and changing experiences of the apostles; but rather find the full orbed teaching of the New Testament in order that you may experience the teaching of the apostles.

Having established this seven-fold relation of the Holy Spirit to the believer, and having noted the variable experiences of the growing church, we are prepared to move on to the expanding work and ministry of the church and growth of the believer. But before we do this, let us look at a peril which may come to anyone in his attitude to the Holy Spirit. It is revealed in the experience of a man in Samaria named Simon Magus with whom originates the sin of simony, which is the buying or selling of ecclesiastical preferment or religious privilege. Simon wanted to buy the power that came with the Holy Spirit so that he might use it gainfully to his own profit.

The sin of simony is historically and scandalously portrayed in the building of St. Peter's Cathedral at Rome. It was begun by Pope Julius II but left unfinished. His successor, Leo X, was involved in debt and the papal treasury exhausted, so he turned to the selling of indulgences. For sums of money it was possible to purchase the pardon of sins and the ransom of souls from purgatory. It brought in vast sums of money from which St. Peter's was built. It resulted also in the Reformation when Martin Luther protested the sale of indulgences by John Tetzel in Germany.

Simon Magus had been a sorcerer, and a user of divination, and had established a great following for his occultism. Now he made the mistake of turning from the false to the true and desiring it at a price. God speaks against it, not only in terms of simony, but in terms of the possession of spiritual power for personal advantage. It is the wrong of seeking spiritual blessing and power to achieve fame, or to achieve spectacular healings, or to enrich himself with large audiences, and the performance of miracles or deeds of lesser stature. It is the desire for spiritual power for the sake of carnal ends. This was an abuse of the blessings and powers related to the experience of the Holy Spirit, and this no doubt has been multiplied innumerably in the course of the church. But this abuse of blessing must not obscure our eyes to the great blessing which comes through a healthy spiritual relationship between the believer and the Holy Spirit, as viewed in the Holy Spirit's seven-fold relation to the Christian.

22

A DISTINGUISHED CONVERT

Acts 8:26-40

When Paul wrote his first letter to the church at Corinth he said, among other significant things, "For ye see your calling, brethren, how that not many wise men after the flesh, not many mighty, not many noble, are called . . . " (I Cor. 1:26-29). Yet at almost the very outset of the process of calling men, we have the instance of a very distinguished convert. He was an official of the Court of Queen Candace of Ethiopia, who reigned in Northeastern Africa on the Upper Nile River where we now have the Sudan and modern Ethiopia.

The circumstances of the conversion of this distinguished convert begins in Samaria, where Philip, one of the seven deacons of the Jerusalem Church, has been doing evangelistic work. Philip had remarkable success in this first missionary effort. Miracles of healing had established the divine nature of his mission, while the preaching of the kingdom of God had brought a multitude of converts so "there was great joy in that city."

During the ensuing excitement which followed these remarkable events, Philip received a most unusual visitation. It was from an angel. The commentators completely ignore this visitation or else speak of it as some nebulous form of divine guidance. But none seems to be impressed with the visitation as if it were not of any great significance. There had been one prior mention of an angel in the Book of Acts. It was at the time of the apostles' deliverance from prison (Acts 5:19). Surely this cannot be ignored and passed over as some natural event. We must pause and account for the appearance of the angel, both here to Philip and before to the apostles when they were in prison. If we have no way to prove their appearance it is at least certain we have no way to disprove their appearance and ministry. We are told elsewhere (Heb. 1:14) that angels are "ministering spirits sent forth to minister for them who shall be heirs of salvation."

Since we are dealing with two worlds, this and the next, we must be prepared to encounter some things beyond the powers of sense and sight to prove. Ours has been described as a walk of faith, and faith must accept what it cannot prove or else it would not be faith. Anyway, we are dealing with a sovereign God in the acts of redemption, and in such things we must be prepared to move into the realm of the spiritual where proof is not left to sight. We must assume, without proof, that this angel was a real person and this visitation was a valid event in a time when God was manifesting Himself in redemptive power. The angel gave Philip a remarkable directive — "Arise, and go toward the south unto the way that goeth down from Jerusalem unto Gaza, which is desert." This was a most amazing command and it must have staggered the faith and credulity of Philip who, apparently, had never been acquainted with or even heard of angels. Here he was in a Samaritan city with his hands full of prosperous work; he was summarily told to leave it and go to the desert, which was both dangerous and completely devoid of people. To reason, and in good planning, this was not a sensible thing. Yet it was a directive that came to Philip who was not told or even given a hint of the real and important nature of the assignment. The fact is that Philip went in obedience to the angel's directive and at Gaza, in the desert, made contact with a most remarkable man who is described as "a man of Ethiopia, an eunuch of great authority under Candace Queen of the Ethopians, who had the charge of all her treasure. . . . "

Let us observe a number of things about this man and the things that took place at Gaza.

I. HE WAS A GREAT MAN (verse 27)

He is described as "an eunuch of great authority" who had charge of all the Queen's treasure, acting in the capacity of the crown's treasurer, or chancellor of the exchequer or secretary of the treasury or minister of finance. As such he was no doubt a member of the Queen's council and helped weigh questions of state and decide matters of national policy. But great as he was, he was not great enough to be saved by his position. He could not be saved by position, power or wealth. In spite of all his position and honors he was a sinner in the sight of God and needed conviction enough to recognize it and humility enough to acknowledge it. Being a high born man he needed something more than noble birth; he needed the new birth.

II. HE WAS A RELIGIOUS MAN (verse 27).

Here was a Gentile proselyte to the Jewish faith who had made a tremendously arduous journey of several thousand miles in order to worship in Jerusalem at the Jewish center of worship at a feast time, perhaps Pentecost. Here he had witnessed, some six years after the fulfillment of Pentecost and the severing of the temple veil and the obsolescence of the Jewish priestly system, the ritualistic observance of the Old Testament worship which had now lost its significance through its fulfillment in the events of the crucifixion and the resurrection. He was obviously disappointed and disillusioned, for all the religion in the world and all the religious pageantry without a personal Savior will never save or satisfy the human soul.

III. HE WAS AN INQUIRING MAN (verse 28)

No doubt, at Jerusalem he had heard many things about the comparatively recent events of the crucifixion and resurrection. He heard of the miracles of Jesus. He was told of His message. He was intrigued by descriptions of His form and actions. And then he was completely overwhelmed when details of the crucifixion were given him. What do you suppose he thought when he went into the temple and found its veil, gorgeous in color and incredibly thick, which had excluded the people from the Holy of holies, rent from the top to the bottom? He must have been deeply moved and disturbed for what he thought was reflected by what he was reading from the Prophet Isaiah, who was the prophet of the suffering Messiah and who had written a remarkable picture of that Messiah as a Lamb of slaughter.

When Philip contacted this man on the way to Gaza he found him reading the Septuagint, the Greek version of the Old Testament. He was making an effort to satisfy the unsatified inquiries of his mind and longings of his heart, for what he saw of a religious nature in Jerusalem did not satisfy and apparently now could not be reconciled by what he was reading in the Old Testament scriptures. At this strategic and crucial moment in a hungry soul's search for religious reality Philip, God's chosen instrument, makes his approach, for Philip had been told by the Holy Spirit to join himself to the chariot.

It is at this point that we notice another characteristic of this distinguished convert to the Christian faith.

IV. HE WAS A HUMBLE MAN (verse 29-35)

It was customary to read the scripture scrolls aloud, and when Philip heard what he was reading he identified its source and asked, "Understandest thou what thou readest?" His answer was, "How can I except some man should guide me?"

Although wise enough to be a royal counsellor and astute enough to be entrusted with the financial affairs of a nation, here was a man humble enough to say he needed help. No one will find God with the same wisdom with which he achieves success in the world. The scientist will never find God with the same wisdom with which he discovers the mysteries of the universe. The philosopher will never find God with the same wisdom with which he discovers the mysteries of knowledge. The rich man will never find God with the same wisdom with which he acquires the secrets of wealth. In fact, one of the earliest questions of the Bible has to do with this very matter. It is in Job 11:7, "Canst thou by searching find out God?" The ultimate answer is in the Biblical axiom, "The fear of the Lord is the beginning of wisdom." In other words, the wisdom that finds God is the wisdom of faith and the New Testament formula identifies this faith as faith that is associated with the scriptures, for "faith cometh by hearing and hearing by the word of God." (Rom. 10:17).

Futhermore, this faith of the Book is faith in a personal Savior, for when Philip was asked to guide the Ethiopian to a knowledge of God he used the Old Testament passage of Isaiah's prophecy and "preached unto him Jesus." Philip took the Ethiopian into the presence of Jesus Christ by way of Isaiah. This man's mind had been deeply moved by what he had heard and seen at Jerusalem, six years after the crucifixion. His reading of Isaiah's description of the suffering servant of God had also prepared him for a personal introduction to the Savior.

V. HE BECAME A SAVED MAN (verses 36-39)

The Ethiopian court official became the first negro convert to the Christian faith. This is another of the many "firsts" found in the Book of Acts. His conversion was based upon his personal encounter with a personal Savior through the triple agency of the Holy Spirit, the Word of God and the human interpreter.

The Ethiopian's conversion is not described in terms of its emotional intensity, but only through his statement about the desire for baptism — "See, here is water; what doth hinder me to be baptized?" Apparently he had not understood the full meaning of baptism for having, undoubtedly, witnessed a Christian baptism at Jerusalem, he had associated it as a rite involved in salvation. Philip proceeds to tell him that faith and personal commitment to God precedes the act of baptism so that it becomes believer's baptism and not a saving rite by itself; and he says, "If thou believest with all thine heart, thou mayest." Whereupon the eunuch made a frank and bold confession of faith: "I believe that Jesus Christ is the Son of God." All the elements of a saving faith are found in this incident. The Holy Spirit is present. The Word of God is employed. Christ is preached. Faith is exercised and conversion is the concurrent result of these elements.

Something else follows the Ethiopian's conversion — he is baptized. We have no hint of the circumstances. It was not in a church building for there was no church in Gaza. It must have been at a convenient site suitable for immersion, for the whole circumstance points to the bodily immersion of the eunuch, following the example of Christ. It further follows the most assuredly common practice of the earliest Christians in observing bodily immersion as the most perfect identification of the believer with the death and resurrection of Christ. It was in a body of water of such size as to accommodate both the eunuch and the evangelist. It was of sufficient depth so that they could go "down both into the water." The act of baptism was performed in so evident a fashion and in so much a quantity of water that they came "up out of the water."

The eunuch of Ethiopia was so thoroughly converted and so satisfyingly baptized that it is said, "he went on his way rejoicing." There are three emotional states that will result from all true preaching which faces man with his responsibility to God. It will either make him mad or sad or glad. The Ethiopian was made glad.

Here was a convert whose religious experience did not depend on his teacher. His joy did not depend on Philip, for the Spirit of God caught him away. There are too many people whose teaching depends upon their teacher and when their teacher goes they go all to pieces. There are too many people running around after teachers instead of after teaching. They are peripatetic teacher-tasters. One week they are running after this teacher and another week after another teacher. They are those of whom Paul spoke, "ever learning and never able to come to a knowledge of the truth."

This man retained his joy in the absence of his teacher because he was the Lord's convert and not Philip's. He was undoubtedly able to verify the reality of his own conversion by the inner witness of the Holy Spirit for, "The Spirit beareth witness with our spirit, that we are the children of God."

23

CHRISTIAN BAPTISM

Acts 8:36

Baptism is an ordinance of the Christian faith. It was practiced as a pre-Christian rite by the Qumram Community which lived at least one hundred and fifty years before Christ. This pre-Christian community observed the baptismal rite of immersion. It was practiced as a pre-Christian rite by John the Baptist. He too practiced immersion. It was experienced by Jesus who was baptized by John the Baptist in the River Jordan, obviously by immersion. It was instituted by Jesus as one of the two New Testament ordinances. "Go ye therefore and teach (disciple) all nations, baptizing them . . . " (Matt. 28:19).

Although there is but one baptism for the church today, there are five kinds of baptism mentioned in the New Testament.

I. The Baptism of John

This was the first of the New Testament baptisms and was pre-Christian. It is described in Matthew 21:25 as being "from heaven," which means that it was authentic, genuine and of God's appointment. It was a baptism "of repentance for the remission of sins," and as such was a visible and physical means by which these people could turn to God and receive forgiveness. Since this baptism was before the cross it could not be a baptism of justification, and had only the efficacy of a rite and ceremony, which needed authentication in Christian baptism as later practiced by the church. It was a baptism of anticipation and preparation for the coming of Christ and was fulfilled with the coming of the Messiah. "Repent ye: for the kingdom of heaven is at hand" (Matt. 3:1-3).

This baptism had special significance for the Jews and served a nationalistic purpose. Acts 13:24 tells us that John had preached "the baptism of repentance to all the people of Israel." Apollos made the mistake of preaching this baptism to the Ephesian Gentiles; and Paul had to correct it by proclaiming the full gospel and baptizing them in the name of Jesus after which they received the Holy Spirit.

John's baptism can be summarized by saying that it was the equivalent of a pre-Christian rite by immersion in water, for the purpose of announcing the kingdom of heaven and giving the ceremonial conscious Israelites a means of repentance and cleansing from sin.

II. The Baptism of Jesus

This refers to the actual baptism of Jesus by John and is referred to in Matthew 3:11-17. It is clearly indicated that Jesus had been wholly and totally immersed in the waters of the Jordan. This constituted a precedent and sets the mode by which all believers are to be baptized, namely, by the total immersion of the body in water. It further reveals Jesus' approval of baptism and requires our obedience by following Him, not merely in baptism, but in this specific form of baptism, that is, immersion.

There were divine phenomena associated with the baptism of Jesus. First, "The Spirit of God descending like a dove . . . " (Matt. 3:16). Second, a voice from heaven which said, "This is my beloved Son, in whom I am well pleased" (Matt. 3:17).

III. The Baptism of Fire

This is spoken of by John the Baptist on the occasion of the baptism of Jesus in the Jordan. "I indeed baptize you with water . . . he shall baptize you with the Holy Ghost, and with fire" (Matt. 3:11). This is a baptism by Jesus and plainly refers to the coming of the Holy Spirit. It was historically fulfilled at Pentecost, never to be repeated again. It was a once-for-all occurrence. It stands in contrast to the baptism performed by John.

In the baptism by John the agent was human (John). In the baptism by Jesus the agent was divine (Holy Spirit). In the baptism by John the purpose was repentance. In the baptism by Jesus the purpose was purification. In the baptism by John the means was water. In the baptism by Jesus the means was the Holy Spirit (here described as fire). In the baptism by John the symbol of the Holy Spirit was a dove. In the baptism by Jesus the symbol of the Holy Spirit was tongues of fire. In the baptism by John the water was literal and actual. In the baptism by Jesus the fire was spiritual and symbolical. In the baptism by John it was by immersion in water. In the baptism by Jesus it was immersing or uniting into the Body of Christ. In the baptism by John the purpose was salvation. In the baptism by Jesus the purpose was service. The baptism of fire by Jesus in the upper room was the fulfillment of a promise made by Jesus who said, "For John truly baptized with water; but ye shall be baptized with the Holy Ghost not many days hence" (Acts 1:5). The baptism by John is obsolete. The baptism by Jesus is current for it is described as a continuing experience associated with the regeneration of the soul. "For by one Spirit are we all baptized into one body . . . " (I Cor. 12:13).

IV. THE BAPTISM FOR THE DEAD

This is described in I Corinthians 15:29, 30 and constitutes one of the most difficult passages of the New Testament. It appears to have been an actual practice of water baptism, in which one person (living) was baptized for another person (dead). This is practiced today in the Mormon Church. It is secretly performed in their temples by the use of immersion. The modern Mormon version is a variant of this early Christian rite because their baptizing for the dead is done for persons who never made any profession of faith; whereas in the New

Testament instance it was done for believers who, because of peculiar conditions maintaining in the beginning days of the church, had not been baptized before they died. It thus appears to have been a temporary custom peculiar to the early church. In the present-day version of this baptism, baptisms for the dead will run into the thousands and hundreds of thousands. Genealogical records will be searched for the names of ancestors for the sake of saving them posthumously through baptism.

This was not the case in this early Christian rite which was performed in rare and infrequent instances for some believer who had lost his life at the hands of pagans because he had embraced the Christian faith. Every baptism in this early Christian rite was undertaken for a dead person who had been a believer. It was believed that this baptism by proxy would be counted as their own and, while it in no way affected the salvation status of the dead believer, it did give consolation and comfort to the living baptismal participants.

Baptism for the dead, as practiced posthumously today for whole lines of indiscriminate ancestors, is neither scriptural nor Christian. In fact, it is a heretical practice common to certain heretical sects in the First Century, such as the Cerinthians and the Marcionites and was not continued as a general practice by any of the New Testament churches.

Paul was using this briefly observed practice to illustrate a truth. He argues that the practice of baptizing for the dead in order to insure their being raised up from the dead is useless if the dead rise not. This baptism was founded on a magical belief that one person could confer the grace of God from a living person to a dead person. This was a variant of the idea of a second chance and that through baptizing for the dead the deceased could have a second chance, which is an idea totally foreign to the Bible's concept of salvation.

V. The Baptism of the Believer

Christian baptism when practiced in its purest and fullest New Testament meaning is reserved for believers. It is for adult believers, or children who have come to the age of accountability and can receive baptism by their own will and responsibility. It is given only after one has made a profession of faith in Jesus Christ and has manifested evidences of a genuine salvation. This is what we term "believer's baptism" or baptism after one's confession, and at an age when the candidate can make a conscious and discriminate personal choice of Jesus Christ as Savior. It is never, in its New Testament form, given in order that people may be saved or in anticipation of a later profession of faith.

There can be no scriptural or historical doubt that the first and usual mode of baptism was by immersion. The variant to this was affusion and affusion is two-fold, either the pouring of water or sprinkling of water on the head of the candidate. The first historical reference to baptism by affusion is in the year 120 A.D. In the early writing called, "Teaching of the Twelve Apostles" direction is given, in case there is not a sufficiency of water, to pour water on the head three times.

By the time of Iranaeus in 180 A.D. the practice of infant baptism was an established custom. But there is no New Testament authority for its practice and certainly no precedent in the rite of baptism as practiced by John the Baptist, Peter and the rest of the apostles, and as observed by Jesus.

One might reluctantly compromise on the amount of water employed, whether it be by immersion or affusion; but one could not rightly compromise on the issue of believer's baptism. Every instance of baptism in the Book of Acts is believer's baptism. "Then they that gladly received his word were baptized . . . " (Acts 2:41); the Eunuch by Philip (Acts 8:36); the Samaritans by Philip (Acts 8:12); Simon by Philip (Acts 8:13); Paul (Acts 9:18); House of Cornelius (Acts 10:47, 48); Lydia (Acts 16:15); Jailer and family (Acts 16:30); Crispus and many Corinthians (Acts 18:8); . . . Acts 19:4, 5). There is even the case of the Ephesians who were re-baptized. Having first been baptized with John's baptism, they were re-baptized in the name of the Lord. These Ephesians were in effect the first Anabaptists. Anabaptists were Christians in Reformation times who rejected infant baptism and administered the rite only to adults, so when new members joined them they were re-baptized. It was because of this second baptism that they were called Anabaptists, a term no longer used.

What is the significance and meaning of believer's baptism?

1. *It is a Confession of Faith.* This is a conscious act with the full responsibility and knowledge of the person being baptized. It is not performed for the candidate by the will of another.

2. *It Follows Conversion.* This is established by the fact that every instance of its occurrence in the records of the early church in the Book of Acts, is the case of believers being baptized after their profession of faith.

3. *It is By Immersion, in Obedience to the Example of Jesus.* We are "baptized into Jesus" (Rom. 6.3). Water is the symbol of death or grave. Immersion in water is the symbol of burial. Lifting from the water is the symbol of the resurrection. The object is to emphasize the "new life" (Rom. 6:4).

Because of the unique and distinct scriptural nature of believer's baptism by immersion, its candidates, when properly instructed and prepared, may look forward to an exhilarating spiritual experience.

When the Ethiopian eunuch rode with Philip and had been instructed concerning salvation, his question was, "See, here is water: what doth hinder me to be baptized?" Whereupon Philip insisted on one thing, a confession of faith and upon this confession of faith he was forthwith baptized. What hinders anyone to be baptized? There are numerous hindrances such as, unbelief, not being a Christian, disobedience to Christ or ignorance of its meaning.

24

CHRISTIANITY'S MOST REMARKABLE

CONVERSION

Acts 9:1-19

There lived in England, many years ago, two distinguished antagonists of the Christian faith. They were Lord Lyttelton and Gilbert West. They established between themselves the conviction that if they could disprove two things they could destroy the Christian faith. These two things were the resurrection of Jesus and the conversion of Paul. In pursuance of their conviction they set out to accomplish their aims. They had agreed to meet later to discuss their findings; and when they did meet years later, it was to make a startling discovery. They were both converted, for in their respective studies of the resurrection of Jesus and the conversion of Paul, they were convinced of the divine nature of the Christian faith and submitted themselves to the claims of Christ.

The conversion of Saul of Tarsus was the most dramatic and remarkable conversion in all the annals of history. In the background stands Saul of Tarsus who belonged to an aristocratic Jewish family of which the father possessed the rights of Roman citizenship, making Saul a free-born Roman. Saul of Tarsus was a learned scholar and theologian. He had been sent to Jerusalem as a boy, where he had a married sister, in order that he might be trained in the school of Gamaliel, the leading Rabbinical scholar of the times. From this training and his family background he acquired a remarkable religious pedigree which he was later to describe to the Church at Philippi in these words, "Though I might also have confidence in the flesh. If any other man thinketh that he hath whereof he might trust in the flesh, I more: Circumcised the eighth day, of the stock of Israel, of the tribe of Benjamin, an Hebrew of the Hebrews; as touching the law, a Pharisee; Concerning zeal, persecuting the church; touching the righteousness which is in the law, blameless. But what things were gain to me, those I counted loss for Christ" (Phil. 3:4-7).

He was one of the most fanatical persecutors of the Christians. He had cast his vote in favor of the murder of Stephen and stood by at the execution, holding the young martyr's clothes. And now in pursuit of his fanatical religious concepts, he had gone to the president of the Sanhedrin at Jerusalem, whose rulings had the force of civil law, and asked extradition rights to go to Damascus to apprehend some Christian refugees in order to return them to Jerusalem for execution.

A remarkable thing happens at this juncture of his gruesome business. We call it his conversion, or turning; for when he had almost reached the gates of the city of Damascus at noon, a blinding, flashing light which outshone the sun, came upon him and he fell to the ground. As he lay prostrate by the side of the Damascan road a voice, speaking in his Aramaic tongue, said, "Saul, Saul, why persecutest thou me?" And when Saul cried out for identification of the voice, he is told, "I am Jesus whom thou persecutest." Four times in the New Testament there are instances of appearances of Christ in glory: once on the Mount of Transfiguration, once to Stephen, once to Paul and once to John in the Revelation.

In the foreground of the picture of this conversion stands its product, Paul the apostle of Jesus Christ, incomparable preacher, intrepid missionary, prolific founder of churches, author of fourteen New Testament books and faithful witness to the saving grace of Jesus Christ. Above all, his is the most remarkable conversion in the annals of the Christian faith. But it is in no sense a pattern of the conversions which were to follow, for Paul's experience contained elements that have never been reproduced in the conversion experiences of others. For example, he saw a vision and heard a voice and fell unconscious under a blinding light. This has not been true of others. These, again, were the unusual evidences of divine and supernatural power that were to be credentials for the apostle who was to become God's spokesman to the Gentile world. And in this respect they were peculiar and unique to Paul's experience and would never be repeated again. A good deal of Acts is of a similar nature.

But there are elements here that point up the essential nature of a real and genuine conversion experience for all men and women.

I. CONVICTION

If at the background of this remarkable picture stands an intransigent Jew, proud and unyielding; and if in the foreground stands the product of this remarkable experience in terms of a mellowed, regenerated disciple and apostle, then at the center is the conversion experience itself which changes Saul into Paul. It is this conversion and what it involves which interests us.

We notice that it takes place at Damascus. Damascus was in Syria and was famous for two very important products, silks in the form of Damasks, and swords in the form of the renowned Damascene blades. To these are now added a third — the place of a notable conversion.

The first step in Paul's conversion, as in any other, is his conviction. This was accomplished by the vision and its attendant wonders on the road to Damascus. This was Paul's arresting or apprehension. It was his conviction of sin at which time he saw himself a sinner, lost and undone. All of the proud items of his religious pedigree fell away, and he saw himself for what he really was in the eyes of God. Here his proud nationalism vanished, his traditions became nauseating and corrupt, and his rabbincial righteouusness but filthy rags. No doubt, what he wrote later to the Christians at Rome were the things he saw and felt on the Damascus road. "For all have sinned and come short of the glory of God" (Rom. 3:23). There must be something to be changed from before there can be anything to be changed into. And Paul saw here the man he really was, condemned, lost and loathesome.

Conviction must precede any conversion or else it is not conversion at all. It may be a religious experience in the sense of involving religious ideas, but no real conversion can take place without conviction of sin. Conviction is the sense of one's need —a need that one recognizes he cannot supply for himself. Conviction is the feeling of being utterly and helplessly lost. Only with this feeling and conviction does one truly turn to the Savior in order to be the recipient of His saving grace. We must begin our approach to conversion from one of two positions. Either man is inherently and essentially good and whatever is wrong with him will yield to education, evolution and religion; or man is inherently and essentially evil and whatever he needs must be done by God and cannot be done by man. This was Paul's position and it arose out of his personal conviction at the time of his conversion.

II. CALL

If conviction is the human element that reveals deep concern for one's helpless and untenable position before God, then calling is the divine element that reveals the divine initiative in salvation. Paul's own words tell us what this calling consists of: "For whom he did foreknow, he also did predestinate to be conformed to the image of his Son, that he might be the firstborn among many brethren. Moreover whom he did predestinate, them he also called: and whom he called, them he also justified: and whom he justified, them he also glorified" (Rom. 8:29, 30).

God's call is the first element in any person's conversion. None can answer who is not called. This call is purely of divine grace and goodness, and precedes all human feeling and effort. But although the call is God's, conversion requires the human choice so that the human will is made to correspond to the divine will.

The unusual factor in God's calling of Paul was in the fact that his call to conversion also involved his call to be an apostle. He is described as "a chosen vessel unto me, to bear my name before the Gentiles."

The calling of God is emphasized in the conversion experience of Paul to remind everyone that salvation is not something which can be desired or sought or experienced at will. It is something which depends on the call of God through divine election. In other words, we cannot be saved when it is convenient to our disposition or choice; only when God chooses to save us.

III. CONVERSION

To convert means to turn; and Paul's conversion was his turning away from all that he was racially, nationally and religiously. It was not only a turning but a becoming, for in words that he later wrote to the Church at Corinth he said, "Therefore if any man be in Christ, he is a new creature: old things are passed away; behold, all things are become new" (II Cor. 5:17). He would also describe it to the Colossian Church as a translation "into the kingdom of his dear Son" (Col. 1:13).

This conversion experience would involve something more than an emotional outburst at a mourner's bench, or an expressed desire to be reformed, or an intention to join a church. This would be an act of God and this act of God would involve a number of things which Paul would incorporate in the teaching of his New Testament epistles.

1. Justification. This would be an act of God in which the sinner was declared to be free from guilt and would have imparted unto him the righteousness of Jesus Christ through faith (Rom. 4:5).

2. Forgiveness. This would be a divine act which dealt with sin in the past, present and future, and make it possible for the recipient of salvation to enjoy freedom from guilt and a place of fellowship with God.

3. Sonship. This is described as the process of adoption in which the justified and forgiven sinner is brought into the family of God and made an heir of the divine estate. The proof of this

sonship is in the presence of the Holy Spirit for "the Spirit itself beareth witness with our spirit, that we are the children of God" (Rom. 8:16).

4. Translation. As an experience simultaneous with those just mentioned, we are brought into the divine kingdom. This is by the only process through which it is possible—translation. This implies a change from one environment of life into another, so that we have a totally new and different set of stimuli for the living of a new life.

5. Glorification. The ultimate end of our conversion experience is found in our glorification in which we will come to the perfection of the spiritual, the moral, the intellectual and the physical. The ultimate conformation of the convert will be "to the image of His Son."

The total process of conversion, from the divine side, would be the equivalent of what Jesus called the new birth.

IV. CONFESSION

This was associated with Paul's baptism (verse 18) which was performed, we assume, by Ananias who had previously prayed for him to receive the Holy Spirit. This was Paul's confession of faith before men, although we are not told where or how it was performed. But we are forced to believe by practice and circumstances, that it was by immersion and that it was the occasion for bearing witness to Jesus Christ as Lord. In all the recorded instances of conversion in the Book of Acts the universal formula of a person's confession of faith was to acknowledge Jesus Christ as Lord (8:37) and upon such confession baptism, as an open avowal and expression of the divine Lordship of Christ, was administered. The confession of Christ puts one on record before God and his fellow man. It is a form of commitment in which he has formalized his intention to follow Jesus Christ as a way of life. It is an act of obedience by which one has revealed his innermost convictions and intentions to walk and live in a way that is different from that which was his former manner of life. No professed conversion is complete without this confession. While confession is not necessary to save us, it is necessary if we wish to fulfill our total obligation to God and man.

25

JESUS CHRIST THE SON OF GOD

Acts 9:20

Although the Gospels carry numerous accounts of Jesus as the Son of God, and although the one article of faith at the outset of Christianity was that Jesus was the Messiah, now, for the first time, Jesus is proclaimed publicly and openly in a synagogue as the Son of God. He had been previously acknowledged as the Son of God in a semi-public baptismal confession of faith by the Ethiopian eunuch; but in this instance we have the first general and public proclamation of this unique and essential nature of Jesus. It marks a milestone in the gradual development of Christian truth. Here is the cornerstone of the whole Christian structure. If this is true the claims of Christianity are unique, authoritative and binding. If this is not true then Christianity takes its place with the religious system of Buddhism and others as natural developments of the human spirit.

Does it not seem an astounding thing that for almost two thousand years after He lived, we are still discussing the life, words, deeds, death, resurrection and continuing influence of that man called Jesus of Nazareth? What is the reason for this continuing interest? Why has He not been completely forgotten? He came from no prominent family, no great nation and no important segment of earth's soil. But He lives today in the lives of men as the most important factor of human existence. We naturally ask, why? The answer lies in the answer to another question: Just who is this man? At the close of the Gospel of John it is written, "But these are written, that ye might believe that Jesus is the Christ, the Son of God; and that believing ye might have life through his name" (John 20:31). Paul would later write unanimously to all the churches he founded and say as he did to the Romans (Rom. 1:4), that Jesus was the Son of God; to the Corinthians (II Cor. 1:19); to the Galatians (Gal. 2:20); to the Ephesians (Eph. 4:13).

To consider the fact of Jesus Christ the Son of God is to consider —

The wonder of a pre-incarnate eternity in which Jesus Christ lived before He was born.

The profound mystery of a virgin birth by which He came from eternity into history.

The humiliating limitations of an incarnation during which He lived our life and suffered our death.

The inexpressable concept of one who was the brightness of God's glory and the express image of His person.

The staggering idea of a man containing "the fulness of the Godhead bodily."

All of these stupendous things are involved in the concept of Jesus Christ as the Son of God.

You are asked to think of four things:

I. The Divine Nature of Christ's Person—Who He Is

It is an incredible feat of intellectual legerdemain by which men try to turn the profound evidences of scripture into innocuous religious sayings and end up by saying that Jesus Christ is nothing more than a great man. Yet when you open the Gospel of John you are greeted with these incomparable words: "In the beginning was the Word and the Word was with God, and the Word was God . . . and the Word was made flesh . . . ."

Toward the end of His earthly career Jesus asked His disciples this question: "Whom do men say that I, the Son of man, am?" By asking this question Jesus indicated a number of things. In the first place, it made a difference, in His judgment, what men believed about Him. Belief was the important prelude to life. Second, Jesus knew that men could not be right followers of Him if they were wrong thinkers about Him. As it developed, those who were His closest followers and most intimate friends were the two who more than all the rest held high views of His divine nature. We refer to Peter and John. Third, the difference between right and wrong thinking about Jesus revolved around His deity. The wrong thinkers said He was a great man like an Elijah or a Moses. The right thinkers said that He was "the Christ the Son of the living God." Fourth, the concept of His unique person was not an incidental item of faith to be vowed or disavowed. It was made the cornerstone on which the future church would be built. And so solid would it be, the gates of hell would not prevail against it.

There is no way that you can separate the life of Jesus and the record of the Bible which sets forth that life. For a written Word and a living Word go hand in hand. In fact, these are the two hands God holds out when He approaches man. The Bible is as much the inspiration of God, or the clothing of God with words, as Christ is the incarnation of God, or the clothing of God with flesh. Jesus Christ is no better than the record that reveals Him; and as this record takes shape through the early years of the church, it sets forth the unique and unassailable nature of Jesus Christ as the divine Son of God.

II. THE DIVINE NATURE OF CHRIST'S MESSAGE—WHAT HE SAID

Jesus assumed world leadership through His spoken word. In it He set forth the facts of His gospel and the nature of His kingdom. All that He said was made valid by His death and proved by His resurrection. When men heard Him speak they said, "Never man spake like this man." When His disciples considered other alternatives to Christ they were forced to say, "Lord, to whom shall we go? Thou hast the words of eternal life."

What are the estimates that we must make of this message?

First, it is God's message. "Believest thou not that I am in the Father, and the Father in me? the words that I speak unto you I speak not of myself: but the Father that dwelleth in me, he doeth the works" (John 14:10). Second, it is a finished message. Jesus

Christ has said the last word there is to be said in answer to the human dilemma. When He was about to leave His disciples, He gave them an idea of how complete and final His answer was: " . . . I am the way, the truth, and the life: no man cometh unto the Father, but by me" (John 14:6). Third, it is the only adequate message. For two thousand years men have striven under the benefits of expanding knowledge to improve on the message of Jesus and their efforts are as pitifully inadequate as is a candle before the sun.

George Bernard Shaw said this about Jesus: "I am not a Christian any more than Pilate was . . . . But I am ready to admit, after studying the world of human misery for sixty years, that I see no way out of the world's troubles but the way Jesus would have found had he undertaken the work of a modern practical stateman."*

III. THE DIVINE NATURE OF CHRIST'S MINISTRY—WHAT HE DID

Jesus added works to words and said to contemporary skeptics, if you do not believe in me because of what I am saying, then believe in me because of what I am doing. And from His hands there flowed a beneficent stream of wonderful deeds that caused men to stand in awe and say, truly this was the Son of God.

The ministry of Jesus included two classes of works. First, what He did for man's physical needs—the lesser. Second, what He did for man's spiritual needs—the greater. The former are the most desired. The latter are the most necessary. The former are temporary. The latter are permanent. Men applauded Jesus for the former and they crucified Him for the latter.

The works of Jesus were not essentially social or economic or political, although He did many things to better men socially, economically and politically. But what was of prime importance was the fact that Jesus' ministry was essentially redemptive. It is said that the whole rationale of Christianity is found in thirteen words: "In the heart of man a cry, in the heart of God

---

*"Christian Century" Jan. 19, 1928.

supply." The ministry of Jesus is continuing today in the lives of those who have been redeemed by His blood, regenerated by His grace, and made new creatures in Him. This ministry will be consummated when He shall come the second time to rearrange, readjust, renovate and regenerate our entire national and international structure in all its political, religious, social and economic phases.

IV. THE DIVINE NATURE OF CHRIST'S CLAIMS—WHAT HE DEMANDS

It is possible to generalize Jesus in such fashion that what He has said evaporates into religious fantasy. It becomes like a religious atomizer, sprayed on the congregation once a week. But to face the claims of Jesus is to realize that He has spoken for God. "God, who at sundry times and in divers manner spake in time past unto the fathers by the prophets, hath in these last days spoken unto us by his Son, whom he hath appointed heir of all things, by whom also he made the worlds" (Heb. 1:1, 2).

The divinity of the claims of Jesus are proved by their audacity. He said, "Come unto me, all ye that labour and are heavy laden, and I will give you rest" (Matt. 11:28). He said, ". . . If any man will come after me, let him deny himself, and take up his cross, and follow me" (Matt. 16:24). If Jesus is God, and if as God He has spoken, than what He has said has the force and compulsion of deity and constitutes a legitimate obligation for every man and woman. His claims upon us are:

> The claims of a God — fear Him
> The claims of a Savior — accept Him
> The claims of a Teacher — learn of Him
> The claims of a Master — follow Him
> The claims of a Sovereign — be subject to Him

The claims of Jesus Christ are the double claims of creation and redemption. His rights to our lives are because He has both made us and bought us. It is utterly inconceivable that man as a created being is turned loose in this world as a free moral agent without answering to anyone or without restraint from law.

Man is responsible to God and God has decreed that that responsibility must be discharged through His Son, the Lord Jesus Christ. So in the last analysis man is answerable to God through Christ. The question that will be asked of all men is not to what political party they belonged, or of what race they were a member, or what deeds they accomplished, but this: "What think ye of Christ, whose Son is He?" This will be the determining question, for our answer to it will put us on the side of God and life or leave us without adequate hope and help.

Jesus Christ is not only adequate for the needs of man but He is available. But all that He is, has and has done is unavailing unless by a conscious act of faith and will we submit to Him as our Savior. The purpose of this kind of faith is that we might have the only kind of life that can survive in the presence of God. It is Christ's life. And the only place to get this life is from Him. "But these are written, that ye might believe that Jesus is the Christ, the Son of God; and that believing ye might have life through his name" (John 20:31).

26

WHY DO CHRISTIANS SUFFER?

Acts 9:21-31

Paul's conversion is followed by adversity, suffering and persecution. It brings into view the problem of suffering that must be answered in the lives of all Christians.

The Christian answer may be found in the Apostle Paul's words, "For, when we were come into Macedonia, our flesh had no rest, but we were troubled on every side; without were fightings, within were fears. Nevertheless God . . . " (II Cor. 7:5, 6). Two words stand out against the black background of Paul's adversity, *"nevertheless God."* These may not be the reason or the explanation, but they are the remedy for and the preventive against despair and surrender to whatever may be harassing our life or jeopardizing our peace.

When Paul went to Macedonia he found no rest for the flesh. Trouble was on every side, fightings were without and fears within; "nevertheless God that comforteth those that are cast down" was His refuge against defeat and despair. And we may write into Paul's experience any condition or circumstance we wish. We may change the geography from Macedonia to North America. We may color it with the complexion of our present personal problems and then may add, "nevertheless God" and it will be adequate and sufficient for anything.

In thinking about adversity, ours and others, there are usually two questions we are troubled over — why and how?

I. WHY IS ADVERSITY?

Job knew a little bit about adversity. Ask him for an answer to this question. He was stripped of his fortune and his family. He lost his health and most of his friends. In the book that bears his name it speaks about adversity on this wise: "Although affliction cometh not forth of the dust, neither doth trouble spring out of the ground: yet man is born unto trouble as the sparks fly upward." Trouble is a common incident of life. Man is born into it and this is so because sin is a fact of life and has disordered the world. The world is not now in the perfect state it was when created. An upward flying spark and a downward looking man are proof of it.

But a Christian's faith does not date with Eden; it dates with the cross. While the effect of Adam's Edenic sin is still in the world, we are living under the provisions of the cross. And while we, like all men, must suffer adversity we do not suffer it hopelessly. We have Christ's power of the cross. He said, "In the world ye shall have tribulation but be of good cheer, I have overcome the world." Trouble is inevitable, but not defeat. Christ overcame that we might overcome in the common troubles of life. Some are like the man who was accosted by a friend who said, "I didn't know you suffered with rheumatism!" "Sure! What else can you do with it?" Adversity may be either an instrument of pain to suffer, or it may be God's shaping tool.

Notice some things that are true in a Christian's attitude to adversity:

1. Adversity is a Great Leveler.

Prosperity has a tendency to make men self-sufficient. Men draw apart into classes and castes. But how different when adversity comes. Let a great catastrophe sweep into a community and all men become alike. Sorrow wipes out distinctions. Reduction to the same common denominator comes to all men when adversity strikes. Then none feel the importance of his previous distinctions. All need a common thing — comfort.

2. Adversity is a Great Reminder.

God gave Israel a warning as it was about to enter the land of Canaan with its vineyards which they had not planted and its wells which they had not digged and its cities they had not builded. "When thou shalt have eaten and be full; then beware lest thou forget the Lord." There was not much danger of forgetting the Lord when they were empty; but when they were full it would be a different matter. One of the greatest crimes of prosperity is man's forgetfulness of God. Most people can pray when they are in adversity; but few seem to realize the necessity of it in prosperity. A pastor once received an unusual request for prayer. It was from a man who earnestly desired the prayers of God's people because he was prospering in business. Few feel this need.

3. Adversity is a Great Purifier.

Adversity builds purging fires to purify our lives. It is expressed this way by Peter: "Wherein ye greatly rejoice, though now for a season, if need be, ye are in heaviness through manifold temptations: that the trial of your faith, being much more precious than of gold that perisheth, though it be tried with fire, might be found unto praise and honour and glory at the appearing of Jesus Christ" (I Pet. 1:6, 7). In this view adversity is not a detriment but an advantage. God uses it as a smelter to purify faith.

4. Adversity is a Great Teacher.

Adversity becomes a day of much doubt and great despair to most people, when God intends it to be a day of learning. The Psalmist saw this and said, "It is good for me that I have been afflicted; that I might learn thy statutes." The principal purpose is learning. God uses pains to teach us. In the physical realm God might have made the body so that cuts would not hurt and broken bones would not pain and organic disorders would not distress; but think of the mischief that would result from cuts uncared for and bones unset. Pain is a warning against infection and it is God's means of preventing physical ruin. God might also have made our bodies without the pangs of hunger and thirst but think what would result. Hunger and thirst are painful reminders of physical need. They have a good purpose. Without pain and pang we could die. Nerves were not placed in bodies for the purpose of torture, but for a wise and benevolent reason.

Abuse and neglect and accident will bring pain, but their chief purpose is warning and prevention. It is identically so with adversity. It is a great teacher and reminder. Through it God speaks by a language we cannot misunderstand. It is used to remind us of a deeper need.

We must learn to live. Even birds which were born for the air must learn to fly. The air seems to be the natural element for birds, but just the same flying is something they have to learn by hard practice. It has been said that young swallows are able to fly without any teaching or persuasion, but if this is true they are very much the exception. Other young birds learn the hard way, and their parents often have to use force as well as persuasion to get them started on their first flights. Thus mother sparrows are sometimes seen coaxing their youngsters by showing them bits of food and then carrying it out of their reach to tempt them into following. Mother storks will push their young off the edge of the nest or chimney stack where they are perched. Other birds, too, give the young ones a push when persuasion fails and then fly along with them. Often they will fly under the fluttering tyro and give him a boost if he seems to be losing altitude too rapidly. The martins are one species who often do this. Even when the young birds get well started, it takes a long while for them to achieve the perfect control and skill in the air shown by the adults. That can be acquired only by constant practice. That also is the only way in which they can gain the endurance necessary for the long migration flights they must soon make. Endurance is equally necessary for such birds as the martins who catch their insect food in the air. The old birds seem to know this, and if one has a chance to watch a colony of martins, for instance, the parents will be seen sitting in front of the nests watching their families circling around in the air again and do this time after time until they think the youngsters have really earned a rest.*

The Christian life is like the wing of a bird; it is given to us as the gift of God, but it must be developed. You could scarcely

---

*"Our Dumb Animals" by John H. Spicer

call the wing of a newly born bird either beautiful, protecting or powerful. It must be developed. The best illustration for the development of a bird's wing is found in Deuteronomy. The illustration is to the effect that the mother bird rears her children in her nest, on some high cliff, where the young birds receive the attention of their mother. The nest is built of twigs, some of them hard and thorny, but covered over with lamb's wool and other soft material, and the eaglets are very comfortable. Here they enjoy themselves in the protection of mother in the continual supply of the best of food, perched in mid-air. The time comes when the mother bird thinks it proper that they should do a little for themselves. She pulls away the wool from beneath the birds and makes them feel for the first time that the nest is uncomfortable. Then it is an easy matter to get the eaglets to shift. Mother pulls one of them over the edge of the rock and now it struggles in its native element, two thousand feet above the ground. And in struggling, it suddenly discovers it has wings; but those wings are undeveloped and incapable of bearing up their burden. The mother who is watching the career of her offspring swoops beneath the struggling mass of eagle nature, and bears it triumphantly on to the ledge again. With one after the other of the eaglets the lessons are repeated, until at last the lessons are learned. Then they can fly, and rise until they can look the sun in the face.

God has been trying to get some people off the nest for a long time!

5. Adversity is a Great Blessing.

This does not always appear upon the face of our tragedy. One cannot see at the moment how death may be a blessing or how disappointment can be a profit. But think of this —

> "Ill that God blesses is our good,
>   And unblest good is ill:
>   And all is right that seems most wrong,
>   If it be His sweet will."

The blessing may not be apparent now, but remember the Christian has a future and in that future all the present will be perfectly apparent. "Our light affliction which is but for a moment worketh for us a far more exceeding and eternal weight of glory" (II Cor. 4:17).

The present affliction may not be our choice but it is God's choice. It may be similar to the purpose which He chose for Paul when he was put in prison, and of which he writes in Philippians 1:12-14. "But I would ye should understand, brethren, that the things which happened unto me have fallen out rather unto the furtherance of the gospel; so that my bonds in Christ are manifest in all the palace, and in all other places; and many of the brethren in the Lord, waxing confident by my bonds, are much more bold to speak the word without fear."

II. How is Adversity Overcome?

Paul's remedy was found in two words, "nevertheless God." He is the answer to everything that is wrong and the reason for everything that is right. "In the world ye shall have tribulation: but be of good cheer; I have overcome the world" (John 16:33).

Someone has said, "If our circumstances find us in God, we shall find God in all our circumstances." If you are a Christian and "hid with God in Christ" you should capitalize on that fact. Since you are with God you have a right to expect God to be with you. That fact is not something to wait for but to realize right now. It is your legitimate, Bible-promised right as a Christian. There is enough legitimate authority here to lift you out of your despondency and sorrow. The question is, do you believe it?

You frequently hear of people who have "lost everything." This is an expression that usually means their fortune. But when has a person really lost everything? Not when he has lost his job or even his health, and certainly not when he has lost his property. He has lost everything when he has lost his reason, the love of his family, the pangs of conscience, the movings of the Spirit, faith in the Bible, trust in God and hope of heaven. And until then he may lose his job, his money, his home, his property, his friends; but if he has God he has not lost anything of lasting consequence.

We admire the faith of the Prophet Habakkuk. "Although the fig tree shall not blossom, neither shall fruit be in the vines; the labour of the olive shall fail, and the fields shall yield no meat; the flock shall be cut off from the fold, and there shall be no herd in the stalls: Yet I will rejoice in the Lord, I will joy in the God of my salvation" (Hab. 3:17, 18). A similar situation may be ours and when it is, put two words into it, "nevertheless God." We might not choose adversity or hardship. We would have put an olive wreath on the brow of the Son of God, as the Prince of Peace, rather than the thorn crown for the Lamb of God. But God saw the need of the cross. He may see that need in our lives too. It is the cross always before the crown.

27

THE HEALING MINISTRY OF THE CHURCH
Acts 9:32-43

There is no doubt that the church, at its very beginning, had a healing ministry. There is also no doubt that the church, as we know it today, has a healing ministry. But the great question is, are these healing ministries the same in their scope and purpose? If they are the same then the church ought to be performing miracles of healing that include all kinds and manners of disease. It ought also to be raising the dead. Moreover, the Lord is just as good an occulist as He is a physician and just as good a dentist as He is a surgeon.

Healing, as we know it in the Gospels and Acts, fell into a special category of events called miracles. These miracles were general and not restricted to a few people or a few forms of sickness. It should also be established that these miracles were for a specific purpose. That purpose was not primarily to cure disease or reverse death. It was to bear witness to the divine nature of Christianity as a means of salvation. The great and important ministry of the church was spiritual and not physical; for the soul and not for the body; for eternity and not for time.

We should always remember that healing was never a permanent experience like salvation, for healed people became sick again and later died. There was always one sickness from which they were never healed, the sickness from which they died. The same was true of the resurrections, three of them in Jesus' experience, one in Peter's experience and one in Paul's. In every one of these five instances irreversible death ultimately came to the individuals.

The reason we say these things is to be able to say that if the healing of the sick was on the agenda of the early church on the same basis as the salvation of the soul, it would have been directed to the cause of sickness and not merely to its effects. Sickness and death remain among us as perpetual reminders of God's judgment upon sin, and they will never totally disappear until God's new redemptive order comes into being.

Today when we speak of the healing ministry of the church we are using a term which does not have a common definition, and consequently means many things to many people. The faith healer gives it one meaning; the Christian Science practitioner, another meaning; the Episcopalian missioner, another, and the average pastor, still another. To one person it is the performance of an outright miracle by a person-to-person meeting between God and man and the achievement of such miraculous events as are described in the Gospels and the Acts. To another person healing is something metaphysical, with mind achieving superiority over matter. To another, it is something psychosomatic, with an inter-play of the mental and physical. To another, it is spiritual therapy through counselling, faith and prayer. But none of these, except the first, describe the healing ministry of the church in the Book of Acts, for here it is the direct and immediate effect of prayer and faith upon the body, resulting in a miracle of healing.

The healings described in the four gospels are innumerable. They cannot be tabulated because there were some mass healings. In the Book of Acts the healings were far less in number, including Peter's healing of the lame man at the Gate Beautiful in the temple, Peter's healing of Eneas, Paul's healing of the cripple, Paul's healing of many at Corinth through the blessing of handkerchieves and aprons, Paul's preventive healing of himself from contact with a viper, and Paul's healing of the father of Publius.

And in the rest of the New Testament there are only four instances of sickness situations mentioned and each one is different in its effect. In the case of Epaphroditus, he was prayed for and healed (Phil. 2:25-27). In the case of Trophimus, he was prayed for and not healed (II Tim. 4:20). In the case of Timothy, he was advised to use physical means because he apparently endured delicate health throughout his whole lifetime as the result of congenital sickness (I Tim. 5:23). In the case of the Apostle Paul, he prayed for himself three times, for the removal of a physical handicap, and was not healed; but was given God's grace to bear his handicap with great distinction and usefulness (II Cor. 12:7-10).

Judging the healing ministry of the church by these facts we come to certain conclusions. First, on the basis of numerical incidence, the original character of the church's healing ministry was a diminishing one. That is, there was a lessening need for the performance of miracles in terms of physical healings, for once the divine nature of the church was established it did not need the continuance of these miracles of healings. Second, when the church passes out of this period of signs and wonders, the treatment of sickness, while always being by prayer, does not always have the same results. In one instance a sick man is prayed for and healed. In another instance a sick man is prayed for and not healed. In another instance a sick man is prayed for, plus the application of means in a medicinal sense, and he is sustained in delicate health. In yet another instance, the most outstanding Christian in the New Testament being afflicted with a distressing physical defect, prays for himself and is answered by being given God's grace. Is anyone going to say that he has an open and closed formula for healing, that embraces all sickness and achieves a healing effect in every case?

It is apparent from these observations that the healing ministry of the early church and today's church are not the same. As we know healing in the Gospels and Acts it was promiscuous; everyone prayed for was healed. But healing as we know it today is providential; it is a selective experience according to the will of God. While the healing ministry of the church is not on the same basis of promiscuous miracles of healing as it was in the early church, God is not limited in His right or ability to perform miracles by healing. There is a continuing precedent for this in the continuing history of the church; for while the same numerous miracles of the early church have not continued in the succeeding church, yet every age of the church has had its valid miracles of healing. Personal experience bears unqualified witness to three such miracles of healing in my own ministry. None of these miracles were in public, under television cameras, but were achieved either in the quietness of a hospital room or the home, and in one instance without physical contact with the sick person. But we must also say that we have prayed for many other people without the same dramatic, death-reversing, miraculous effects. We believe according to the pattern of experience which follows the events of the Book of Acts, that prayers for the sick may in some cases result in healing, in other cases not result in healing, in other cases justify the use of means such as modern medicine and surgery, and in all instances see the manifestation of God's grace so that sickness is born with distinction and blessing.

How are we going to conduct the healing ministry of the church today? Should the sick be encouraged to believe that they will be healed if only they have faith? No, because this might be raising hopes that may lead to cruel disappointment. But, we should always pray for the sick that God's inscrutable will be done.

Should we assume that God wants everybody to be well? If we do we are contradicting the experience of the Apostle Paul. We are also contradicting the triumphant experiences of some of the choicest saints. And we are assuming something that cannot be verified by the normal lives of God's people.

Is it God's will to heal all sickness? Not in a general sense. God is able to heal all sickness or He would not be God; but God's will may permit the experience of sickness for the higher good of the sick person.

Is sickness always due to sin and does it come as God's punishment upon the sinner? No, emphatically no. This is contradicted by Paul's experience and Job's experience, and the experience of many others. It is the normal consequence of being alive in an abnormal world where sickness is a universal experience for good and bad alike.

To summarize the answers to all these questions someone has said, "While there is a strong presumption in favor of the fact that it is the will of God for people to have sufficient health to do that to which God has called them, still we cannot be sure that it is always His will to answer every prayer to heal sickness." That is on the negative side. On the positive side we can confidently believe in the available power of God, in response to the prayers of His people; for "although we cannot fully comprehend the way in which God uses intercessory prayer as a channel for His blessing, there is every reason to believe that power for healing is often thus released."

The church has a healing ministry and it should include the following:

1. Healing For the Whole Person.

We are body, soul and spirit and any healing which is available to us is available in the spiritual, mental and physical levels of life. Triumphant living does not depend on perfect health, for while the outward man perishes the inward man may be renewed day by day.

2. Faith Health as Well as Faith Healing.

Faith health is preventive, while faith healing is corrective. Faith health can be the normal consequence of living the Christian life at its highest levels of faith, and respect for the laws of God. This brings freedom from worry and fear, deliverance from tensions and the conquest of the effects of a mechanical civilization. Faith health is one of the dividends of a clean life with its freedom from destructive habits. It is the result of the understanding and application of faith to everyday living.

3. Prayer For the Sick.

After you get past the Book of Acts there is only one New Testament writer who gives any instruction regarding the healing of the sick. That writer is James who says, "Is any sick among you? let him call for the elders of the church; and let them pray over him, anointing him with oil in the name of the Lord: And the prayer of faith shall save the sick, and the Lord shall raise him up . . ." (James 5:14, 15). This must be read and practiced within the context of the four cases of sickness to which we have already referred. This does not make healing mandatory in all cases even though it says, "the prayer of faith shall save the sick." It means that we should pray in all cases of sickness for God's will to be done. Prayer for the sick is definitely in order. It is the church's spiritual therapy. It has accounted for multitudes of known cases of healing, apart from the use of means. It has resulted in healing forces being released upon the sick that cannot be measured. Prayer for the sick is the instrument which the church possesses for what we properly call spiritual healing or divine healing. It may be with or without the use of means. It may or may not result in the visible healing of the sick person. It may, as it did in the case of the Apostle Paul, result in the release of a sufficient measure of divine grace that life may be a triumphant experience of service in the face of adversity, handicap and affliction. In any case we have access, through prayer, to God's power to heal when that healing is in accordance with God's will.

28

THE YIELDED VALUE OF LITTLE THINGS
Acts 9:36-43

Everything has two values. The obvious value is the intrinsic, inherent or natural value. The less obvious value is the yielded value. Money has two values. One is the hoarded value of the miser, who keeps it locked up within his selfishness and never lets it reach the place of useful and productive investment. The other is the yielded value, in which in the form of a tithe, an offering, or a sacrifice, it is surrendered for use in the propagation of the gospel or the alleviation of human need. Talents have two values. One is the useless value of an unused talent, in which some choice ability is shut up within a selfish life. The other is the useful value of a yielded talent in which it is given to God, and used for the blessing and benefit of all whom it reaches.

Most of us are little people. Our names never reach the headlines of newspapers. Our lives are submerged in the desperate monotony and mediocrity of everyday living. We never attract great attention or do great things. But little people are the people God needs. In fact, they are the people He can use to the greatest advantage. This is what Paul had to say about little people: "For ye see your calling, brethren, how that not many wise men after the flesh, not many mighty, not many noble, are called: But God hath chosen the foolish things of the world to confound the wise; and God hath chosen the weak things of the world to confound the things which are mighty; and base things of the world, and things which are despised, hath God chosen, yea, and things which are not, to bring to nought things that are: That no flesh should glory in his presence" (I Cor. 1:26-29).

Just where does the value of little things lie? To be sure the intrinsic value of little things will always be littleness. But the yielded value of little things is greatness, usefulness, achievement and incalculable blessing. Yes, the yielded value of a little thing is a great thing.

The true value of the things we possess, or the person we are, does not consist in what they or we are, but solely in what they or we are, yielded and in the hands of God. Littleness will never be any more than littleness; but when the ordinary talents or possessions of ordinary people are yielded to God for His sanctification and blessing, they possess the potential of greatness.

Did you ever pick up an ordinary paper clip and examine it? It is just a piece of coated wire whose value is not in the little strip of wire, but in the shape into which that wire has been bent. It is so with our lives. The value and usefulness of life is not in what we are intrinsically or inherently, but in the shape of character and the form of usefulness into which God has brought us. The piece of wire we call a paper clip is a very insignificant and common implement. It is the commonest, most ordinary thing we possess, yet because of its shape it performs a service for us that we could not do without. Take paper clips out of the world and business would be stopped in its tracks. The common paper clip prevents the loss of valuable papers. It provides efficiency in keeping order. It saves time and expense and has a thousand and one uses; yet the paper clip is scarcely noticed and never honored simply because it is a paper clip. However useless or insignificant we may feel or seem to be, there is a place and use for each of us and it lies solely in the yielded value of what we are and possess.

Speaking of usefulness, everyone has some useful purpose in life, even if it is only to serve as a horrible example. It lets others see what they ought not be.

Do you recall the story of the Chinese student who was discovered in a church attic in Ann Arbor, Michigan where for four years he had hidden from the world? Driven by shame of failure in his studies at the University of Michigan, he took refuge in the attic of the church, coming out only at night to get scraps of food left from church dinners. Perhaps if we found the right attic we might hide from some of the things that trouble us, like taxes and rock and roll music, and freeways, and so forth. But what is to be seriously observed in this attic epic is that there is more than one person hiding in our churches. They are hiding behind creedal professions and liturgical ceremonies. They are hiding their light under the bushel of business, the bed of leisure and the table of pleasure. They are hiding from useful, productive and fruitful lives. They have allowed the intrinsic value of what they are to be obscured by the lack of yielding themselves for useful living for God.

A flock of geese once lived together in a barnyard. Once a week they gathered in a corner of the yard and one of the more eloquent of their number mounted the fence to speak of the wonders of geese. He recounted the exploits of their forefathers, who mounted on wings and flew the trackless wastes of the sky. He spoke of the goodness of the Creator who had given geese the urge to migrate and wings to fly. And as he spoke the geese would nod their heads and marvel at these things and comment on the eloquence of the preaching goose. All this they did. But one thing they never did; they did not fly. They went back to their waiting dinner, for the corn was good and the barnyard secure.

The principal character of reference in this sermon is Dorcas. Dorcas lived in Joppa and was a consecrated disciple of Jesus. Her name and fame have survived the centuries. This survival was not because Dorcas died and was raised from the dead by the power of God through Peter. It was because she owned a needle, and with that needle she clothed the bare backs and naked bodies of the needy of Joppa. By her needle she spread the love of Christ as effectively as Apollos did by his eloquent speech. Certainly there was no magic in the needle of Dorcas, yet it sewed love with every stitch it took. Instead of the "dolorous song of the shirt" with its sewed-in misery and grief, it was, for Dorcas, the joyous song of the Christ with prayers and love and deeds of generosity and sacrifice. The needle of Dorcas of Joppa became more powerful than the sword of Caesar and the pen of Celsus, simply because she yielded it to God. The intrinsic value of Dorcas' needle was ordinary craftwork but the yielded value was love, mercy, comfort and salvation.

But Dorcas does not stand alone in the Bible to display the yielded value of little things. There are others and among them there is a list of distinguished names.

I. MOSES AND HIS ROD

On the backside of an Arabian desert God found a fugitive Hebrew tending sheep in his lonesomeness. Out of the strange phenomenon of a burning bush Moses is called to emancipate a host of Hebrew slaves from Pharaoh's bondage. He protests on the basis of personal incapability. God calls his attention to what he held in his hand, a shepherd's rod. Cast on the ground, at the command of God, it became a serpent. Retrieved, it was a rod once more. And this rod was to become the emblem of power and symbol of strength. With it Moses would bring plagues of deliverance upon Egypt. And with it he would part the waters of the sea and later produce water in the desert.

There was no magic in a shepherd's rod. Power of that sort did not lie in the fibres of a piece of wood. But there was yielded value in Moses' rod, for when he yielded it to God the man and the rod became instruments of God's use. Yes, and there is a rod like that in every life. God is looking at you and saying what He said to Moses, "What is in thine hand?" It may be a meagre talent. Yield it to God, cast it at His feet and let Him invest it with power and blessing.

II. GIDEON'S THREE HUNDRED AND THEIR PITCHERS

To rid Israel of the marauding Midianites God chose a young man named Gideon. A call to arms by the dynamic leader brought thirty-two thousand volunteers. But God said these are "too many." The fearful and fainthearted were dismissed, leaving ten thousand. But still there were "too many." And then by a test of alertness three hundred were chosen from the ten thousand. By these three hundred God proposed to deliver Israel from an army of Midianites described as numerous "as the sand of the seaside." In the dead of night they went out armed only with pitchers; and at the sound of the trumpets they broke their pitchers and three hundred hidden lights flared in the darkness and, appearing from every quarter of the hillsides, they sent the Midianites into riotous defeat. The effectiveness of this strategy was not in the smallness of their number, nor in the fact that they concealed lights in their pitchers. It was only when the pitchers were broken that the hidden lights appeared and sent the enemy in fearful flight.

As Christians we are said to be "the light of the world." But this light is of no value if concealed in selfish, useless, unwitnessing lives. The light is of no value until the vessel that holds it is yielded and broken so the light can be displayed.

III. The Lad and His Lunch

The possession by a boy of a lunch of five loaves and two fish was an insignificant thing until an emergency arose by a lakeside. That lunch was scarcely enough for any normal boy, let alone for a multitude. But the yielded possession of that boy strangely multiplied in the hands of Jesus, until He fed five thousand with basketsfull remaining for further use. The power of multiplication was not in the molecules of bread and fish, for had that boy used it for himself it would have remained five loaves and two fish. But when he yielded it to the hands of the strange Galilean it multiplied into what might have well become infinitude.

IV. The Widow and Her Mites

The story is too well remembered for repetition, but when the widowed worshipper placed her two mites in the temple treasury Jesus said, "This poor widow hath cast more in than all they which have cast into the treasury." Two mites, or leptons, valued at one tenth of a penny each, outweighed and outvalued the gold of the rich. But the value of the gifts was not in their metals. Gold was still gold and copper still copper. The vault of the treasury affected no strange alchemy upon the gifts. The difference lay between intrinsic value and yielded value and the yielded value made copper worth more than gold.

It is so with the mites of talent, service, time and treasure that you may possess. Yielded, they outweigh the deeds of the mighty. Yes, there is greatness in the yielded value of little things like a needle, a rod, a pitcher, a lunch, a mite and a life like yours.

29

WHO CAN BELONG TO THE CHURCH?
Acts 10:1-48; 11:19-30

We are concerned in this portion of the Book of Acts with an important matter of church polity which involved a Roman centurion of Caesarea, by the name of Cornelius. The events centering in Cornelius, and also involving Peter, settled a very important question—who can belong to the church?

There is both a prelude and a sequel to the story of Cornelius.

1. The Prelude (Acts 9:31)

The prelude is described in the words, "Then had the churches rest throughout all Judea and Galilee and Samaria, and were edified; and walking in the fear of the Lord, and in the comfort of the Holy Ghost, were multiplied." This was rest from the great persecutions which came when the Jerusalem disciples were "scattered abroad throughout the region of Judea and Samaria, except the apostles" (Acts 8:1). Now that the chief persecutor, Saul of Tarsus, had been converted, persecution died out and gave the church occasion for the consolidation of its position. It did so by "walking in the fear of the Lord." This resulted in "the comfort of the Holy Ghost," and all of this spiritual progress resulted in their multiplication.

Up to this time the church had been located at Jerusalem and was involved almost entirely with its Jewish neighbors, and concerned almost solely with its Jewish converts. Now that it was scattered abroad it was brought into contact with the pagan Gentile world from which it was drawing converts. The question now was, what was to be done with these converts? Who had a right to belong to the church? Is it a place exclusively for converted Jews with their Hebraic traditions, or are converts from the pagan Gentile world entitled to a place in the church? There was a growing party in the early church that wanted to make the church a suburb of Judaism. They wanted it to be a Jewish sect identified with the Old Testament system of ceremonies, food laws, sabbath worship, and so forth. On the other hand, there were others called Hellenists (Gnostics) who wanted the church identified with Grecian culture and philosophy. Who would prevail?

2. The Sequel (Acts 11:1-18)

The news of what happened in Caesarea had reached the apostolic council in Jerusalem, so Peter went up and gave an account of the things that had transpired because he had already been called into question concerning his breach of the traditional Jewish religious practice of exclusiveness by sitting down with uncircumcised Gentiles. He related the events and their lesson, namely, that God had established a new order of grace in the church; that ceremonial laws were abrogated; that converted Gentiles were to be as welcome to the new community of Christians as converted Jews. This was indeed a momentous decision and marked a milestone in the history of the church, which was to be neither an ecclesiastical suburb of Judaism, nor a religious adaptation of Grecianism. It was to be the church, established in grace, and separated from all other forms of religion and philosophy.

The determining events of this momentous decision centered around two personalities, Cornelius the Gentile and Peter the Jew. You could not have had anyone more Gentile than Cornelius, nor anyone more Jewish than Peter.

I. CORNELIUS THE GENTILE

That this man was a centurion in the Roman Army was of lesser importance to other things said about him. He is described as a "devout man, and one that feared God with all his house." He "gave much alms to the people, and prayed to God alway" (verse 2). The question is, was his religious piety a saving credential? Could he belong to the new community of the church because he was an inquirer of the Jewish faith, and because he was an alms giver and a man of prayer? The answer is, no. He may have had a beginning faith and an inquiring faith and a sincere faith, but he did not have a saving faith. This is evident from the fact that he was directed in a vision to send for Peter, the messenger of God and the preacher of the gospel; and find out from him what he must do to be saved. It is further evident that he was not saved, because when he heard Peter's message of the gospel, he and his household believed, had the experience of the Holy Spirit and were baptized, his piety, alms-giving and prayers notwithstanding.

It is therefore established that the basis of belonging to the new community of Christians, called the church, is neither Judaism nor Grecianism, piety nor good works. The basis is faith in God through Jesus Christ. Jesus had previously said to a religious Jew, "Verily, verily, I say unto thee, Except a man be born again, he cannot see the kingdom of God." Is the church different from the kingdom of God? The church is the present, visible manifestation of the kingdom of God. If piety alone was a criteria of fitness then almost any religious devotee would qualify for the kingdom of God.

II. PETER THE JEW

Peter was not an ordinary Jew. He was the leader of the Jewish party in the infant church. He had held out for the observance of the externals of Jewish practice, as a part of the Christian faith. But now he is presented with a singular situation. He is asked to forego his convictions and break down the racial barriers which kept him from association with Gentiles. What is even more startling, he is asked to accept these people into the church on an equal footing.

It happened this way: While at Joppa, Peter stayed with a leather merchant named Simon. As was Peter's custom, he went to a secluded portion of the house to pray. It was to the roof top, for it was a flat roof with parapets on four sides and afforded excellent seclusion. While praying he had a vision in which he saw a giant sheet-like object being lowered from heaven on which were all manner of beasts and birds and other animals. Of course, from a strictly Jewish standpoint, some of these were unclean, because they were forbidden by law. Then a voice entered the vision and Peter was told to kill and eat at his pleasure. He instantly rebelled and rejected the instructions of the heavenly voice because his Jewish ceremonial sensitivity told him he could not eat what was "common or unclean." Even clean animals must be butchered according to rabbinical ritual before they could be eaten. Then came the precedent shattering verdict of the divine voice which said, "What God hath cleansed, that call not thou common" (verse 15). The meaning of this experience was very plain. In the new order of the church, God not only destroyed the barriers of the food laws which separated one animal from another; but He also destroyed the racial barriers which separated one race from another. Gentiles, heretofore considered unclean and unfit for contact with Jews, were made acceptable to God. The basis of this acceptability was the new order of grace in the church. And the new order of grace made provision for personal and racial cleanness and acceptability through regeneration. So Peter was confronted with a momentous revision of principle. He could no longer stand within the select circle of racial exclusiveness. He could no longer depend upon ceremonial cleansing. Now it was the cleansing of grace, the washing away of sins by the blood of Christ, sanctification by the Holy Spirit, and the fitness that came, not through ceremonial righteousness of the law, but through the righteousness of Jesus Christ which becomes ours through faith in Him.

Peter had already been summoned by both man and God to go to Caesarea to the house of Cornelius. Through the impetus of this revelation of the new order of grace and the new standing of all men before God without racial barriers, he went to Caesarea and entered the house of the Roman Gentile Cornelius. This was a man whom Peter, before his vision, would have considered common and unclean. The house was full of people, including Cornelius' kinsmen, neighbors and friends; for they were anxious for a revelation from God.

Although Cornelius was a devout man full of good intentions and noted for his deeds of alms, his righteousness was still imperfect and insufficient "for it did not spring from the highest motive, namely, conscious faith in Christ, of whose work of redemption he was ignorant."*

Peter asked them to state more fully the reason for summoning him, and Cornelius proceeded to describe the vision he had in which he was directed to send for Peter at Joppa and added, "now therefore are we all here present before God, to hear all things that are commanded thee of God." Whereupon Peter preached the first sermon ever given to an exclusively Gentile audience in which he told them that "God was no respecter of persons" (verse 34). Then Peter went on to recount the coming of Christ, his crucifixion and resurrection and His work of salvation for all men and concluded by saying, "that through his name whosoever believeth in him shall receive remission of sins" (verse 43).

God did not accept people into the church just because they were Jews or Gentiles, Romans or Grecians, freemen or bondmen. He accepted them on the basis of their faith in Jesus Christ and their spiritual fitness by God's work of regeneration.

The upshot of all this was the Gentile Pentecost. These people received the Holy Spirit in exactly the same manner that the Jews did at the Jerusalem Pentecost and evidenced it by speaking in tongues, after which they were baptized.

What are we to deduce from this momentous event concerning the question of who can belong to the church? Belonging to the church in the sense of entering the kingdom of God is based on these things:

1. Confession of Faith

Here is the word: "that through his name whosoever believeth in him shall receive remission of sins" (verse 43).

---

*R. B. Rackham

We must first of all understand what this confession of faith is. It is confession of faith in Christ crucified and risen from the dead, who died for our sins that He might bring us to God. It is confession of faith involving repentance of sins so that we no longer live as we once did, but forswearing all the past and forsaking all sin, we follow Jesus Christ as our supreme Lord and Master. I am afraid that sometimes confession of faith means what it did to a man who once joined the the church on "confusion of faith." We must dissipate this confusion by understanding the scriptural formula of confession of faith.

2. Christian Experience

The church is not a place for perfect people, but for those who, upon confession of faith, have entered into that personal experience in Christ which sets them on a new pathway of life. We are not entitled to enter the church on the experience of others, like our parents. Christian experience is something personal. It is what happens to us. It is something we find out for ourselves. I knew a father who submitted the name of his married son for church membership. After considering the case it was decided that this son should not be admitted. It greatly angered the father, and he left the church, because he thought it was the duty and obligation of the church to receive everyone who wanted to belong. But when we are dealing with the church we must remember that the standards are not ours to set; they are God's. Christ is the Head of the church and no man can either open or shut the door.

3. Baptism

This seems to have been a universal requirement in the first church. It is something that followed the confession of faith and acceptance of Christ by the early believers. It is what we call believer's baptism, or the baptism of believers who are conscious of their own personal act of confession of Jesus Christ as Savior.

Should people unite with the church? If the precedent established at the beginning is any criteria, this seems to be what they did then. It seems quite evident that these were organized churches; that there were church officers; that there were prescribed ordinances; that there was a body of faith to be believed by a body of believers; that when both Jews and Gentiles, religious and pagan, accepted this body of faith, they were baptized and were recognized as a part of the body of believers. Belonging to the church is no assurance that you belong to the kingdom of God; but when a person belongs to the kingdom of God he most certainly has the most urgent reason for belonging to the church which God established to nurture our faith and provide a channel for our service and give opportunity for our witness to others.

30

WHAT DO WE MEAN BY THE CHURCH?
Acts 11:19-30

The unfolding story of the church brings us to Antioch in Syria which scattered Christian evangelists had reached in their effort to extend the base of the church. They had chiefly confined their preaching efforts to Jewish communities; but at Antioch they found a large Greek population, and emboldened by their growing successes, they presented the claims of Jesus as both Lord and Savior of all mankind to these Gentiles. The results were astounding because these Gentile Greeks, or Hellenists, eagerly received the message and embraced the Savior, resulting in "a great number" turning to the Lord.

This was to be the first test of the principle of church membership established at the house of the centurion, Cornelius, when Peter came and preached the gospel. It was established that "God is no respecter of persons" (Acts 10:34) and that God also granted repentance to the Gentiles.

Now, with vast numbers of Gentiles believing and turning to the Lord, what would be the attitude of the church, for the church up to this time was largely made up of Jewish believers. This was settled when the church in Jerusalem sent Barnabas to Antioch to investigate the nature of this Gentile revival. On his arrival Barnabas was overjoyed at what he observed. This, he said to himself, was truly of God; for he saw Gentiles and Jews alike hearing and believing the good news of the gospel. Consequently he gave his approval and encouraged both Gentiles and Jews to dwell in Christian love and unity. Losing their racial identity as Jews and Gentiles, they would soon have a common name to bind them together. They would soon be called Christian, which would be the source of their new identity and unity (Gal. 3:26-28).

Now the question was, of what did they become members when they became members of the church? What is the church? From now on the word "church" would be very prominent in the record of events and the vocabulary of the Christians. Soon there would be churches springing up all over Asia Minor, made up of thousands upon thousands of members, both Jews and Gentiles. The best way to answer this question is to say that the church is a body. It is obvious that it is a body of people; but it had a mystical nature for it is described as "the body of Christ." This is not an attempt to define this body, which is the church, but rather to describe it. When you define a thing you are involved almost exclusively with words. But when you describe something it involves action and Acts is the church in action. It is the body of Christ in terms of life, experience and activity.

Taking our cue from the concept of the church as a body, we notice that the existence of a body involves birth; that members of a body have to be born with it; that a body has functions; and that the over-all purpose of a body is to give expression to someone who dwells in it. This is what we find in the church.

I. THE FORMATION OF THE BODY

This happened at Pentecost when the coming of the Holy Spirit marked the beginning of the church. This was the equivalent of birth. Bodies are born; they are not assembled or organized. This was in the very nature of the case, a local church, but it was also a universal church. As a local church it was known as "the church which was in Jerusalem." It is never called the church of Jerusalem. There was also a "church in Rome" but there was never a church of Rome. The church of Rome is an ecclesiastical accretion and a theological invention. As a local church it functioned autonomously, electing officers, sending out missionaries and determining its own affairs. As a local church it was also a part of a universal church that would comprise many churches with certain interrelated functions such as determining doctrinal standards, establishing principles of action, and ministering to the material needs of others. This universal church became the total expression and extension of Christianity throughout the world; but it never swallowed up or destroyed the local identity of believers assembled for worship and service on a community basis.

II. MEMBERS OF THE BODY

If the church, as a body, is the present expression of the kingdom of God on earth then we remember that Jesus said, "Except a man be born again he cannot see the kingdom of God." So then, whoever will be a member of this body can be so only on the basis of birth and in this case, the new birth. This means that the church must insist upon a regenerate membership. It is not a religious society embracing the whole community. This experience is individualistic, for we are born again as individuals. But it does not remain an individualistic experience, for those so born are described as "being baptized into one body" by one Spirit. Thus a true Christian experience is shared with other Christians in a body of faith and a body of experience, called the church.

It is emphasized by the experiences and teachings of the first Christians that members of this body, called the church, were:
1. Believers

They were believers in the gospel. This gospel contained very specific elements including the divine nature of Christ, the crucifixion as means of atonement, and the resurrection as the means to life and immortality.
2. Baptized Believers

All thoughout the Book of Acts the baptism of adult believers by immersion in water was practiced with a universality that points up the significance and importance of baptism as a means of confession and identification with the Christian community.
3. Separated Believers

When a pagan became a Christian he immediately separated

himself from all contacts with paganism that he might maintain his witness without compromise.

There was the divine-human nature in this body. Its head was Jesus Christ; its motivating force and power was the Holy Spirit; but its members were human. They were brought out of all the racial, social and religious categories that exist among men. And while they were regenerate people, there would always be about this body, which they comprised, the weaknesses that would be true of human beings. The elimination of human weaknesses would depend upon the individual members' growth in grace, and submission to the Holy Spirit, and commitment to Jesus Christ.

III. Functions of the Body

The physical body functions as a means of expression for the man who lives in it. That is, it is not an end in itself to eat, sleep, walk, work and indulge itself for its own sake. It is a means to an end. It exists that the man who occupies it may express himself through the mental, physical and spiritual facilities which his body possesses. So, likewise, the church as a body is a means of expression for God who is said to inhabit the church corporately and the Christian individually. When Jesus Christ came God gave Him a body through which to express Himself and function as the God-Man. But when the Holy Spirit came He was not given a body through which to function, therefore He requires that body which is the church, and that body which is the Christian. So it is said, "I beseech you therefore, brethren, by the mercies of God, that ye present your bodies a living sacrifice, holy, acceptable unto God, which is your reasonable service. And be not conformed to this world, but be ye transformed by the renewing of your mind, that ye may prove what is that good, and acceptable, and perfect, will of God" (Rom. 12:1, 2).

How does God express Himself through the function of the body, called the church?

1. By the Ordinances

These are two: baptism and the Lord's supper, and they constitute the visible means by which the faith and fellowship of the believer is set forth and maintained.

2. By Preaching the Gospel

This is the charge of the Great Commission, the intent of which is the proclamation of the good news and the disciplining of men.

3. By Social Service

The members of the church were to be mutually helping, sharing their means and abundance in the time of need (verses 28, 29). This is the second reference in the Acts to the Christian's social obligations. The first was the emergency measure of communal sharing created by the emergency conditions which arose when many new Christians lost their means of support upon their profession of faith in Christ. Here the situation is different. It is no longer a communal arrangement, but based upon the principle of individual ability. It says, "Then the disciples, every man according to his ability, determined to send relief unto the brethren which dwelt in Judea" (verse 29). This was relief for Christians by Christians on a voluntary and free-will basis. This is a far cry from the social gospel of modern times which is so closely related to the welfare state. The social gospel as it is preached today makes it the business of the church to resort to governmental regulation, police power, taxation and governmental control of economic activities in an effort to promote what is termed social justice and a more equitable distribution of wealth. In other words, the church uses the facilities and resources of the state to do its work. This is not what was done by the early church. It used its own resources, gathered by its own people, according to their own ability, and distributed by their own organization.

4. By Teaching

One of the great functions of the church is to teach men the Word of God so they might know how to do the will of God. When great numbers of converts overwhelmed the church at

Antioch, Barnabas sought help in the person of Saul, a Hellenist Jew, who had been converted seven or eight years prior. He was ideally suited to help Barnabas instruct these new Christians, and so was brought to Antioch where he and Barnabas worked together for one year.

All of this functioning of the church was to be in the manner of a body. A body exists and functions as an organism, that is, it is organized. A physical body is a unit of organized physical members all co-ordinated by the head. The church is also a unit of organized, spiritual members co-ordinated by Christ, its Head. The organization of the first church included apostles, deacons and now, for the first time, elders are mentioned. But the church was not organized around these offices. It was organized around the laity and not the clergy. It was not a new sacerdotal order of priests that took the place of the Old Testament order of priests. It was, instead, the priesthood of the believers that made up the church. When the Bible speaks of the church it means a body of believers composed of people. It knows nothing of a church of clergymen, constituting a hierarchy. The church is the people, saved, baptized and separated unto Christ who function in the capacity of members of the body through which God sees, hears, walks and works.

Count Zinzendorf, that great Moravian, said the church is "a disciplined, dedicated company of radiant, liberated, confident crusaders of vital religion."

31

FAITH TAKES A NAME

Acts: 11:26

"And the disciples were called Christians first at Antioch."

Up to this time Christians were chiefly identified as those who belonged to "the way" (Acts 9:2).

A book has recently been written bearing the title "Faith Takes a Name." Its thesis is that faith was given a name when the disciples were called Christians at Antioch. Faith has to have a name. It has to have a name to indicate what form and what course it takes.

Our Christian faith has been organized around a series of names, which in each case indicate certain states of character, certain courses of action, or certain forms of service. It can be assuredly set down that unless one has in his life the characteristics, the action, and the service that are indicated by these names, he does not have a Christian faith. The Christian faith is not impassive and inactive creeds and ideas; it is life, action, experience, work, achievement and victory.

If we are ever anxious to know what we believe we can find out by noting the things about which we organize our lives. Everyone of us would say we believe in God; but how much time do we spend seeking to know God's will for our lives, and then living in accordance with that will? We say we believe in the Bible; but how much time do we spend reading and studying and translating the Bible into deed and act? We say we believe in prayer; but how much time do we spend in prayer? We say we believe in worship; but do we spend any time at all in our everyday life in contemplation and meditation? We say we believe in the church; but how much do we really believe in the church, when we are only in our pews when we have nothing to do that we consider more interesting, or when it is not raining, or when we can take off for the mountains or the beach to satisfy a greater interest and urge than we have in the church? Yes, we can get a much better idea of what we really believe by checking on what we do and not on what we say.

We can also find an accurate index of our faith in the names that attach to the Christian. The word Christian was given at Antioch and while it was derisively invented, it serves to gather all the other meanings of our faith into one name and is adopted as a badge of glory. Each of the names of the Christian presents a distinct facet of meaning to describe the various aspects of the Christians' faith.

I. DISCIPLE

This meant a "learner" and it was given to the Christian to indicate his need of knowledge. To be called a disciple is to be known as a novice, one who is immature and unskilled. It indicates a period of apprenticeship in which we are learning the ways and the skills of the Christian life. It is not a mark of distinction that one should bear this name for a whole lifetime, though of course there is a sense in which we are always learning; but the time of maturity should come when we would be able to bear adult Christian responsibilities.

II. BROTHER

This is the name of unity. It reveals the common origin of all Christians. That common origin is not the origin of the natural birth in which some are Americans and some Europeans and some Asiatics and some Polynesians and some Africans. It is the spiritual birth, or the new birth, in which we are Christians. It is a mistake to associate the fatherhood of God and the brotherhood of man with our birth as Americans and Europeans. God is not our Father because we are Americans, and men are not our brothers because we are Europeans. The brotherhood of man is a spiritual relationship that comes with the new birth. It is a Christian identity and not a racial identity.

Just before the battle of Trafalgar, Nelson inquired of Admiral Collingwood where his captain was, and learned that he and Captain Rotherham were not on good terms with each other. Sending a boat for the captain, he placed the hands of Collingwood and Rotherham together, pointed to the enemy's ships, and earnestly looking them both in the face, he uttered the simple words: "Look — yonder is the enemy!" The effect was instantaneous. Disagreements were forgotten, harmony was established, and victory was ultimately achieved.

III. BELIEVER

The Christian is the product of faith. The Christian is sustained by faith. The Christian walks by faith. The Christian is identified by faith, that is, by what he believes. The Christian is not a person who believes anything he chooses to believe. His faith is marked out for him in the Bible. The Bible constitutes the source of our faith. It is our constitution of faith and life.

IV. WITNESS

Jesus said immediately prior to His ascension, "Ye shall be witnesses unto me. . . . " The duty of a witness is to testify what he has seen or experienced. The spread of Christianity in the first centuries was not due to its great preachers such as Paul, Apollos, Polycarp, Augustine and Chrysostom, but rather to its witnesses. These witnesses were common people, speaking in a personal and unprofessional way of their encounter with Jesus Christ and of their changed lives.

The cause of Christ languishes today and is hung up on dead center, because it lacks witnesses. The pastor is expected to win the converts, whereas God's method was through witnesses. If we returned to the New Testament principle and practice of evangelism, we could change the face of civilization and could quickly evangelize this generation. The people who call themselves Jehovah's Witnesses may be far from the truth in their message, but their method is right. We would not go so far as they do in street corner paper peddling, and so forth; but the person to person encounter is what God intended us to do in proclaiming Christ.

V. SAINT

This was a common name used as a form of address in the New Testament Epistles. Those addressed were called "saints." It was a term which applied to the people of these New Testament churches. All such were saints. It was not given to a few. It was not applied after they were dead. It was not an indication of a special class. It was a universal characteristic. A saint is a person who by character is a son of God. It was therefore an indication of character. It did not mean that such a person was always saintly in his behavior; but sainthood was the mould of character and the direction in which one was traveling.

VI. SON OF GOD

This was the family name. It was the name of those who by reason of their new birth were members of God's family and were His children. "But as many as received him, to them gave he power to become the sons of God, even to them that believe on his name" (John 1:12). This means the authority to be called the sons of God. This authority is not given to the church. It is only given by the Holy Spirit. You will discover in all these names of the Christian that it never identifies a Christian by the name, "church member." This is a relationship that can be real or unreal; it can be genuine or artificial; it can be true or untrue.

VII. STEWARD

This is the Christian's relationship to time, talent and money. He is called a steward because in this capacity he manages and uses the resources which God has placed at his disposal. He is a capitalist who has been given a certain capital for wise use and investment. This capital consists of time, talent and treasure.

VIII. GOD'S ELECT

This is an indication of our origin. The source of our salvation is divine election. It is also an indication of our manner of life; we are described as "the elect of God." Israelites were committed to a particular way of life because they were God's elect nation. They were forbidden inter-marriage with their pagan neighbors. They were forbidden religious identity with pagan practices. This identity of life continued in Christian practice, for he was expected to reveal his identity as God's child by the difference in his behavior.

IX. A HOLY NATION

This was the designation of a new classification of people. Christians come from every nation, every tongue and every race, but they are put into a new classification — a holy nation. This is not a form of segregation in which Christians become anti-social, and in which they refuse to engage in the accepted forms of social and political relationship. It does indicate their peculiar identity; in fact, they are called "a peculiar people." This means a purchased people or a different people.

They make up the church. "The church is never a place, but always a people; never a fold but always a flock; never a sacred building but always a believing assembly. The church is you who pray, not where you pray. A structure of brick or marble can no more be a church than your clothes of serge or satin can be you. There is in this world nothing sacred but man, no sanctuary of God but the soul."

X. MEMBER OF THE BODY OF CHRIST

This is the Christian's mystical relationship. He is a member of the mystical Body of Christ. The total number of believers in Jesus Christ are considered in terms of a body of which Christ is the Head, and each believer a member. All of the members function in and through the head and therefore should not act independently or selfishly. It is an indication of the inter-relationship of all believers. When one member suffers, all members suffer. It is an indication of the importance of every member functioning by doing his part in the body.

Once when Sir Michael Costa was having a rehearsal with a vast array of performers and hundreds of voices, one man who played the piccolo far away in some corner, said within himself, "In all this din it matters not what I do," and so he ceased to play. Suddenly the great conductor stopped, flung up his hands, and all was still; and then he called out, "Where is the piccolo?" Every member of the church, large or small, old or young, rich or poor, has a part to play in the symphony. The call of Christ now is to every member of every church, "Go make disciples." This is his timeless mandate.

XI. STRANGERS AND PILGRIMS

Christians are strangers in relation to earth and pilgrims in relation to heaven. Here the Christian has "no continuing city." This is not his permanent or ultimate home. The final abode of the Christian will be "the house of the Lord forever." The Christian is a person who is "en route." Often when traveling by train or air or ship we identify our place on the letterhead by the word "en route." We were in no certain place, either between continents or between airports. This is our position as Christians. We are to act as persons en route:

1st – By the ticket we carry.
2nd – By the destination we are to reach.
3rd – By our traveling companions.
4th – By our baggage. "Lay not up for yourselves treasures upon earth. . . ."

When faith takes a name, it is something more than a name. It is a way of life. When faith takes a name, it works, it speaks, it gives. When faith takes a name, it is lifted out of the category of formal, superficial, one-day-a-week religion, into an encounter with Almighty God for every day and every situation of life.

Has your faith taken a name? Have you become a disciple to learn, a brother to love, a believer to stand, a witness to speak, a saint to edify, a child of God to belong, a steward to give, an elect of God to be sure, a pilgrim whose destination is sure and certain?

32

THE POWER OF PRAYER

Acts 12:1-25

It is about eleven years after Pentecost with its manifestation of the Holy Spirit. The principle relationship of the Holy Spirit to the church is that of an intercessor in prayer. The Holy Spirit came while the church was gathered in Jerusalem in a ten day prayer meeting. Following this significant prayer meeting there were numerous instances in which the disciples engaged in prayer to meet conditions arising in the church and the world about them.

We observe the church in peril. Herod, a notorious enemy of the Christians, begins a grievous persecution of the church. His first victim is James, the brother of John. James is given special executional treatment for he is beheaded with the sword. Being pleased with his work and encouraged by the pleasure of the Jews, Herod thinks to strike a decisive blow at the Christian cause, by striking down its prime leader, Peter, whom he has incarcerated. Since it was the Passover time, Peter is held in prison, waiting for the passing of the holy days, so he can be properly and inoffensively executed.

This is the occasion for the first crucial test of the power of prayer as experienced in the early life of the church. The occasion for prayer, then, was the peril of the church. This peril was represented by Herod Agrippa I, grandson of Herod the Great, who was on the Judean throne when Jesus was born. Here were strong political forces, impregnable prisons, implacable judges, inhuman soldiers, angry Jews and bloodthirsty pagans. Against these forces, conditions and powers the beleaguered church arrayed itself upon its knees in prayer.

The center of this crucial test of the power of prayer, and consequently the strength of the new Christian community, was Peter. He had been imprisoned twice before and this was his third imprisonment. It accounted for the unusual precautions taken for his safe incarceration. He was placed in an inner prison area, with four quaternions of soldiers charged with his keeping. Under these circumstances it seemed certain that nothing could defeat Herod's purpose to execute him, and nothing could deliver Peter from so impregnable a fortress. But there was one thing Herod had not counted on. In fact, there was one thing he was not acquainted with — the power of prayer. He undoubtedly knew the pagan rituals, but nothing of the new and tremendous force that lay in the hands of the Christians he was seeking to exterminate.

It was against this background that we read, " . . . but prayer was made without ceasing of the church unto God for him" (verse 5).

The story of this great triumph of the Christians' new power of prayer can be told something like this: It was the eleventh anniversary of Easter (Passover), a most significant day in the calendar of the church that records the triumph of Christ's resurrection. Here is renewed proof that their beloved Leader is alive and able to succour them in need and aid them in trouble. On the very night before Herod intends to execute Peter, he is in the inner prison sleeping between two prison guards and manacled with double chains upon his wrists, while two more guards maintain a strict watch outside the cell door. But while Peter is in this seeemingly impossible situation, surrounded with the might and force of the Roman Empire, the church goes to prayer. By the church we mean its people, meeting in the house of a well-to-do member of the Jerusalem church. It was the house of one of the illustrious Marys of the early church. This Mary was the mother of John Mark, who was to have such a prominent place in the affairs of the church for the next thirty years. In response to these prayers God sets divine and supernatural forces in motion that converge upon the sleeping Peter in his prison ward. An angel reaches him first with a bright and blinding light, and then an awakening blow upon the prisoner, with a command to dress and follow his deliverer. Peter thinks he is in a trance or a dream; but, however it may seem to be, he follows his shining guide through three successive prison gates, the last of which opens automatically; and then out into the street.

When Peter is delivered he is left alone and is on his own, and it says he came to himself. He realizes at last that he has not been dreaming. This is real. This was a supernatural deliverance. This was a great moment in the life of the church, as it pits its new power of prayer against the human and physical forces of its enemies. Whether Peter knew it before hand, or whether he is divinely directed to the house of Mary the mother of Mark, we do not know; but Peter goes to this prominent disciple's home where many are gathered together in prayer for his deliverance. He knocks at the outer gate of the wall that surrounds the house and his knock is answered by Rhoda who recognized Peter's challenging voice. But instead of opening the gate to allow Peter to enter, she runs for sheer joy into the house and almost incoherently shouts out to them that their prayers are answered and Peter, in person, is at the gate. It is too much for the disciples. This sudden answer makes them respond with incredulity. They cannot believe in so dramatic and sudden an answer. They charge the damsel with madness, and when she steadfastly holds to her story they attribute her account to a vision, and say it must be an angel, but surely not Peter. However, when the din of the inner excitement, created by Rhoda's announcement, subsides, they hear the persistent, clamorous knocking of Peter at the gate; and, convinced at last that it must be true, they rush out to find the answer to their praying standing in flesh and blood before their very eyes.

The church has met its first crucial test of the power of prayer with a great victory; and it is the beginning of a succession of events that caused the poet to say:

"More things are wrought by prayer
Than this world dreams of. Wherefore let thy voice
Rise like a fountain for me night and day.
For what are men better than sheep or goats,
That nourish a blind life within the brain,
If, knowing God, they lift not hands of prayer,
Both for themselves and those who call them friend?
For so the whole round earth is every way
Bound by gold chains about the feet of God."

This story of Peter's deliverance serves as a lesson of the power of prayer.

1. We Find the Church in Peril

In this case it was the peril of the political and military power of the Roman Empire. In our case it may be different. It may be the peril of ordinary life with its physical dangers, common sicknesses, inevitable death, human frustrations and satanic oppressions. As the response of the early church to its peril was prayer, so the response to our peril is prayer; for our position as Christians in the family of God gives us access to this divine privilege and power. We must not think that prayer becomes an Aladdin's lamp which we can rub whenever we want something. This is not the nature of prayer. Prayer is not a weapon like a sword or a gun. Prayer is an attitude, an approach, a means of communication between man and God. The Westminster Shorter Catechism says, "Prayer is an offering up of our desires unto God for things agreeable to His will." This is a reminder that the emphasis of prayer is not on the things we want but rather on the will of God.

2. We Find the Church in Prayer

It says here that "prayer was made without ceasing." This means earnestly or "stretched out." Their peril created an urgency in praying that gave real meaning to their prayers. Here were people who were not asking for foibles or trinkets or palatable experiences or good times. One of their own was in danger and their prayers had awesome meaning. This, it must be admitted, was an emergency. Not all life is an emergency. Not all life situations are dangerous. Therefore, we ought to remember that prayer is a continuous attitude of fellowship with God. This was what Paul must have meant when he said, "Pray without ceasing."

3. We Find that Prayer was Answered

Not all prayers will be answered as dramatically and decisively as in this case. In fact, it will appear many times in our experience of praying that not all prayers will be answered. We have an example of this in the incident at hand, for in one instance Peter was delivered from prison in answer to prayer, whereas James was beheaded. It is a fact, however, that in principle all prayers are answered, for a "no" can sometimes be better than a "yes." We will not always be able to understand the mystery of God's will. But this is precisely what faith means because faith recognizes that "no prayer can be right that makes God wrong." And the prayer which demands our will without regard to God's will would result in God not being God. Faith says, "Thy will be done." It is to be noticed here that while prayer was answered in the deliverance of Peter, the praying disciples were not conscious of it. They prayed importunately and confidently so that presently the answer to their prayers was knocking at their own door. And when the answer came they could not believe it. There is just as much of faith involved in receiving the answer as there is in praying the prayer. This is where most of the problem of prayer lies. We may find many reasons for praying. They may never be as dramatic and urgent as those experienced by the church at prayer in Jerusalem. But none of us is ever beyond the need of prayer, even for the ordinary and common things of life.

Whatever the reasons may be for praying, the most important thing about prayer is praying and not just talking about it.

4. We Find the Answer was Supernatural

Prayer is not a psychological gimmick that plays tricks on our mental processes so that we believe to be true what is not so. Prayer is an exercise of mind, but it is also an exercise of the spiritual nature of man, based upon his personal relationship with God. It therefore involves the divine as well as the human, the supernatural as well as the natural. In the case of Peter's deliverance all the elements of the supernatural were present; an angel appeared as the deliverer; the prisoner's handcuffs and chains fell away as if they were made of sand; the gates were opened without benefit of keys. It was the supernatural at work. Prayer, and its effects, is not something you can rationalize. It will forever be hidden in the inscrutability of divine sovereignty. If this is not true then the answer to our religious devotions is found in the mechanics of psychology or the ritual of religion.

What we find as a prime lesson in this incident of the power of prayer is that prayer is greater than prisons; the church is bigger than Caesar; the prayer of the smallest Christian puts him in league with God.

33

FIDELITY IN SERVICE
Acts 13:1-3

One thing which grows increasingly evident in the growth of the early church is the fact that it was an organized body of people. When we come to this point in Acts we enter its second and last division, extending to the end of the book. In the first division the church was centered in Jerusalem. In the second, it was in Antioch. In the first, the church was made up largely of Jews; in the second, of Gentiles. In the first, the leading figure was Peter; in the second, it was Paul. But neither Peter in the church in Jerusalem, nor Paul in the church in Antioch were by any means the only principals, for by this time the church had such offices as apostles, elders (bishops) and deacons; later, evangelists and pastors. Nor must we forget that the rank and file members belonged to the New Testament order of the priesthood of believers. There were still others who, while not having elective offices, had an important part in the development of the church. They are the "prophets and teachers" mentioned here as the leaders of the church at Antioch.

The five leaders who are mentioned here are described as those who "ministered to the Lord," that is, they performed rites of Christian worship. To them also the Holy Spirit gave authority to ordain Saul and Barnabas for the first missionary work of the church. They were in effect the leaders of the Antiochene Church. How did they become "prophets and teachers"? Who made them such? What is the basis of their authority to prophesy and teach? Their authority originated with "the gifts of the Spirit" that came out of Pentecost, and were practiced in both the Jerusalem and Antioch churches, and would later be described by Paul in his first letter to the Corinthians. Here you will find nine gifts of the Spirit, including three gifts of the intellect, three gifts of the will and three gifts of the emotions. By these divinely distributed gifts you have the ability and authority for such men as the five prophets and teachers at Antioch. What you have now is an organized church with recognized offices. You then have power and energy proceeding from the pentecostal experience of the coming of the Holy Spirit to flow through the organized body of believers. Here is a comparatively simple arrangement. There is not much theology and very, very little ecclesiasticism, with the rank and file membership considered as priests, and with the ministerial work of the apostles recognized as the function of teachers.

How then did the church become catholic and after it became catholic how did it become Roman Catholic? This is the unfolding story of church history that goes beyond the Book of Acts. At this time, after eleven years of existence, there were just two churches, Jerusalem and Antioch. But soon Paul and Barnabas would take off on their first missionary journey and when they would return to Antioch, they would gather the church together and tell them of the churches they had founded. From this point on you have a burgeoning church situation. But "how did it happen that from the simple message and unpretentious life of Jesus of Nazareth, as we find these described in the gospels, there came an international organization, fully equipped with priests and bishops and patriarchs, with rites and sacraments and pomp, with the power of discipline for this world and the control over grace for the next"?* That is a question which only church history can answer. By the catholic church we mean just what the word means, "world-wide." At this point the church stands poised at Antioch for its world-wide venture. This was the launching platform for the missionary activity that would take Christ and His gospel into all the world and make the church catholic.

---

* Pelikan

It was not Peter who gave the church its catholicity; it was Paul. Peter violently opposed extending the church beyond its early Jewish borders. He wanted to keep it Jewish, and make everyone who came into it somewhat of a Jew. It was Paul, in the company of Barnabas, who not only nurtured a church made up of Greek Gentiles and Hellenist Jews, but he also took the Christian message out to the Gentile world and gave it its catholic character. How this catholic church became the Roman Catholic Church is another and much longer and more complex story, which must be reserved for a later time, for it goes far beyond the history of the Book of Acts.

Apparently church organization is not sacred, for the church exists in many forms with many varieties and combinations of offices and members, with stewards, vestrymen, deacons, elders, bishops, priests almost ad infinitum. When one becomes acquainted with the church in these many governmental forms he is aware that the essence of real Christianity can exist in any form that exists today. The reason for this is that the continuity of true Christianity is not in the form. It is in the presence of the Holy Spirit and in the truth. In fact, this was precisely what Jesus said to the Samaritan woman, "But the hour cometh, and now is when the true worshippers shall worship the Father in spirit and in truth . . . " (John 4:23). Following this pattern we have the "spirit" in the coming of the Holy Spirit at Pentecost and the "truth" in the revelation of the New Testament. This is the "spirit and the truth" that comprises the true church and not the form of church organization into which it is arranged.

What is important to us in the continuing church today is not its organizational forms, buildings and ecclesiastical structures, for God, by the Holy Spirit, does not indwell these forms. He indwells people. When the Holy Spirit came at Pentecost there was no church, only one hundred and twenty people. And when He indwelt these people the next step was to give them truth. This truth came in the gradually increasing truths which ultimately became the New Testament.

The next important thing for us in the continuing church is

the proclamation of the truth by the Holy Spirit through the existing forms which the church has taken. This is where events and responsibilities find us today with our various forms of church organization. The question is, what are we doing with them? Are we glorifying the forms or magnifying the Lord? Are we bogged down in tradition and organization and forms, or are we vital and alive and productive?

What are the proofs that a church is alive? Well, what are the proofs that anything is alive? Life is something which is self-evident and self-proving, and one of these is life itself. A thing is alive because it has life. A church is alive when it is activated by the breath, or life of God, which is the Holy Spirit. The specific evidences of this spiritual life will be in its manifestations. There is no question about the life of the church at this time and when we look at it we see certain specific manifestations of this life.

A church is alive —

1. When It Is In Communion With God

Life is described as the correspondence of an organism with its environment. If this is what life is, then a church is alive when it is in a state of agreement and adaptation with God, who is the environment of the soul. The means of this correspondence is communion.

2. When It Is Providing Fellowship For Man

Communion is the direction of the spirit toward God, while fellowship is the direction of the spirit toward man. There cannot be any valid fellowship with man without a vital communion with God. Both communion and fellowship depend on "spirit and truth."

3. When It Has Functioning Members

In any living organism its life is proved by its functioning members. Sometimes these members may be temporarily immobilized by forms of paralysis; but in any normal existence, life is revealed in the manifestation of functioning members. There is no question of this in the church whose double portrait we are looking at in Jerusalem and Antioch. The members of these churches were functioning, for life flowed out of its members in terms of witnessing, prayer and social service. It was the members who performed the services and functions of the church. Charity was not dispensed by professionals, but through the loving and merciful attention of the people, who at one time had all things in common and at another time gave each man "according to his ability."

4. When It Is Led By Faithful Leaders

We have seen something of the leadership of the early church, chiefly in terms of the offices they occupied. But the occupation of these offices depended upon the faithfulness and fidelity of their occupants. When we look at these occupants we see, by the qualifications with which they were chosen, something of the importance of their offices. One of these qualifications was wisdom or good judgment. Someone wrote to Wesley, "God can get along without your knowledge." Wesley wrote that he knew it — "But God can also get along without your ignorance."

The most important qualification was fidelity. This balances up any deficiency in knowledge or ability; for faithfulness will be shown to be more important than anything else, for it will enable ordinary people to be conspicuous and extraordinary in their accomplishments in life. Proverbs 25:19 says, "Confidence in an unfaithful man in time of trouble is like a broken tooth and a foot out of joint." Here is something of functional importance. Whoever has had a broken tooth or a foot out of joint knows the pain, discomfort and malfunction of such members. It is the same in the church with malfunctioning leaders. They stand out as broken teeth and disjointed feet. You may remember that some years ago one of the major oil companies used a national slogan for its gasoline. It claimed for it: "no knock, more power, smooth performance." This is to be coveted for the church and it is found when there is faithful leadership.

5. When It Has a Missionary Vision

This was certainly characteristic of the first church. There was an outflow of life, and an outreach of truth to the uttermost parts of the earth. Any other church than a missionary church will become self-indulgent and self-satisfied, and will limit itself to a body of self-admiring people whose chief contribution is what it does for itself. The life of the church is in the life-line of its missionary activity. There must be an inflow of spiritual life through the Holy Spirit, and there must be an outflow of life through the propagation of its message. It seems that as one personalizes this matter of the Christian and his relationship to the church that it can be expressed in these contrasting poems:

I HAVE A RENDEZVOUS WITH DEATH

I have a rendezvous with Death
At some disputed barricade
When Spring comes round with rustling shade
And apple blossoms fill the air.
I have a rendezvous with Death
When Spring brings back blue days and fair.

It may be he shall take my hand
And lead me into his dark land
And close my eyes and quench my breath;
It may be I shall pass him still.
I have a rendezvous with Death
On some scarred slope of battered hill,
When Spring comes round again this year
And the first meadow flowers appear.
God knows 'twere better to be deep
Pillowed in silk and scented down,
Where love throbs out in blissful sleep,
Pulse nigh to pulse, and breath to breath,
Where hushed awakenings are dear . . .
But I've a rendezvous with Death
At midnight in some flaming town,
When Spring trips north again this year,
And I to my pledged word am true,
I shall not fail that rendezvous.*

---

* From "Poems by Alan Seeger" — Copyright 1916 by Charles Scribner's Sons.

ANOTHER RENDEZVOUS

"I have a rendezvous with Christ . . .
And that time is not far away,
When all I am and do and say
Will counted be, and weighed by Him.
I have a rendezvous with Christ,
Ere days are run, and eyes are dim.
It may be He shall take my hand
And lead me into some dark land
Of burdened souls, and say to me,
'This is the work I have for thee.'
This life of mine, now His, must be
Obedient to His will, not mine —
Set in the way His hand shall find.

It seemed 'twere better to be free
To follow the career I'd choose,
And let no mighty Power be
Turing my course at His high will,
And all for self my own days fill.
But, I've a rendezvous with Christ;
All other aims in that must pale,
And fatal is it if I fail!
And I to my pledged word am true;
I shall not fail that rendezvous!"

34

THE SAVING MESSAGE
Acts 13:4-43

At Cape Canaveral there are launching pads on which rockets are periodically poised for our conquest of outer space. But a conquest far more important to the advance and destiny of life on this planet stood poised in the persons of two men at the middle of the First Century, when Saul and Barnabas were about to leave on their first missionary journey to the Gentile world from Antioch. What importance the conquest of the moon has for us is at the present moment not quite clear; but it did seem to have some significance to an old Indian who stood on top of a hill with his son, looking over the beautiful valley below them. Said the old Indian, "Some day, my son, all this land will belong to the Indians again. Paleface all go to the moon."

It is at this point that the church becomes catholic, entering into its world-wide phase and spreading itself throughout the length and breadth of the entire world. Four things are to be seen in connection with this projected venture from Antioch:

I. THE NEW MISSION (verse 4). "So they, being sent forth by the Holy Ghost, departed into Seleucia and from thence sailed to Cyprus."

This is the beginning of the missionary era of the church. At this time Paul, in company with Barnabas, sets out on the first of three missionary thrusts into the ancient world. What this world owes to the missionary ministry of the Christian church cannot be calculated. "When the keen scrutiny of skeptics has found a place on this planet, ten miles square, where a man can live in decency, comfort, and security, supporting and educating

his children unspoiled and unpolluted, a place where age is
reverenced, infancy respected, womanhood honored, and human
life held in due regard, where the Gospel of Christ has not gone
and cleared the way and laid the foundations, and made decency
and security possible, it will then be in order for the sceptical
literati to move thither, and then ventilate their views. But so
long as these men are very dependent on the religion which they
discard for every privilege they enjoy, they may well hesitate a
little before they seek to rob a Christian of his hope and humanity
of its faith in that Saviour who alone has given to men that hope
of eternal life which makes life tolerable and society possible,
and robs death of its terrors and the grave of its gloom."*

In the face of forces even more formidable than the might
and spread of the Roman Empire, the only hope of survival for
our civilization lies in a resurgence of missions in order that the
saving message may reach present generations of the world's
people. We are confronted notably with the fanatical zeal of the
communists whose recent conquests have been more missionary
than military. What they did in China is a case in point. The
strategy for the conquest of China was a missionary strategy.
Every year for ten years the Russian communists in the Soviet
Union trained fifteen hundred Chinese and sent them back to
China to work and teach. In ten years that meant fifteen thousand missionaries, each one creating converts and each one sowing
the seed of the communist gospel of world revolution. And yet
there are people in our churches today who do not believe in
missions. It was the very first maneuver of the early church. It
accounted for the advance of Christianity in the world. It is
our best defense against communism today. It is the best
hope we have for survival, and it is something that belongs
to the whole church and not just to women's missionary societies.
It is the first business of the whole church.

II. THE NEW NAME (verse 9) "Then Saul, (who also is called
Paul,) filled with the Holy Ghost, set his eyes on him,"

Paul is making his first thrust into the Gentile world of Rome,

---

*James Russell Lowell

and it is fitting that the name by which he is to be henceforth known is his Roman name, Paul, rather than his Jewish name, Saul. His old name was associated with a dead past, both national and religious. His new identity is with the living present and the glorious future and, while it is a Roman name, it is something that transcends Roman significance. It includes all that Paul hoped to be by the power of Christ. It was the name of his future and not the name of his past.

III. THE NEW POWER (verses 8-12)

When Paul and Barnabas, in the company of their companion John Mark, reached Paphos on the island of Cyprus, they were confronted with a challenging situation. It was in the person of a sorcerer who professed occult powers that were a challenge to the new missionaries at the very outset of their missionary journeys into the very realms of Satan himself. It was at this point that Paul, the man of the new name, now demonstrates the genuineness of his new office as apostle. It is done by a demonstration of divine power which strikes the sorcerer, Bar-jesus, blind. So impressed was the Roman proconsul that he is persuaded to believe and become the first known convert of this missionary operation.

This miracle, at the hand of Paul, was not an incidental event, but one among many remarkable evidences of divine power in Paul's brilliant career as an apostle. It was the first of such events, but it was proof of what Paul later would point to as "the signs of an apostle." Enemies in the church would call his apostleship into question and he had but to point to such events as this to show his legitimate claim as an apostle of Jesus Christ.

IV. THE NEW MESSAGE (verses 14-43)

This is Paul's first recorded sermon, and the first recorded presentation of the gospel to the Roman world. It is significant for what it contains, because it contains the heart of the Christian faith and the hope of the world. It is in fact its saving message, because Paul calls it "the word of salvation."

Here are two men with a new idea — an idea that can change the world and did in fact change the course of human history. The core of this new idea was expressed by the first missionaries in these words of their missionary message: " . . . that through this man is preached unto you the forgiveness of sins: and by him all that believe are justified from all things, from which ye could not be justified by the law of Moses" (verses 38, 39). Christianity is not taking the best out of paganism. It is not a readaptation of Judaism. It is not even a compilation of men's best thoughts. It is something new. It is a new revelation.

A convocation of scientists, which met in Chicago to re-study and evaluate Darwinian evolution, has stated that a new religion will inevitably evolve out of man's continuing evolution. Of this we have no fear, for while religion, as such, has been of man's creation, it has also been man's effort to circumvent divine revelation which we have in its finality in Jesus Christ, who is declared to be "the way, the truth and the life." Here is a finished and final faith as sufficient for the age of the space man as for the age of the cave man.

It was the custom of Paul and his companions to attend the local synagogue services, as they did at Antioch. And since there were no definite ministers attached to the synagogue for the specific function of preaching, the ruler of the synagogue offered the Christians an opportunity to speak. Their part was the last of a three-part service. The first part was the recital of a creed called the Shema. The second was the reading of the Scriptures, first from the law and then from the prophets. The final part of the service was an exposition or exhortation. For this part Paul went forward, ascended the bema, beckoned the people to attend his words, and launched into his message.

Paul's message had three parts:

1. Christ Predicted (verses 14-22)

It is to be remembered at this point that Paul did not have even one book of the New Testament in hand when he set out on his mission to the Roman world. The New Testament was in the making, but it was of God's making, not man's. Paul would later write to the Thessalonians, the first of his fourteen New Testament epistles, and say, "For this cause also thank we God without ceasing because, when ye received the word of God which ye heard of us, ye received it not as the word of men, but as it is in truth, the word of God . . . " (I Thess. 2:13).

Paul undertakes in this first portion of his sermon to refer to the past. He is saying that the roots of the new idea he has come to present lie in ancient Jewish history. It is not something lately invented, such as a new religion would be. It is of God's doing and it goes back to the earliest recollection of the forefathers. No people can outlive the usefulness of the past. All of us are indebted to it for our present knowledge. Think what would happen if every bit of knowledge now known to our minds and found in our books, should be obliterated. We would immediately be thrust back into the darkness of pre-historic ages when man, having lost his consciousness of God, was slowly inching his way out of primeval darkness and ignorance. Every bit of present progress is based upon knowledge bequeathed to us by previous generations. The Christian faith, too, has its roots in the past. It is found in the predictions of the promised Messiah who would come as the fulfillment of the divine plan to provide man with an adequate and sufficient salvation. In fact, it all began with the promise of Genesis 3:15, "And I will put enmity between thee and the woman, and between thy seed and her seed; it shall bruise thy head, and thou shalt bruise his heel." In the progressive revelation of the Old Testament it comes to its ultimate fulfillment in Jesus Christ: Galatians 4:4, 5, "But when the fulness of the time was come, God sent forth his Son, made of a woman, made under the law, to redeem them that were under the law, that we might receive the adoption of sons"; and Hebrews 1:1-3, "God, who at sundry times and in divers manners spake in time past unto the fathers by the prophets, hath in these last days spoken unto us by his Son, whom he hath appointed heir of all things, by whom also he made the worlds; who being the brightness of his glory, and the express image of his person, and upholding all things by the word of his power, when he had by himself purged our sins, sat down on the right hand of the Majesty on high."

2. Christ Presented (verses 23-37)

When the announcing angel came to Mary in anticipation of the incarnation, he said to her, "And behold thou shalt conceive in thy womb, and bring forth a son, and shalt call his name Jesus. He shall be great, and shall be called the Son of the Highest: and the Lord God shall give unto him the throne of his father David" (Luke 1:31, 32). It was precisely this that Paul said had happened, for "of this man's (David's) seed hath God according to his promise raised unto Israel a Saviour, Jesus" (13:23). Christ came not only as the fulfillment of God's promise, but in the precise manner and of the particular lineage that had been predicted. This was important for no sinful son of Adam would have qualified as the Redeemer. It took one who was unlike all others and without taint of sin, for this would disqualify him from being the Savior from sin.

Paul was now announcing, first to the Jews and then to all the Gentiles, that the Messianic promise had been fulfilled. It had been fulfilled in the recent events which transpired in Judea. Here the Son of God was born. Here the Messiah presented Himself with the words and works of His office; but He was rejected and crucified, yet God had raised Him from the dead and now the glad tidings of this salvation were being brought, not only to Jews, but to all who feared God and would heed His word. The two compelling reasons for faith in such a Redeemer was His crucifixion and His resurrection. These were the evidence that this was the work of God, and these would forever remain as the reasons why men could believe and trust Him as their Redeemer.

3. Christ Proclaimed (verses 38-43)

Here is the offer to personal salvation and this offer included two things: the forgiveness of sins and justification. No salvation is complete without these elements, because forgiveness deals with our present and justification with our past. Forgiveness relates to what we do and have done, and justification to what we are.

Paul says that these, in the fullest sense, are impossible upon the basis of any law of works. They are only possible through grace and such grace is what is revealed and offered in Christ. This is the ultimate. We can go no further than this.

Attached to the offer of salvation is a warning. Paul uses the word "beware" and refers his synagogue hearers to the Prophet Habakkuk who referred to Israel's unbelief and unwillingness to accept God's work in their behalf. The moment of faith had come. God had acted and the Messiah had come. God had spoken and the message was proclaimed. The offer was made of forgiveness and justification. Israel and all others thereafter were called upon to believe in an act of faith which called for the laying down of the whole life of the believer. If there was not this evidence of faith and obedience there could then be but one alternative — judgment. Judgment is really self-judgment for we judge ourselves when we refuse God's salvation.

The peasants of northwestern Spain tell a legend about Lake Sanabria. At its bottom, they say, lies the village of Villa-verde de Lucerna. It was drowned a long time ago, when Jesus, dressed as a pauper, came begging alms and the villagers turned him away. Only a few women who gave him bread were saved, as well as the oven in which the bread was baked — and the oven survived as a small hermitage on the western shore of the lake near the village of Ribadelago.

One night recently all was quiet in Ribadelago. In the tavern men were playing cards. At the church Father Placido Esteban Gonzalez had just arrived on his motor scooter from the provincial capital of Zamora. An electrician named Rey was working late in his shop. Shortly after midnight the lights in the village flickered out. At the tavern irritated card-players lit candles and went on with their game. Suddenly, a distant, muffled roar was heard. To wood-cutters in the mountains it sounded like a "great stampede." To one villager the noise resembled "a continuous dynamite blast." Father Placido went worriedly into the street, as did the electrician and some of the men from the tavern.

The thunderous rumble came from up the valley where, three

miles distant and sixteen hundred and ninety feet above them, the Tera River, swollen by a fortnight of rain, was held in check by a stone and concrete dam built two years ago. The only explanation of the now deafening thunder was that the dam had burst. Electrician Rey scrambled up the church tower and began ringing the bell in alarm. Father Placido started waking his neighbors. Some few fled with him across the only bridge and climbed the opposite hillside. Others raced to the church tower or to high ground.

A wall of water, with the weight of two hundred thirty million cubic feet behind it, came surging down the narrow ravine, smashed into the village in a wave twenty feet high. The stone bridge was swept away. The church was cut in two, and only the tower remained standing. All but twenty-five of the town's one hundred fifty houses were wiped out.

Slowly the flood subsided and lost itself in the waters of Lake Sanabria. On the surface floated the bodies of men, women and children. Dead cows, pigs and chickens were mingled indiscriminately with tree trunks, telegraph poles, rooftops, household goods. A man caught in his home floated to safety on the inflated rubber mattress on which he was sleeping. The innkeeper, who escaped to the hillside, went back to empty his cash register and was drowned. Just before the water hit, an elderly couple dashed back for their life savings. They disappeared. Of the village's five hundred inhabitants, two hundred and one were drowned or missing, and rescue workers estimated that the toll would pass two hundred and fifty.

This time the legendary oven hermitage of Villa-verde de Lucerna was not spared; it too was swept away. In this manner, they believed judgment had come for their ancient rejection of Jesus. This may have been what men call "an act of God," but it is certain that ultimate judgment comes to all for their rejection of salvation in the person of Jesus Christ.

35

TRIAL AND TRIUMPH
Acts 14:1-18

It could be assumed, because these men were the servants of God, that they were immune to abuse, danger, hardship, persecution and death. But this would be a false assumption because their leader, the Lord Jesus Christ, had said, "In the world ye shall have tribulation: but be of good cheer; I have overcome the world" (John 16:33). It could be assumed that because many are Christians, who have made great sacrifices, that they are not to be subjected to the same difficulties, diseases and disasters that come to others; but are to enjoy a sort of cosmic immunity to life's common troubles. This, too, would be a wrong assumption. There is no promise in our Christian faith which gives immunity to the followers of Jesus from the sufferings, adversities and disabilities of life. In fact, when Paul and Barnabas were returning to their home base at Antioch, at the close of their first missionary thrust into the Gentile world, they stopped at the cities where they had founded churches on their way in and confirmed these believers in their faith and exhorted them to continue in their newly found faith, saying, "that we must through much tribulation enter into the kingdom of God" (verse 22).

The story of this first missionary thrust into the Roman world was one of trial and triumph. Because they were divinely chosen messengers of God, they had no special immunity to abuse from men, opposition from Satan, or suffering from natural forces. They met tribulation in every conceivable form wherever they went.

The story of their trial and triumph reads something like this: When Paul finished his memorable first sermon in the synagogue at Antioch in Galatia the people were divided in their response. Some Jews and Gentiles were for him and some against him. But whatever the outward response may have been "as many as were ordained to eternal life believed." However, the Jews attached to the synagogue agitated violence among the city leaders and the two missionaries were expelled from Antioch.

They made their way eastward into barbarian country to Iconium, where they found another Jewish synagogue where their message resulted in "a great multitude both of the Jews and also the Gentiles" believing. Persecution broke out again, but in spite of this opposition they stayed in Iconium for a long time, engaged in preaching God's Word while being supported by "signs and wonders."

Finally the opposition at Iconium became so intense that they were compelled to flee to other Lyconian cities, such as Lystra and Derbe. At Lystra a very notable miracle was performed. It was the case of a congenitally crippled beggar whom Paul healed with such dramatic results that these barbarians assumed that their gods, Zeus and Hermes (Luke gave Latin equivalents), had favored them with a divine visitation; and had come down in the likeness of these men, Paul and Barnabas. So the Lystrans prepared for a public sacrifice. When Paul and Barnabas saw this they protested with horror and vehemence, and succeeded in turning the Lystrans away from their blasphemous pagan intensions.

This, however, was not the end of their problems at Lystra because the antagonized Jews from Antioch and Iconium came to Lystra and incited the pagan Lystrans against Paul and Barnabas. Although so lately worshipped as "messengers of the immortals," they were now made the targets of a violent assault. Paul was stoned and left for dead; but a notable miracle of God's power took place and he was raised from apparent death to continue his missionary efforts.

This is the story of trial and triumph, crowned with victory for those who had suffered every conceivable form of opposition and anguish. If one wants to know the extent of the trial of these early founders of the church and their followers, he has but to read the record of their experience in the language of Hebrews eleven where it gives an extended account of all sorts of experiences.

Let us retrace our steps to the place where we find the apostles, the victims of assault at Iconium, and inquire into the meaning of their trial. Trial has a place of great advantage in the experience of God's servants and God's people.

One of the purposes of trial is that it gives us identification with our Lord. This is precisely what He promised to His disciples. He said, "Remember the word that I said unto you, The servant is not greater than his Lord. If they have persecuted me, they will also persecute you . . . " (John 15:20). Paul would later say to the Philippians, "That I may know him and the power of his resurrection, and the fellowship of his sufferings, being made conformable unto death" (Phil. 3:10). Here is the "fellowship of his sufferings" in the trials of life which are related to faith and service. The natural consequence of being alive in the experience of the common ills of men is not what is meant here by the "fellowship of his sufferings." His sufferings were redemptive and ours must be those associated with our redemptive faith and service. A redemptive faith must be followed by a redemptive service.

Another purpose of trial is that it links the crown with the cross. Jesus had laid down an inviolate principle for discipleship when He said, "If any man will come after me let him deny himself, take up his cross and follow me." If the cross brings trial, the crown brings triumph. Paul would later write to the Christians at Rome where, in a few decades, the spectacles of Christians slaughtered in the arenas would shock the world; and to them he would say, "if so be that we suffer with him, that we may be also glorified together. For I reckon that the sufferings of this present time are not worthy to be compared with the glory which shall be revealed in us" (Rom. 8:17, 18).

Another purpose of trial is that it purifies faith. When Peter wrote his first epistle to the Hebrew Christians who had passed through every conceivable kind of suffering for their faith, he said, "Wherein ye greatly rejoice, though now for a season, if need be, ye are in heaviness through manifold temptations: That the trial of your faith, being much more precious than of gold that perisheth, though it be tried with fire, might be found unto praise and honour and glory at the appearing of Jesus Christ" (I Peter 1:6, 7).

Another purpose of trial is that it strengthens and enhances character. Character is improved by hard things, not soft things; by trials, not blessings; by testing, not resting. Opposites produce opposites for as one has said, "I have learned kindness from the unkind, silence from the talkative, toleration from the intolerant; yet strange to say, I am not ungrateful to those teachers." We Christians are altogether too prone to ask God to provide us our crown while sparing us our cross. We want the triumph without the trial, and the victory without the battle. It does not come that way. We want spiritual tranquilizers that make us immune to pains of life, and remove the normal tensions and strains that are a part of a competitive and combative life.

Another purpose of trial is that it is a means of overcoming evil. The Christian principle of overcoming evil is not force, but good. Jesus said that we are to "overcome evil with good." We are not simply to overcome evil, but overcome it with good. This illustrates the operation of the laws of the spiritual world when a higher law overcomes the effect of a lower law. In this case it is the higher law of good against the lower law of evil. In the natural world the law of evaporation is stronger than the law of gravitation, for tons of water lifted out of an ocean must be done so against the pull of the law of gravitation which tends to keep all things tied to the earth. Good is greater than evil, and when the Christian endures trial he has illustrated its power to overcome evil forces. Truth is greater than error, and will ultimately triumph. The church is greater than the world, and the gates of hell cannot prevail against it.

Paul illustrated this principle during his experience of physical sickness. His prayers for healing were answered by God saying, "My grace is sufficient for thee: for my strength is made perfect in weakness." To which Paul said, "Most gladly therefore will I rather glory in my infirmities, that the power of Christ may rest upon me. . . for when I am weak, then am I strong" (II Cor. 12:9, 10).

The forms of trial are very many, including physical, spiritual and satanic, adversities and adversaries. But you will notice that the chief source of trial for the apostles was human. Human opposition in the outside world will be a major form of trial. But it is also true that it will come from inside the Christian community from immature, carnal, and uncommitted believers.

There is a fable about an old man, a boy, and a donkey. Going through a village, the old man rode the donkey, the boy walked. The people in the village criticized the old man for riding and making the boy walk. So the boy rode and the old man walked. In the next village the boy was criticized for letting the old man walk. So they both rode the donkey through the next village. Again they were criticized for both riding the poor little donkey. So the old man and the boy carried the donkey. But they were again criticized, so the old man and boy said they would pay no attention to anyone's opinion and proceeded as they had originally started out. The moral being, you cannot please everyone, so why not please yourself?

What we have in the experience of the apostles can aptly be called "the big story." It is the headline story of the experience of the first missionaries in their brave efforts to advance the cause of Christ. Few of us will ever occupy a place of distinction with them. Our lives will be lived in the shadow of the big story in the deeds of everyday living.

Harry Golden, a Jewish immigrant who became famous as an editor, writes this story in his book, "Only in America": "As a boy, I kept a scrapbook of the leading news story of each day from July 1, 1914, to November 11, 1918. It filled fifteen notebooks. In later years, I discovered that the Big Story in every instance was on the other side of my important clipping.

"On the other side of the clipping which told of the loss of Lord Kitchener on the H.M.S. Hampshire was an announcement by the Borden Milk Co. that it would put up milk in sanitary bottles, no more dipping out of the can at the grocery.

"On the back of the photo showing Kaiser Wilhelm and his five younger sons on parade, I found an advertisement of John Wanamaker calling attention to boys' 'going-back-to-school' wool suits at $7.95.

"Behind the news story of a new offensive in the Meuse-Argonne, I read that Father Francis Joseph O'Brien, a recent graduate of a seminary in New Rochelle, had been appointed to his first parish, on 116th Street.

"This was the real news of those war years. Because this was the everyday life of the people.

"Thirty-five years from now, despite the Khrushchev pronouncements, the twirling sputniks and artificial planets, the Big Story will still be about people who struggle to pay the rent and get up tuition for a girl in college. The story is about people who lose jobs and find better ones. How they go off to hear a first sermon of the new priest, and how they raise their families, and how they die."

The end of the first missionary venture was triumph. On their way back to Syria, whence they departed some twelve to eighteen months previously, the apostles stopped at the places where they had left little colonies of Christians. Here they confirmed the believers, arranged for the election of elders or presbyters, and when they returned to Antioch the whole church was assembled, and the story of their triumphant missionary trip was told. It must have been a great occasion, giving a foretaste of heaven with its resumé of earth's triumph in the trial and conquest of faith.

36

WHAT HEAVEN IS LIKE

Acts 14:19-20; 2 Corinthians 12:1-12

Heaven ranks high in the anticipations of the Christian. He is led to anticipate it at the consummation of life, not only because of his natural desires for a place of surcease from evil and trouble, but also because of the promises which the scriptures contain.

The subject of heaven and what it is like is brought to our notice in an experience of the Apostle Paul while at the city of Lystra, and is described in these words: "And there came thither certain Jews from Antioch and Iconium, who persuaded the people, and, having stoned Paul, drew him out of the city, supposing he had been dead. Howbeit, as the disciples stood round about him, he rose up, and came into the city: and the next day he departed with Barnabas to Derbe" (Acts 14:19, 20).

This bare historical record says nothing whatever about heaven. The only hint that it has anything to do with the future is in the words, "supposing he had been dead" and their sequel, "Howbeit, as the disciples stood round about him, he rose up. . . ." But Paul himself has something to add to this incident by way of personal experience, for when he wrote his second epistle to the Corinthians he gave this elaboration of what happened at Lystra: "It is not expedient for me doubtless to glory. I will come to visions and revelations of the Lord. I knew a man in Christ above fourteen years ago, (whether in the body, I cannot tell; or whether out of the body, I cannot tell: God knoweth;) such an one caught up to the third heaven. And I knew such a man, (whether in the body, or out of the body, I cannot tell: God knoweth;) How that he was caught up into paradise, and heard unspeakable words, which it is not lawful for a man to utter" (II Cor. 12:1-4).

The meaning of this miracle at Lystra is two-fold:

1. It Was a Credential

When Paul wrote his second letter to the Corinthians he was concerned about his standing as an apostle, since, as you know, he was not among the first apostles who actually walked in the company of Jesus. There were those who were questioning Paul's apostleship, since he had not been present at the resurrection of Jesus, and this had been made a condition for apostleship. But in this miracle at Lystra Paul speaks of the remarkable and unusual experience vouchsafed to him in which he has a preview of heaven; as once before on the Damascus Road he had met and seen the risen Christ at the time of his conversion. This, then, was his credential as an apostle.

2. It Was an Experience

What Paul describes in II Corinthians is apparently and undoubtedly his own experience. There is no other place in Paul's life to position what he relates about heaven, but at the time described in Acts 14 of events which took place at Lystra.

What Paul has experienced is a preview of heaven at the death of a Christian. Paul had been stoned to death according to the observation of his companions; and later, according to the testimony of these same companions, he was raised from the dead. But, in between his death and resurrection, he had an experience which appears to him as "visions and revelations of the Lord." He is as a man "caught up to the third heaven." This heaven is the heavens beyond our immediate earth and not the atmospheric heaven which is an envelope of air in which the earth's inhabitants live. Nor is this the sidereal heaven of sun and stars. It is heaven as a place of life and existence for the ongoing race of redeemed men and women upon the consummation of redemption.

What happened to Paul at Lystra in terms of resurrection parallels the three instances of such resurrection miracles performed by Jesus in the Gospels and the two instances in Acts beside this one. This miracle falls into the category of what is termed perpendicular miracles, occurring once or a few times and never repeated. This power is not possessed by the church today any more than the power of absolute healing. The church's power in these things is relative and not absolute. Our Lord's power is absolute and not relative.

Paul describes his experience as that of a man who entered a place of life called "paradise." This word is used three times in the Bible to indicate the future life. It is found in Luke 23:43 concerning the penitent thief. It is found in Rev. 2:7 to describe the heaven which later appears in view at the end of Revelation. And it is found here where Paul uses it to describe his own experience of death and the preview of heaven. It means garden or, more specifically, a king's garden, or a large park abounding with all sorts of flora and fauna. Kings' gardens, such as Hampton Court in London and Versailles Palace outside of Paris, are beyond description for their beauty and grandeur. This is precisely what Paul says about his experience. It was beyond description. He says that he "heard unspeakable words, which it is not lawful for a man to utter." That is, it was impossible with what he knew of earth to tell earth-people what he saw in heaven. It was too beautiful for description. Words failed him. Men would think him mad, or visionary, should he attempt to tell them what he saw.

We notice that he both saw and heard. Here were things both of sight and sound. Apparently Paul retained, during this experience, the faculties of body which enabled him to see and hear, smell and feel; but he retained these in a state of spiritual exaltation that enabled him to appreciate the greater beauties and glories of the heavenly state which he could not describe in the language of earth.

Let us say first of all, from this experience at Lystra, that heaven has reality. Although Paul thought his experience had its source in "visions and revelations" and although he could not exactly say what he saw, or whether he was in the body or out of the body, nevertheless it had substance. It was as real as a garden. Jesus taught the reality of heaven. He said, "I go to prepare a place for you." Furthermore, it was to be a place to which He would take His disciples.

Then, of this place called heaven, let us say that it undoubtedly is a place of beauty. We would not expect less than this from the God who made earth so beautiful. Heaven will far exceed earth in its beauty. It is an architectural principle that the exterior should be secondary to the interior; that is, the inside of a building should always be more beautiful than the outside. We should always move from the better to the best. And heaven, which will be the heart and center, the very interior of the universe around which it revolves, will be more beautiful than all the rest of the universe.

When John saw the new heavens and earth he said, "And I John saw the holy city, new Jerusalem, coming down from God out of heaven, prepared as a bride adorned for her husband" (Rev. 21:2.). Is there anything more beautiful than a bride? Think of all the care and expense involved in the preparation of a bride: her dress, her coiffure, her adornments, her bearing, her smile, her transparent joy; all combine to make her wedding moment the most transcendent event of life. And the Bible uses this as the simile and symbol of heaven.

When Paul describes his experience of heaven, he likens it to a king's garden, and when he does so he borrows a figure which represents the ultimate in space, arrangement, beauty and variety. Yes, heaven is a very beautiful place.

There are not many descriptions of heaven in the Bible, and when there are such descriptions, they are usually symbolic, such as a bride, the Father's house, and a king's garden. The reason for this is that the Bible must be understood by people who live over a span of thousands of years, during which conditions of life on earth pass through great change. For instance, in John's description of the holy city he speaks of the food source of its inhabitants as a tree of life. Here is something that is understood by people of all generations. A tree bears fruit; fruit is both beautiful to look at and tasteful to eat. Furthermore, this tree has variety for it has twelve manner of fruits, which says to us that the food source of heaven will be in great abundance, of sufficient variety, and will be tasty and pleasant.

As man moves on in his mechanical achievements he talks more and more about synthetics, so that now it is possible for him to compound capsule food. Perish the thought! This would make a dull heaven.

If man's diet were determined by strictly scientific considerations, what would it cost him to live? Brown University researchers fed the problem to an IBM 650 electronic computer, and reported the answer—twenty-one cents a day. Caring nothing for variety or any other of life's spices, the computer solemnly accepted the facts that a man must have certain minimum quantities of protein, calcium, iron, phosphorus and five vitamins. Then its nerve cells went to work and concluded that only four foods are needed to sustain life: lard, beef liver, orange juice and soybean meal. With less culinary than mathematical skill, the researchers could not make the stuff into a palatable meal. Even a laboratory dog was reluctant to put the mess away. The only conclusion: a computer could live cheaper than a human because it has no taste buds.*

In the Bible's description of heaven there is the negative aspect as well as the positive. It tells us that heaven will be beautiful because of the absence of everything unlovely. There will be no night there; neither will there be death, disease, sickness, sin, ignorance, sorrow or tears. All the things that make earth an unlovely place will be missing from heaven. But heaven is not built upon the negative. It has the positive too, for here will be health, knowledge, symmetry, redeemed men, happiness, the presence of God and His Son Jesus; all of which combine to make heaven the most attractive place of time or space.

Heaven will be dominated by a capital city called the New Jerusalem. This will be filled with places called mansions, for

---

* Time, Dec. 7, 1959

Jesus said, "in my Father's house are many mansions." It will be arranged that the kings and the nations of the earth have access to it and bring their glory and honor into it.

When we combine the Bible's descriptions of heaven we have everything we know of that impress us with its beauty. It has a city, a park, gardens, palaces, trees, flowing fountains, sea, fruits, candelabra, robes, palms, music, crowns, precious stones, light, the colors of the rainbow, water, knowledge, friendship, holiness and the presence of God.

PARADISE

Once in a dream I saw the flowers
　　That bud and bloom in Paradise;
　　More fair are they than waking eyes
Have seen in all this world of ours.
And faint the perfume-bearing rose,
　　And faint the lily on its stem,
And faint the perfect violet,
　　Compared with them.

I heard the songs of paradise;
　　Each bird sat singing in its place;
　　A tender song so full of grace
It soared like incense to the skies.
Each bird sat singing to its mate
　　Soft cooing notes among the trees:
The nightingale herself were cold
　　To such as these.

I saw the fourfold River flow,
　　And deep it was, with golden sand;
　　It flowed between a mossy land
With murmured music grave and low.
It hath refreshment for all thirst,
　　For fainting spirits strength and rest:
Earth holds not such a draught as this
　　From east to west.

The tree of Life stood budding there,
　　Abundant with its twelvefold fruits;
　　Eternal sap sustains its roots,
Its shadowing branches fill the air.
Its leaves are healing for the world,
　　Its fruit the hungry world can feed
　　And balm indeed.

I saw the Gate called Beautiful;
　　And looked, but scarce could look within;
　　I saw the golden streets begin,
And outskirts of the glassy pool.
Oh harps, oh crowns of plenteous stars,
　　Oh green palm-branches, many-leaved—
Eye hath not seen, nor ear hath heard,
　　Nor heart conceived.

I hope to see these things again,
　　But not as once in dreams by night;
　　To see them with my very sight,
And touch and handle and attain:
To have all heaven beneath my feet
　　For narrow way that once they trod;
To have my part with all the saints
　　And with my God.

— Christina Rossetti

There is one more thing of great importance concerning heaven. It is how to get there. It has imposed upon it a great restriction, for it says, "And there shall in no wise enter into it any thing that defileth, neither whatsoever worketh abomination, or maketh a lie: but they which are written in the Lamb's book of life" (Rev. 21:27). This is on the negative side but on the positive side there is this word: "Blessed are they that do his commandments, that they may have right to the tree of life, and may enter in through the gates into the city" (Rev. 22:14). The commandments are not the commandments of the

Law, for these have been superseded by John 3:16 which says, "For God so loved the world, that he gave his only begotten Son, that whosoever believeth in him should not perish, but have everlasting life," and John 14:6 which says, ". . . I am the way, the truth, and the life: no man cometh unto the Father, but by me," and Revelation 22:17 which says, "And the Spirit and the bride say, Come. And let him that heareth say, Come. And let him that is athirst come. And whosoever will, let him take the water of life freely."

37

RELIGIOUS CONTROVERSY IN THE CHURCH
Acts 15:1-35

Growth is always the occasion for change. There is a difference between a child's attitude to life and an adult's. Between the child and the adult has been a lot of painful growth and agonizing change. This has been true of the church. For the first twenty years of its existence it did not have any part of the New Testament in its hands for guidance or reference. For the first sixty years it did not have the complete collection of New Testament books in its hands. For the first three hundred years it did not have any of these twenty-seven books in an assembled and canonical New Testament. During this time there was much controversy and discussion. At last, through the councils and the creeds, we have a well defined body of truth.

There is a difference between religious controversy and religious contention. Controversy is healthy and inevitable in growth and development. But contention is to be deplored because, since it is not under the Holy Spirit's guidance, it can only result in diversion from the true mission of the church and in division, by fragmentizing and fracturing the body of Christ. When there is controversy there is the sincere desire of people to know the truth, under the guidance and direction of the Holy Spirit, who was given for this specific purpose. But when there is contention there is carnal desire to promote sectarianism and almost always a lack of open mindedness, because these people usually have pre-judged an issue and determine their course of action before the verdict is in. This was not the attitude at the Jerusalem council. It is not the attitude of true controversy, and it is not the result of the guidance of the Holy Spirit; for the

Holy Spirit is on the side of those who want to find the truth and on the side of those who want to preserve the united nature of the Body of Christ.

The occasion for religious controversy in this first instance at the council at Jerusalem, which occurred about fifteen years after the formation of the church at Pentecost, was a fundamental issue of what really constituted conditions of salvation and entrance into the church. For convenience let us divide this into four parts: The Council, the Participants, the Issues and the Conclusion.

I. THE COUNCIL

The council met at Jerusalem. It had been decreed that when the disciples were scattered abroad by persecution, the apostles would remain at this base and hold the scattered, expanding and growing church on its God-given course. The council was brought about because of a controversy at Antioch, where certain teachers had expounded the idea that no Gentile could be saved without adhering to Mosaic regulation. This is what we call Judaizing Christianity, making it a Jewish sect or advocating legalism. It had happened before when Peter, under revelation of God, had preached the gospel to the house of Cornelius; and it had been concluded there that these Gentile believers were to be as equally acceptable in the church as were Jewish believers. Now the controversy breaks out anew and with such intensity that it threatens the peace as well as the purity of the church, and also threatens to divide it. How serious and important this controversy was was later explained by Paul when he wrote to the Galatians, who likewise were threatened with this divisive teaching. He said, "I marvel that ye are so soon removed from him that called you into the grace of Christ unto another gospel: Which is not another; but there be some that trouble you, and would pervert the gospel of Christ. But though we, or an angel from heaven, preach any other gospel unto you than that which we have preached unto you, let him be accursed. As we said before, so say I now again, If any man preach any other gospel unto you than that ye have received, let him be accursed" (Gal. 1:6-9), and "Behold, I Paul say unto you, that if ye be circumcised, Christ shall profit you nothing. For I testify again to every man that is circumcised, that he is a debtor to do the whole law. Christ is become of no effect unto you, whosoever of you are justified by the law; ye are fallen from grace. For we through the Spirit wait for the hope of righteousness by faith. For in Jesus Christ neither circumcision availeth any thing, nor uncircumcision; but faith which worketh by love. Ye did run well; who did hinder you that ye should not obey the truth? This persuasion cometh not of him that calleth you. A little leaven leaveneth the whole lump. I have confidence in you through the Lord, that ye will be none otherwise minded: but he that troubleth you shall bear his judgment, whosoever he be. And I, brethren, if I yet preach circumcision, why do I yet suffer persecution? then is the offence of the cross ceased" (Gal. 5:2-11).

Nothing could be more important and vital than to discover, or clarify, the means of salvation and the conditions under which salvation is received. It can be said briefly that the council concluded, although these are not its words, that men are saved by grace alone, through faith without works of satisfaction of any kind.

II. The PARTICIPANTS

It is observed here that it was the whole church, or ecclesia, which assembled, heard and settled the controversy. This means, of course, an important historical and fundamental precedent in that the affairs of the church, either local or general, are not under a select hierarchy without the consideration of the people of the church. This hierarchical development in the church has accounted for everyone of its major errors, heresies and corruptions. When the affairs of the church were in the hands of its people, and when its people were under the dominion and guidance of the Holy Spirit, both the purity and peace of the church were preserved. But when the hierarchical principle developed, corruption prevailed and error developed, until in some bodies Christianity is completely obscured and lost, and doctrine is totally corrupted without a semblance of relationship to New Testament theology.

A composite collection of the participants at the Jerusalem council reveals that it consisted of "the church" or "the multitude," "the apostles and elders," who were presided over by a layman who was not an apostle. He was James, the brother of Jesus. This council, so composed, heard disputations on the one hand by Paul and Barnabas who were sent by the church at Antioch, and on the other hand by representatives of "a sect of the Pharisees" who advocated the ideas that caused the controversy. To these was added the testimony of Peter who spoke of his experience at the house of Cornelius.

What you have in effect was a controversy between a Gentile party of the church at Antioch, which was largely composed of Gentile converts, and a Jewish party of the church at Jerusalem, which was largely composed of Jewish converts. And it was from among these Jewish converts that there arose this "sect of the Pharisees," or Judaizers, who wanted to legalize salvation and make it subject to adherence to the law of Moses. The controversy was not heard behind closed doors by the apostles and elders (verse 6), but before what is described as "the multitude" (verse 12) which, by the terms of its language, implies a large number or, in other words, the whole body of the church.

III. THE ISSUES

We must all be aware of the fact that Christianity grew out of Judaism in the sense that the mould of Christianity is definitely Jewish. But this does not mean that Christianity was intended to perpetuate Judaistic ideas, or that the keeping of its laws and the observance of its ceremonies and sacrifices, are to be conditions of salvation. We know differently, because the cross marks the line that separates Judaism and Christianity completely and forever.

We must also understand the fact that while the cross made this complete separation in principle, the early Jewish disciples continued to observe many Jewish regulations in practice, such as: worshiping in the synagogue, the observance of the Sabbath, abstinence from certain kinds of food, the practice of circumcision, and adherence to the feasts and fasts. But, as the church began to grow and mature and realize the true significance of the cross, it had to face up to some of these continuing practices which the Judaizers, or Jewish party, were now saying were necessary for Gentile converts, if they were to share in salvation and the church on an equal basis with the Jewish converts. This then became the issue: Did the new converts need to observe Moses' law and become somewhat of a Jew if they expected to be Christians?

The issue is another form of an age old problem of the relation between law and freedom, obedience and liberty. And so, the council at Jerusalem must find an answer; how could one be obedient to law and still enjoy liberty and freedom?

This answer is found in the presence of a new law which displaced the old law. It is "the law of the spirit of life in Christ Jesus" which has made us "free from the law of sin and death" (Rom. 8:2). This new law supersedes the old law of ceremonies and regulations, and puts a new standard of life and principle within us through God's work of regeneration. When we become obedient to this new law it balances the matter of obedience to law on the one hand, and freedom from the law on the other hand. This new law of life in Christ Jesus is the gospel that Christ gave His disciples to preach. It is found in the gospels and epistles of the New Testament and is the governing principle of Christianity. It is expressed by such New Testament statements as these: "Knowing that a man is not justified by the works of the law, but by the faith of Jesus Christ, even we have believed in Jesus Christ, that we might be justified by the faith of Christ, and not by the works of the law: for by the works of the law shall no flesh be justified. But if, while we seek to be justified by Christ, we ourselves also are found sinners, is therefore Christ the minister of sin? God forbid" (Gal. 2:16, 17). "I am crucified with Christ: nevertheless I live; yet not I, but Christ liveth in me: and the life which I now live in the flesh I live by the faith of the Son of God, who loved me, and gave himself for me" (Gal. 2:20). "For as many as are of the works of the law are under the curse: for it is written, Cursed is every one that continueth not in all things which are written in the book of the law to do them. But that no man is justified by the law in the sight of God, it is evident: for, The just shall live by faith. And the law is not of faith: but, The man that doeth them shall live in them. Christ hath redeemed us from the curse of the law, being made a curse for us: for it is written, Cursed is every one that hangeth on a tree" (Gal. 3:10-13). "But before faith came, we were kept under the law, shut up unto the faith which should afterwards be revealed. Wherefore the law was our schoolmaster to bring us unto Christ, that we might be justified by faith. But after that faith is come, we are no longer under a school master. For ye are all the children of God by faith in Christ Jesus. For as many of you as have been baptized into Christ have put on Christ. There is neither Jew nor Greek, there is neither bond nor free, there is neither male nor female: for ye are all one in Christ Jesus. And if ye be Christ's, then are ye Abraham's seed, and heirs according to the promise" (Gal. 3:23-29). "But when the fulness of the time was come, God sent forth his Son, made of a woman, made under the law, To redeem them that were under the law, that we might receive the adoption of sons. And because ye are sons, God hath sent forth the Spirit of his Son into your hearts, crying, Abba, Father" (Gal. 4:4-6).

At the Jerusalem council the issues were stated by Paul and Barnabas who were in the minority. They were opposed by the Jewish party which was in the majority. It was Peter who gave the heavy argument in favor of liberty when he referred to his experience in the house of the Gentile Cornelius, where he appeared among uncircumcised Gentiles, preached the gospel and witnessed God's confirming act in the coming of the Holy Spirit upon these Gentiles.

It is good for us to consider some things in relation to this council at Jerusalem as it effects us today. In the first place, it is the first meeting of the catholic church. By this we mean the whole or universal church. Many years after this the catholic church became Roman Catholic and then, by reason of a series of schismatic events of its own causing, the Roman Catholic Church ceased to remain catholic, while still being Roman; so that, by the verdict of church history, it is now in fact the Roman Church but not the Roman Catholic Church. It ceased being the catholic church in the Eleventh Century in the schism of the eastern churches. It became even less catholic in the Sixteenth Century when it expelled and excommunicated reformers like Martin Luther, who became the nuclei of the reformed churches. So now, when Pope John XXIII calls an Ecumenical Council it is not ecumenical at all, for it does not comprise the Catholic Church but can only be a council of the Roman Church.

Let us remember another thing: The controversy at the Council at Jerusalem concerned a central, not a peripheral, matter. It concerned the principle on which salvation rested. Much of what concerns the church today is peripheral and not central. It is concern over the frame and not the picture. You can afford to disagree about details of the frame, but the picture is important. And the church can afford to disagree on its modern frame, which is church polity and church denomination-alism; but it must protect the picture. It may be suspended in a defective frame, but we must not keep fighting over the frame and neglect the picture.

Another thing, let us remember that theology and doctrine do not exist for the sake of theology and doctrine. They must always concern people. They must always be practical and never theoretical. They must lead to conduct and not to conflict. They must not be a hobby, but a habit.

IV. The Conclusion

The conclusion of the council came when its moderator, James, summed up the argument and made a pronouncement to the effect that it was God's purpose to take out of the Gentiles a people for His name and that when these Gentiles embrace the gospel they should not be treated as Jews and made to obey the law. Actually he said, "Wherefore my sentence is, that we trouble not them, which from among the Gentiles are turned to God" (Acts 15:19). This was a victory for Paul and Barnabas and the Gentile party of the church at Antioch, and it set clearly before the church the fact that salvation was by grace alone through faith, without works and without the law. When the moderator's judgment was submitted to the council it was unanimously adopted. A letter, which was the first of such and the fore-runner, no doubt, of the letters which are the New Testament epistles, was dispatched to Antioch at the hands of two members of the Jerusalem council, Judas and Silas. In this letter the findings of the council were stated, and, so far as we know, became final and binding on the Antiochan church. We do not read of the Jewish party separating from the Antioch Church because the verdict was against them, and it is assumed, although Judaistic teaching persisted in the church for years, that all the parties involved continued within the framework of the church. It was not perfect but it was the church.

One of the notable things about the decision of the council and the pronouncement that was made and sent to Antioch, was that it contained a concession. Because of the immediate circumstances which involved Jewish converts coming out of their faith and practice into the church, and were therefore sensitive to their tradition, it was proposed by James that Gentile converts "abstain from pollutions of idols and from fornication and from things strangled and from blood" (verse 20). This abstention was to be out of charity on the Gentiles' part, so that their liberty would not be an offense to Jewish tradition. Strictly speaking, this need not have been done, but, practically speaking, it was a tactful concession that no doubt preserved the unity of the church. It was a concession that was peripheral for it did not involve basic doctrine, truth or practice.

Here is a practical lesson for modern Christians. Life is often a series of adjustments to contrary or perplexing situations.

In many areas of our experience we rarely find a complete solution to our difficulties or a total unanimity of viewpoint among those with whom we work. Therefore, we are called upon to adjust ourselves and our feelings to what we know is the highest good, by submerging ourselves so that the work of God may proceed with a united front.

When the church grows up it learns to seek the mind of the Spirit in all matters of faith, and to seek the mind of Christ in all matters of conduct. In this manner the minds of individuals become united in a common purpose and the church marches on in both peace and purity.

38

PERSONAL CONTROVERSY IN THE CHURCH
Acts 15:36-41

Personal controversy is as inevitable as religious controversy. Religious controversy is the quest after truth. But personal controversy can be the result of a multitude of personal factors all of which have their preventions and remedies.

The church is not a society of perfect people without fault and error. It is a society of redeemed people who must express their spiritual natures through imperfect bodies, limited minds and defective personalities. It is a body of people which is being perfected by the means of grace; and the extent, degree and acceleration of progress in this perfecting process is solely determined by the individual Christian in terms of his own surrender to the inward power of his new nature.

The disputants in the controversy at Antioch were Paul and Barnabas, prominent, well known, and highly respected fellow Christians and missionary companions. For almost two years they had shared the perils and hardships of missionary service in alien lands. Now they stood as antagonists in a personal controversy. It is not a pleasant picture to see. Nor is it any more pleasant to remember that this kind of controversy has shattered the peace of the church on many occasions since, and often divided and disunited it. This was particularly true at the time of the Reformation, when we observe the sad spectacle of the reformers quarreling and disputing among themselves when such great issues were at stake.

The cause of the dispute in this case was a young evangelist named John Mark. He was a cousin of Barnabas, and the son of a distinguished family of Christians in Jerusalem. It was in their spacious home that the disciples prayed for the deliverance of Peter from prison, and to which he came to report his release to a houseful of disbelieving and incredulous disciples.

John Mark had been a companion of Paul and Barnabas on their first missionary journey into Asia Minor. He had defected at Perga for reasons that are not apparent. Paul took great offense at this defection and no doubt considered it either a weakness of character or a lack of devotion, which disqualified him from further trust in the hazardous mission of their recently projected second missionary journey. This brought about the controversy between Paul and Barnabas. It is described by the words "sharp contention." Actually the original language uses the word *paroxysm* which in medical terms means a fit or exacerbation. At any rate it was a violent, sharp and convulsive experience. Apparently it was not an objective difference of opinion but an emotional attack that created an unfortunate separation between two fine friends.

So far as we know, there is not another such occasion like this in Paul's life. He had been a Christian some twelve or fourteen years when this happened. He had not written any of the New Testament epistles in which he expressed the matured spiritual development to which he came in later life. On the other hand, Paul had many antagonists among whom were the enemies of his apostleship. Then, there were the Judaizing teachers who still remained in the church at Antioch in spite of the decree of the council at Jerusalem. But there is not another separation of brethren like this; neither do Paul and Barnabas work together again. Barnabas disappears completely from the work of the church recorded in Acts, although his name does appear later in one of Paul's epistles.

For whatever benefit it may serve, let us personalize this controversy and bring it down to contemporary situations. Being expositors and not merely historians, we draw some valuable lessons from this incident for modern living; and to do so we must take into account the subsequent teaching of Paul in the rest of the New Testament as it relates to believer relationship.

I. THE CAUSE OF PERSONAL CONTROVERSY

There is not enough known of the details of the incident between Paul and Barnabas to pinpoint the specific cause. But there are other instances in the New Testament where the causes can be identified.

There is, for instance, the *party spirit*. It is written about by Paul in his first epistle to the Corinthians. He says this, "And I, brethren, could not speak unto you as unto spiritual, but as unto carnal, even as unto babes in Christ. I have fed you with milk, and not with meat: for hitherto ye were not able to bear it, neither yet now are ye able. For ye are yet carnal: for whereas there is among you envying, and strife, and divisions, are ye not carnal, and walk as men? For while one saith, I am of Paul; and another, I am of Apollos; are ye not carnal? Who then is Paul, and who is Apollos, but ministers by whom ye believed, even as the Lord gave to every man?" (I Cor. 3:1-5). Here was the party spirit of personal preference and contention dividing the Church at Corinth into many camps and segments. Paul attributes this party spirit to spiritual immaturity and speaks of these Corinthians as acting like babes instead of adults, Corinthians instead of Christians, men instead of new men, naturally minded instead of spiritually minded.

Then, there are the *sins of the disposition* like bad temper, selfishness, jealousy and malice. Paul lists some of these in II Cor. 12:20. "For I fear, lest, when I come I shall not find you such as I would, and that I shall be found unto you such as ye would not: lest there be debates, envyings, wraths, strifes, backbitings, whisperings, swellings, tumults." All of these defects of disposition should yield to Christian maturity and growth in grace; but because so many fail to attend to the culture of the soul, and because they think so often in terms of the other person, we have the deplorable spectacle of backbiting, jealousy and their kindred sins, disrupting the peace of the church.

It is not always big issues or great problems which divide us. It is more often the little and more common things of human pettiness which are the cause of controversy. In pursuit of a cure for the common cold it is estimated by medical authorities that it will be at least thirty to fifty times as difficult, complex and expensive as the conquest of poliomyelitis. It seems to be the same in problems of human nature.

Many times the cause of controversy is in the expression of one's feelings and not their suppression. We have all heard people held up as virtuous because they say what they think at whatever expense it may exact upon their hearers. But there is more character involved in controlling one's output of opinion than in the explosive release of feelings. There is a silence which is golden. Brown met his friend Smythe and asked, "Did my wife speak at the meeting yesterday?" Smythe replied, "I don't know your wife, but there was a tall, thin woman there who arose and said she could not find words to express her feelings." "That was not my wife," added Brown.

II. The Prevention of Personal Controversy

It is better to prevent personal controversy than to correct its effects by picking up the pieces and patching up the wounds which are inevitably left in its wake. It is better to "be oil on the water than fat on the fire." The old adage that an ounce of prevention is worth a pound of cure is proper here.

Paul must have remembered his Antiochan controversy with Barnabas when he wrote I Cor. 13, where he said, "Charity suffereth long, and is kind; charity envieth not; charity vaunteth not itself, is not puffed up, Doth not behave itself unseemly, seeketh not her own, is not easily provoked, thinketh no evil; Rejoiceth not in iniquity, but rejoiceth in the truth; Beareth all things, believeth all things, hopeth all things, endureth all things" (verses 4-7).

There is another way to prevent personal controversy. It is in the *sincerity and purity of Christian action*. Paul wrote to the Colossians, "Where there is neither Greek nor Jew, circumcision nor uncircumcision, Barbarian, Scythian, bond nor free: but Christ is all, and in all" (Col. 3:17). And when he wrote to the Christians in the church at Rome he said, "Be kindly affectioned one to another with brotherly love; in honour preferring one another" (Rom. 12:10). Think of all the controversy that could be avoided in this preference of another; in honor and respect rather than in the carnal defense of one's own position and opinion. Then again, "Endeavouring to keep the unity of the Spirit in the bond of peace" (Eph. 4:3). Here is an admonition which is binding on every believer who should consider every personal act in this light — am I keeping the unity of the Spirit? Any other act is either divisive or disruptive and therefore not conducive to maintaining the "bond of peace."

The danger in all instances of personal controversy is the after effects which concern, not only the parties immediately involved, but extends to others. It is inevitable that the party spirit should prevail in these instances and that the Body of Christ be divided into separate companies of sympathizers. The danger is described in Hebrews 12:15, "Looking diligently lest any man fail of the grace of God; lest any root of bitterness springing up trouble you, and thereby many be defiled." Personal controversy is our failure in the realm of "the grace of God." It results in "bitterness" and ultimately "many be defiled" through the party spirit.

Another aspect of prevention is in *personal poise* through spiritual growth. When the world of our cherished opinions seems to be threatened by attack and abuse the one thing that will save it is personal poise. This is patient enduring in its finest form. There is a story told of a little girl who did not want to go to bed when her mother told her to one night, because she "had some thinking to do." Her mother understandingly told her to finish her thinking and then she could go to bed in a little while. Later the mother asked the girl, "What were you thinking about, dear?" The little girl confided, "I was thinking about gravity, Mother, and I decided that gravity is God right at the center of the world that keeps the people right side up when the world is upside down."

III. THE TREATMENT OF PERSONAL CONTROVERSY

Generally speaking, the treatment and cure of personal controversy comes out of spiritual maturity through the inner motivations of the Holy Spirit and soul saturation of the Word of God. Specifically, one of the most prolific sources of cure of this unfortunate problem is the Sermon on the Mount, particularly Matthew 5:17-48 which deals with personal relations. Here is a wealth of teaching to remedy bad personal Christian relations.

Another specific treatment is found in Galatians 6:1, "Brethren, if a man be overtaken in a fault, ye which are spiritual, restore such an one in the spirit of meekness; considering thyself, lest thou also be tempted." Here the idea of restoration relates to the doctor's treatment of a fractured bone. It is to be mended by being adjusted and then splinted so it can heal properly. In fractured Christian relations this same sort of careful adjustment and healing is to be undertaken in the spirit of love and consideration.

Yet another specific treatment of the problem is found in the instructions of Romans 12:21, "Be not overcome of evil, but overcome evil with good." This is the displacement of evil with good as well as the returning of evil with good.

Many times personal controversy can be avoided by forgoing the use of what we call the aggressive impulses like competition, fighting, hostility, insistence on having our own way, and so forth. We usually respond to attack by a show of strength. The apostle Paul learned a very valuable lesson in this connection when he became afflicted with a physical disability. After praying for its removal God responded to Paul's need by saying to him, "My strength is made perfect in weakness." Paul responded to this by taking the attitude that he would not fight his problems. He would accept them and not fight them. He would absorb them and not resist them. So he said, "Most gladly therefore will I rather glory in my infirmities, that the power of Christ may rest upon me" (II Cor. 2:9). His position became one of power and strength but it came out of the weakness of non-resistance.

Too often our attitude is that of the little boy whose mother made him sit in the corner as punishment for bad conduct. His retaliation was a defiant rejoinder that went like this: "I may be sitting down on the outside, but remember, I'm standing up on the inside."

IV. DIVINE PROVIDENCE IN PERSONAL CONTROVERSY

It is a tribute to the versatility and flexibility of the principles and teachings of our Christian faith that the controversy at Antioch was finally resolved without permanent damage to the cause of Christ. In the first epistle to the Corinthians (9:6), Paul speaks of Barnabas and himself being of one mind. And even John Mark apparently won Paul's unqualified confidence and approval, for Paul speaks of him a number of times in his church epistles, Philemon 24, II Timothy 4:11 and Colossians 4:10.

Another mitigating result of this Antioch controversy was the overruling effect of divine providence, for in the separation of Paul and Barnabas two missionary thrusts were made on the pagan world, for Paul chose Silas as his companion and they went in one party to Syria. Barnabas chose John Mark as his companion and they went in another missionary party to Cyprus. Thus, there were two expeditions instead of one, with greatly multiplied results; and there were four missionaries instead of two. This is the working of divine providence, for God can make "the wrath of man to praise him." But it would not be wise if you wish to increase missionary activity to precipitate a quarrel among brethren to do so. It is better that we "keep the unity of the spirit in the bond of peace," for in union one can be better than two and two can be better than four.

39

THE MAN IN YOUR LIFE

Acts 16:1-24

The fullest use and employment of one's life, according to God's will, is the great problem which faces all of us. This was the concern of Paul and his companion, Silas, as they struck out from Antioch on their new missionary venture. What happened to them and how they were guided to the best employment of their lives is the subject matter of the narrative of this chapter.

After revisiting many churches, which Paul had founded previously, he and his companions had a remarkable spiritual experience happen to them. They were forbidden by the Holy Spirit to preach the gospel in Asia, and when they went on further in another direction, they were forbidden again. What was happening, although they did not know it, was that they were being driven by a series of divine preventives to the northwest extremity of Asia Minor so that ultimately they would come to what proved to be the gateway to Europe. All of this was by the direct and immediate action of the Holy Spirit upon their lives, so that they could fulfill the highest purpose God had for them. Another reason was to bring the gospel into a vast unreached area of Graeco-Roman dominion where Grecian culture and Roman military might held sway.

The final impetus and direction of their activities came when Paul had his now famous vision of the man of Macedonia who said, "Come over into Macedonia and help us." This was the man in their lives. He needed their help and without their response he would never know the good news of the gospel. Such a man is in every Christian's life. He is the person who is appealing to us for help and our help stands between him and great loss.

To Paul and Silas this man of Macedonia was the symbol of a whole geographical area, of a whole culture and of an entire generation of people. He became the beckoning hand of God to them. He led them to change their Asiatic preaching strategy, take shipping across the Aegean Sea for this needy area in what is now modern Greece. These Macedonians were forerunners of modern Europeans. They became the dominant power in the Greek world under their great king, Philip of Macedon and later his son, Alexander the Great, who, at the age of thirty-three had conquered the world four centuries before Christ.

The culture of the Macedonians was Hellenic although it was now under Roman dominion and in a semi-barbaric state.

It was here that Paul spent five of the most fruitful years of his life. To the people of this extended area he wrote some of his most important church letters, including Thessalonians, Corinthians, Philippians, Ephesians, Galatians, Colossians and later Romans.

Under the compelling impetus of the Holy Spirit's leading, through the call of the man in their lives, Paul, Silas, Timothy and later Luke, entered Macedonia and went to Philippi, its leading city. Here they would have gone to the synagogue on the Sabbath in order to seek an opportunity to make their message known; but this city had no Jewish quarter. It could not even muster as many as ten Jews which would have been enough to organize a synagogue. Instead, the newcomers went to the water-side where Jews always gathered when they had no synagogue for there they could conveniently take care of their religious ablutions. And on the banks of Philippi's local river they discovered a Proseucha or prayer place consisting of a simple enclosure of branches. Here those inclined to Judaism, as well as devout Jews, carried on their religious practices.

Under these rather inauspicious circumstances Paul and his missionary adventurers began their European ministry. What led to it we have already seen, but what it led to is a story of importance to every contemporary Christian.

I. The Over-ruling Providences

The over-ruling of divine providence in the prohibitions to preach the gospel in Asia is an important factor in the over-all picture of these adventures. Without these providences and prohibitions they could not have reached their most fruitful field of service.

Sometimes Paul attributed the hindrances in his life to Satan, and rightly so, for Satan is a great hinderer and actively tries to prevent the progress of the work of God. But this was not Satan's hindering. It was exactly the opposite for it was the providential work of God.

The Bible speaks of open and closed doors. It speaks of open doors that no man can shut and closed doors that no man can open. It is spiritual wisdom when we can recognize the closed doors as well as the open doors. Both of them are found in the believer's life. It is spiritual wisdom when we can recognize the "stops" as well as the "gos" in a spirit-led life. And there are these too. Not all of life is unhindered progress forward. The heights are reached by the zigzag trails of altered courses.

II. The Divine Call

The call was human in its instrumentation but divine in its nature and authority. It was personified by a representative Macedonian with all his contemporary color and all the urgency of his great need. It was nevertheless the voice of God which spoke to Paul. And this was what they understood for they assuredly gathered "that the Lord had called us for to preach the gospel to them." This sustains the divine nature of the church. It is not being revealed here as a human enterprise conceived and executed by men but as the work of God. It was conceived of God, born of God at Pentecost and now directed by God in the choice of personnel and their employment in strategic areas.

This divine call, as it is understood in the nature of the church, is not confined to a few leaders. It extends to all the discipleship for God has given a place of service to every saved individual. It is well said that "You cannot promote the Christian enterprise adequately by merely being a patron: you have to be a partner." Christians need to move from the spectator stands to the combat arena. They need to change from watchers to workers.

III. THE IMPERATIVE NEED

Few of us will ever be favored by visions like that which came to Paul in his Macedonian call, yet there is a man in each life. He is the person in need of Christ. He is the person for whom Christ died. He is the person whose need will never be met unless we meet it.

The classic call of the Macedonian was the representation of an imperative and compelling need. These Macedonians had a proud history. Their country was the seat of Roman military power. Grecian culture and philosophy were intrenched in Macedonia. But none of these things were enough to meet their total need. And none of the things we have in terms of modern technology are enough to meet our total need. Our needs are deeper than our skin and greater than any technology can supply. Our need is the basic, historic, spiritual need of God. It is as universal as it is personal for "man doth not live by bread alone." Material progress cannot supply us with the basic satisfactions of the soul.

The crisis of America today is not the crisis of poverty, ignorance and want; it is the crisis of plenty. Our problem is what to do with our surpluses. It is our problem socially, economically, agriculturally and spiritually. This seems to be borne out by the fact that people in the most democratic and prosperous countries, where there is the greatest technological advancement, have the highest incidences of suicide, alcoholism, mental illness and divorce. Erich Fromm, world famous psychologist said this, "We find then that the countries in Europe which are among the most democratic, peaceful and prosperous ones, and the United States, the most prosperous country in the world, show the most severe symptoms of mental disturbance . . . . Could it be that the middle class life of prosperity, which satisfies our material needs, leaves us with a feeling of intense boredom, and that suicide and alcoholism are pathological ways of escape from this boredom? Could it be that these figures are a drastic illustration for the truth of the statement that 'man does not live by bread alone'?"

IV. The Ready Response

It is indicated here that when Paul received his Macedonian call there was neither debate nor delay. He did not question the unique circumstances of his call. He did not consider the hardship and dangers involved. He did not ask for compensations or comforts. He and his friends went as swiftly as passage could be arranged and they were on their way with all speed.

One wonders what has happened to the spirit of ready response in the modern church. When General Douglas MacArthur pleaded for missionaries to fill the void in Japan at the close of the war, we failed to respond. Could an earlier failure to sufficiently evangelize China be the reason for the communist conquest? And what about the foment of nationalism in Africa? Have we failed to meet an urgent need? The only place where evangelical forces seem to be fairly adequate is in Latin America where there are now five million Protestants in a diminishing Roman Catholic constituency. But we are losing the battle in America where we are dangling on the precipice of a fearful population explosion. We are unable to match in Christian devotion the incident created by a lost dog in the city of Detroit where the combined civil and civic resources joined in search of a child's lost Alsatian pet. A city's imagination can be stirred to find a dog but we cannot summon enough Christian concern to search that city or any city for the lost souls of men.

The missionary, evangelism and prayer work of any church is almost always the interest of a minority.

Periodically we are stirred by the devotion of some Christian who responds to the call of God such as Miss Frances Aylword. You have seen the film or read the book about this determined young woman who went to London to offer herself for missionary service in China. She was courteously received but told that she had no qualifications. So she took a position as a servant until she had saved sufficient money to go to China by the cheapest route. She made light of hardships and was appointed assistant to an old lady who had spent her life helping the Chinese. Then the Japanese invaded the country. They bombed the city and chased the refugees with their planes, and the woman without qualifications found herself in charge of a crowd of children. They trudged together to what was considered a place of greater safety. When food was running out she shared her rations with boys and girls; when they cried in their weariness the gave them new heart, even carrying some of them. She arrived at last and they were all welcomed by new friends. She responded to God's call and did what she could.

V. THE FRUITFUL RESULTS

The immediate results of this European adventure were represented by three notable converts in Philippi. There was Lydia, who was from a company of Jews and God-fearing Gentiles who came together for prayer and worship at the river side. She was apparently a woman of distinction, perhaps a wealthy widow originally from Thyatira where she belonged to a guild of dyers. Because of this connection she carried on a flourishing business in Philippi, selling dyes and fabrics. Lydia became the first of a company of distinguished women disciples which included among others, such illustrious names as Syntyche and Euodias of Philippi who became valuable assistants of Paul; also Dorcas, Priscilla, Eunice and Phoebe. Here is a tribute to the invaluable place of womanhood in the work of the gospel. It is a place which has been held and filled with many distinguished women in every age of the church.

This prominence and eminence of women in the early church

was a tribute to the nature of Christianity, for it flourished in a day when contemporary religion put little value upon womanhood. Women were little more than chattel and valued only for breeding and work. The place of women in our modern world can be attributed to the Christian faith.

Little Johnnie brought home his report card, and showed it proudly to his father. "This is fine, son," said the father. "This probably puts you at the head of your class." "No," replied Johnnie, "Mary Brown is ahead of me." "What," replied the father in mock horror. "You don't mean to say that you let yourself be beaten by a mere girl." "Oh, but Dad," replied Johnnie with the air of one who knew when he was abreast of the times, "girls aren't as mere as they used to be."

The second convert was the slave-girl who was the property of a company of priests. Because of her occult ventriloquism and fortune telling ability, they were able to make considerable financial gain from her. But when she was converted and her way of life changed, it brought down the wrath of her owners upon the apostles and their ultimate imprisonment and finally expulsion from Philippi. As disappointing as this might seem, for the moment, and as an apparently unjust reward for faithful service, all such incidents worked out for the furtherance of the gospel. In God's plans liabilities become assets.

The third convert was a most unlikely prospect. He proved to be the governor of the Roman prison with the rank of a centurion. When he witnessed the divine nature of the apostles' deliverance from his prison, he asked the way of salvation and brought his whole family to confession and baptism.

All these things put together came as the result of a man in the lives of the apostles. The man in your life is saying with all the over-tones of modern urgency and need, "Come over and help us." What will be your answer?

40

QUESTION AND ANSWER

Acts 16:25-40

Here is one of the greatest evangelistic themes of the Bible. It is one of at least four such themes in the Book of Acts — No Other Name, Chapter 4; The Unknown God, Chapter 17; and Almost a Christian, Chapter 26. It brings us face to face with the most momentous and important decision of life, one's personal relationship to God. After all, evangelism is the recital of the facts of the gospel which is God's overture to man to become reconciled to Him.

There can be many variations in the recital of these facts but the facts themselves never change. These facts consist of something *historical* and something *personal*. The historical is the incarnation, crucifixion and resurrection of Jesus Christ through which He represented God to man and became in turn man's way to God. The personal is conversion, regeneration and justification by faith through which man is brought into right relation to God. The *catalyst* which brings the personal and the historical into reality is the exercise of man's faith. When this faith is exercised it brings into play all the saving effects of the grace of God so that man is forgiven his sins, becomes the recipient of divine mercy, is born into the family of God, is made a member of the Kingdom of Heaven, and is the beneficiary of all the benevolent effects of divine salvation.

This is the theoretical and theological side of personal salvation. But there is the practical side which is illustrated for us in an outstanding and notorious way by the conversion of the governor of the Philippian jail.

1. Its Locale. In this case it was a prison. This is most unusual

because comparatively few people have conversions associated with prisons. But it can be anywhere; and when you sum up the conversion experiences related in the Bible, very few of them are associated with churches. Peter was saved in a boat, Matthew in a tax collector's office, Zacchaeus in a tree, the malefactor on a cross, Joseph of Arimathaea at home, Paul on a highway and the Ethiopian in a chariot. It almost looks as if men could be saved anywhere but in a church. But of course churches, as we know them, did not exist in this period.

2. Its Occasion. It was brought about by the preaching of the gospel to a slave-girl who was employed as a sorcerer by a band of unscrupulous priests. "The burden of the apostle's message was salvation; but to accept it involved a change of life and so the conversions that were made caused some considerable disturbance in social and civic life."* In this case it robbed the priests of their gain and they had the apostles put into jail.

3. Its beginning. The conversion experience of the prison's governor began with a question. A question is the sign of curiosity. Curiosity is a valuable thing. Curiosity leads scientists to the discovery of new things. Curiosity leads explorers to the discovery of new lands. Curiosity leads philosophers to the discovery of new knowledge.

The pity of much of our curiosity is that we seem to be little concerned with our spiritual welfare. Curiosity concerns material and physical things. It is not much occupied with spiritual things. It concerns time but seldom eternity. It concerns man but seldom God. It concerns the world we live in but seldom the world to come. It concerns life but seldom salvation. In fact, one could go through a lifetime without anyone ever asking him the question, "What must I do to be saved?" There may not be the same urgency as that of being in prison; but there are other even more urgent reasons for salvation, like critical illness, deep sorrow, serious trouble, conviction of sin and above all else, life itself.

The careless, thoughtless and incurious man of the world has

* Rackham

been likened to a child sitting on the branch of a fruitful tree which extends over a yawning abyss. This child is thoughtlessly eating the fruit of the tree while two worms called Night and Day are slowly eating through the branch. Finally the branch breaks and plunges the thoughtless child into the abyss. The moral spoken of here is that no one dares to give thoughtless and careless attention to the material and physical so long as his eternal interests are not secured.

There are many famous questions and answers in the Bible. There is the first one which God asked of man in the beginning, "Where art thou?" The answer was, "I was afraid." The fact is man was hiding from God in fear, a fear that has become a universal fright which religion tried to change through ritualistic appeasement, or by barter through good works. It did not succeed, so "In the fulness of time God sent forth His Son. . . to redeem them that are under the law."

Here is a question which applies to all men although the circumstance of its asking may be as different as men are different.

I. THE QUESTION

"Sirs, what must I do to be saved?" (verse 30). This question suggests three things:

1. That Salvation Is a Matter To Be Settled. It says, *"What* must I do to be saved?" By the very fact that he asks the question, the governor of the prison admits to an inherent and instinctive need in his life. He would not desire what he already possessed if he were already saved.

Salvation is a matter to be settled with God's help because humanity is beyond the place of self-salvation. Self-salvation demands absolute goodness, and absolute goodness demands absolute perfection, and absolute perfection demands, among other things, absolute honesty, truthfulness, morality and righteousness. It is impossible for the relative to produce the absolute, and since man can only be relatively good he cannot be absolutely perfect.

2. That Salvation is a Personal Matter to be Settled. It is, "What must *I* do to be saved?" Under the urgencies and exigencies of this critical moment the governor realized that salvation was his own personal responsibility. It belonged to no time but the present.

It is a matter of *personal responsibility*. Men have been introduced to positions of power and prestige by an influential parent or friend. Women have been presented to royal courts by the recommendation of governmental officers. But no one will ever have salvation conferred upon him by virtue of the influence of another. Neither parental piety, priestly praying, or saintly sanction can open heaven's door for anyone. It is a matter of personal fitness.

It is also a matter for the *present time*. The earth is heaven's vestibule and time is eternity's prelude. What we must do for eternity we must do in time. The Greeks had two words to designate time: *chronos* and *kairos*. Chronos is the time we measure by clocks and calendars. Kairos is the kind of time which means opportunity and privilege. In this matter of salvation kairos time must be done in chronos time for our opportunity to to be saved comes to us in time alone.

These Greeks pictured chronos time as an old man, bowed and haggard with the weight of years. Nothing is left to this man but sadness and regret because of the passage of time. But kairos time was pictured as a young man who was a swift runner. The back of his head was smoothly shaven while on the front was a long forelock of hair. In this picture time, as responsibility, was something to be seized as it was coming because it could not be grasped as it was going. Those who hesitated lost their opportunity and failed in their responsibility.

3. That Salvation is a Personal Matter Demanding Decisive Action. It says, "What must I *do* to be saved?" Salvation is more than an attitude; it is an act. It is more than an ancestral posture; it is a personal position. It is something which we do in relation to what God has done. It is our faith in respect to God's grace. It is something personal because of something historical.

II. THE ANSWER

". . . Believe on the Lord Jesus Christ, and thou shalt be saved, and thy house" (verse 31). Here is a question whose answer prescribes action. Personal salvation is an action experience; it is not a passive inheritance of pre-natal goodness. It is something that rests with us as individuals.

There is a three-fold answer to a three-fold question:

1. That if salvation demands definite action that action is to believe. "What must I do?" . . . *"Believe."*

Someone asked Samuel Coleridge if one could prove the truth of Christianity and he replied, "Why certainly, let him try it." The trouble with most people who are unsaved is they would like their questions answered before their position with God is established. Jesus said, "If any man will *do* his will he shall *know* of the doctrine whether it be of God." Here the order is "do and know" and not "know and do." In salvation experience always precedes explanation.

If salvation is an action experience then the action is to "believe." What must one do? "Believe." It is not the action of religious works or moral deeds. It is, "believe." The only thing a person can do to be saved is "believe." This will in turn lead to benevolent action of all kinds to satisfy the demands of moral equity.

2. That if salvation is a personal matter it is a personal matter involving a personal Savior. "What must I do?" . . . *"Believe on the Lord Jesus Christ."* A personal sinner requires a personal savior. A personal sinfulness requires a personal salvation. God has not supplied an institutional salvation to save an individual sinner.

The church is the channel through which salvation is brought to the world but the church does not save. Men are saved by their personal encounter with Jesus Christ. Salvation is something that flows through Christ who is presented by the church. We never consume the cup to have our thirst quenched. It is the water which the cup holds that satisfies the thirsty throat.

3. That if salvation is a personal matter to be settled it will be satisfactorily settled when one believes on the Lord Jesus Christ. Sin is a present need and salvation is a present experience to meet that need. If we believe in time we will be saved in time, and will not have to wait until eternity to be saved or to know it. The notion that one cannot be sure of salvation until he gets to heaven is like saying you cannot know you are alive until you are dead.

The very happy result of this incident was that the jailer not only believed, but also persuaded his family and household to believe. More than this, both he and they identified themselves with the growing Christian community in Philippi by public baptism.

Two things are generally overlooked in connection with the conversion of this Roman official. One is something which Paul and Silas did after the jailer believed. The other is something the jailer did before he publicly professed his faith in Christ through baptism.

Paul and Silas "spake unto him the word of the Lord, and to all that were in his house" (verse 32). In other words, they were instructed more fully in the way of salvation. This instruction consisted of the sum of the things which now constituted the Christian faith. These were the crucifixion, resurrection and ascension of Jesus, things concerning the Kingdom of God, the ministry of the Holy Spirit, justification by faith, salvation in the name of Jesus alone for the remission of sins. This was the whole gospel message in which the jailer, his family, and his servants were instructed.

The jailer then did a gracious thing to indicate the reality and depth of his own conversion. He took Paul and Silas and "washed their stripes." In this manner he made some measure of restitution to indicate the sincerity of his position and the effect of divine grace upon his life. Instruction in the things of God and restitution in the things of man are two important preparations for any man's confession of faith.

41

THE TALE OF TWO CITIES
Acts 17:1-14

The tale of two cities is the attitude of two different communities to the Christian message. Neither of these communities had the Bible as we know it today. What they had was only the Old Testament. Not a single portion of the New Testament had been written by this time. It was the Old Testament which the people at Berea searched daily to see whether the things which were told them were so.

Paul and Silas had been forced to leave Philippi and in consequence went to Thessalonica in upper Thessaly. Here, as was their usual custom, they sought out the Jewish quarter and attended the synagogue. In fact, they spent three weeks here, and each Sabbath "reasoned" with the people out of the Old Testament scriptures, alleging that Jesus Christ was actually the Jewish Messiah. They could prove the messianic claims by His crucifixion and resurrection.

The result of this ministry was the conversion of great numbers of Greeks and many prominent women; but only a few Jews responded. The hostile Jews started a wave of persecution against the apostles and went out into the city and stirred up a malignant segment of unlearned people who proceeded to riot against the visiting preachers. Seeing their danger the apostles found safety, while the wrath of the mob was vented upon a believer named Jason. The upshot of the incident was that Paul and Silas went on to Berea, a distance of about forty miles. Here they found another colony of Jews with a synagogue and, following their usual custom, reasoned with them out of the scriptures.

But these Bereans were of a different sort than the Thessalonians because "they received the word with all readiness of mind, and searched the scriptures daily, whether these things were so."

This text is used constantly as a reason for Christian believers to study the Bible in order to confirm their faith. Such use is a proper accommodation of the scriptures, but this was not the circumstance at Berea. These people were Jews, not Christians. The apostles were bringing a new teaching which was revolutionary and would require a complete reversal of attitude upon the part of the Jews. They could have responded with bigotry, prejudice, intolerance and hatred, as the Thessalonian Jews did. But being possessed of nobility of spirit they "searched the scriptures daily." They examined the apostles' teaching in the light of their own Old Testament scriptures. This is nobility and it is this nobility which is the heart of the message to all of us. When confronted with ideas and situations requiring our decision and judgment, let us be done with bigotry, intolerance and narrow-mindedness and be noble of spirit with reason and open-mindedness.

Had this nobility been followed in the course of the next three centuries, the church would have been saved its great defections and deep corruptions. But failing of this nobility of the Bereans, the church developed forms of rigid formal worship in rituals, ceremonies and symbols instead of continuing its inquiry of the scriptures. The power of the Holy Spirit manifested by the inquiry of the believers, was substituted by the power of a hierarchy which decided what the people were to believe. The church exchanged the scriptures for tradition, divine authority for human authority, spiritual worship for fleshly worship, and a Bible centered church for a ritual centered church. The result is the spectacle of paganism wedded to Christianity in a religious system that repudiates the scriptures as the final authority for faith and practice.

The peril of this kind of substitution is present today in another form. It is religious "additives" to Christian truth.

These "additives" are also found in today's commercial products. There was a time when one bought soap because it contained soap, and tooth paste because it contained tooth paste. Now we are urged to buy tooth paste because it contains Gardol, deodorant because it contains complex K, shampoo because it contains DO44, soap because it contains Aqua-D and shave cream because it contains Lubrasol.* In this manner the American public is bombarded by the pseudo-scientific creations of advertising agents to induce gullible people to buy their nostrums.

But the tragedy is "that this same mentality goes to church."

There are preachers who try to sell the gospel with all sorts of additives. It is Christ plus Freud. It is Christ diluted with "togetherness." It is Christ and metaphysics. These are the pseudo-religious inventions offered gullible church-goers whose only proper response is to "search the scriptures daily, whether those things were so."

The tale of two cities has some pertinent lessons for the modern Christian.

I. There Is a Nobility of Spirit to Be Emulated

This nobility of spirit makes a choice between prejudice, intolerance and bigotry as one attitude of response, and open-mindedness and reason as the other attitude of response. At Thessalonica the Jews showed bigotry and intolerance and refused to consider the facts to be found in their own scriptures and stoned the apostles out of the city. But at Berea they were open-minded and reasonable concerning the new doctrine. They tested it by the one means they had at hand, the Old Testament. It is this nobility which is fitting for all. We should judge ideas, proposals and situations by searching the scriptures and seeking the facts, rather than exercising our prejudice and becoming emotionally unreasonable.

This kind of nobility is for believers as well as inquirers. Often evangelical Christians have responded to liberal teaching

---

* Eternity Magazine

with the bigotry and intolerance of the Thessalonians. They have done the same to their own kind and have ended by "stoning" them out of their fellowship. Proposals and propositions are to be looked at objectively rather than emotionally. We should be willing to find the facts, face the facts and follow the facts. God gives us the source of this noble spirit in the new nature of the Christian and in the scriptures.

We ought to have authority for our viewpoint and not prejudice. The one certain authority is the scripture made attractive by the agreeable spirit of Christian nobility.

II. WE SHOULD BASE OUR CONVICTIONS ON THE SCRIPTURES

"All scripture is given by inspiration of God, and is profitable for doctrine, for reproof, for correction, for instruction in righteousness: that the man of God may be perfect, throughly furnished unto all good works" (II Tim. 3:16, 17).

This puts the burden of responsibility on the pulpit. It must be the provider of scriptural truth. Its preaching and teaching must be the Bible. Even without a complete Bible the apostles used the portion at their command, and constantly "reasoned with them out of the scriptures."

The art of Bible teaching has been lost in the church today. It has happened to the church as happened to Israel when the nation lost the scriptures; it was found in the temple where it had been lost for a generation. The same thing prevails today and we have substituted ritual, ceremony and a host of other things in its place.

There is one book every minister ought to know; it is the Bible. He must know it, not simply as literature, theology, history, Hebrew or Greek, but in terms of its solutions for the human dilemma. Our people must be taught to "search the scriptures," and the minister must know the book his people are searching.

III. The Growth of the Individual Christian Depends Upon His Personal Use of the Bible.

Spiritual growth is not the result of receiving pre-digested scriptural food regurgitated by the minister once a week at a public worship service. It is the result of the individual search of the believer in his own quest for truth. This search begins with the advent of Christian life as a babe in Christ when that babe "desires the sincere milk of the word." But it goes beyond that to personal inquiry, search and study. An adult Christian studies to show himself "approved unto God a workman needing not to be ashamed."

The importance of this search (translated "examine" in the R.S.V.) is found in the biological fact that we are what we eat. Science has found that our eating habits reveal a great deal about our character and personality. Psychologists have discovered that a person's likes and dislikes about food provide an index to how well-adjusted he may be. Not only is this true, but the very composition of our food effects the chemistry of the body and contributes to our health or our sickness. This is equally true in a spiritual sense for our spiritual food is the determining factor in our growth. If the right spiritual ingredients, which can only be found in the Bible, are missing then we are bound to be spiritually deficient and malformed.

IV. The Bible is Worthy of Being Searched Because It is a Confirmed Book.

It is a thoroughly trustworthy source for all truth. It contains all the essentials for faith and action. It is said to be "profitable for doctrine, for reproof, for correction, for instruction in right-eousness: that the man of God may be perfect (complete), throughly furnished unto all good works."

The Bible is confirmed by its *internal evidence*—the text. To examine the text of the Bible is to be assured that it contains, with an infinitesimal amount of error, the intended word of God to man. This breeds trustworthiness and confidence for anyone who wishes to know what God has to say about matters pertaining to faith and life.

The Bible is confirmed by its *external evidence*—the context. The historical accuracy of the Bible is one of the wonders of literature and an evidence of the supernatural transmission of truth.

In commenting on the historical accuracy of the Bible Dr. Wm. F. Albright said, "Thanks to modern research we now recognize its substantial historicity. The narratives of the patriarchs, of Moses and the exodus, of the conquest of Canaan, of the judges, the monarchy, exile and restoration, have all been confirmed and illustrated to an extent that I should have thought impossible forty years ago. The faith of the patriarchs still shines through the stories of Genesis, handed down by oral tradition with surprising accuracy in detail, though this tradition cannot be used to reconstruct a chronological record of events. The background of Moses and his contributions to religion and law take definite form in the light of our present knowledge, and we may rest assured that his towering personality is fairly represented by tenacious oral tradition. We can now date the exodus and the conquest, and can understand the evolution of institutions—if not always of ideas—during the time of the judges and kings of Israel. Exile and restoration have been rescued from the critical controversy of the past generation and appear again in the clear light of history. There has been a general return to appreciation of the accuracy, both in general sweep and in factual detail, of the religious history of Israel. To sum up, we can now again treat the Bible from beginning to end as an authentic document of religious history."

Recent archeological discoveries have revealed the following items of confirmatory evidence concerning the trustworthiness of the Bible. These recent discoveries have confirmed the authenticity of the times when Joseph was in Egypt where he became Prime Minister: the story of the exodus; the miracle of the manna; the Biblical Ark of the Covenant and the Tabernacle; the walls of Jericho; the activities of David and the glories of

Solomon; the ruins of Megiddo (Armageddon) where twenty cities appear, one on top of the other.

V. THE END OF SEARCHING THE SCRIPTURES IS PRACTICE

It is possible to over-emphasize the facts and trustworthiness of the Bible, and become a devotee of doctrine rather than to realize that while right doctrine is important it is not enough in itself. It is only a means to an end and the end is to establish and develop a person's relationship with God. The final test of Christianity is not in the area of orthodoxy or the acceptance of right teaching because faith without works is dead. The ultimate test of orthodoxy is right conduct.

Searching the scriptures can degenerate into theological witch hunting. It can degenerate into a carnal effort to support our prejudices rather than an effort to find God's mind. It can degenerate into a support of sectarianism, factionalism and denominationalism rather than spiritual excellence in both character and conduct.

Searching the scriptures was a mark of nobility in the Bereans who revealed in their acts and attitudes an absence of bigotry, intolerance, sectarianism, theological provincialism, prejudice, jealousy and hatred. They displayed sweet agreeableness which led them to find truth and a noble manner of life. Jesus said, "If ye know these things, happy are ye if ye do them" (John 13:17). James said, "But be ye doers of the word, and not hearers only, deceiving yourselves" (James 1:22).

42

TURNING THE WORLD UPSIDE DOWN
Acts 17:6

Archimedes once said that given a fulcrum strong enough and a lever long enough he could move the world. He did not do this, although it is theoretically possible. However, in another sense it has been done, as is described here. Here are men who moved the world, and their fulcrum and lever was the same instrument, the Cross. When the Cross is turned sideways its cross-arm becomes the fulcrum and its upright, the lever. With the spiritual power of the Cross they were able to enter the world and change it for good.

Here is the story of the early adventures of the first Christians and their tremendous power to move the world. Here is the story of the early conquests of Christianity and its supremacy over the barbarian mind, the religious mind and the cultured mind. Here also is the record of the essential nature of the Christian faith, for here you see in essence what Christianity is by what Christianity does.

What is the essential nature of the Christian faith?

1. Christianity is Revolutionary, not Reactionary. When Christianity confronted its two principle antagonists, Judaism and paganism, it did not react against them with violence or bigotry; nor did it return blow for blow when force was used against it.

True Christianity has never been anti-Semitic or anti-religious. It has never denied freedom of religion to anyone who may have been opposed to it. Any form of intolerance is not Christian in nature. When that system, purporting to be the one true church, limits, abridges and denies freedom of religion to other branches of the Christian faith or to non-Christian faiths, it is not acting in the true spirit of Christianity.

Christianity made no attempt to conquer Judaism and paganism by out-fighting them. Instead, it out-thought, out-prayed and out-lived them. Its weapons were positive and not negative. Christianity never adopted the methods of the world in order to conquer the world. It recognized, first of all, the essential nature of its struggle was spiritual, for "we wrestle not against flesh and blood, but against principalities, against powers, against the rulers of the darkness of this world, against spiritual wickedness in high places" (Eph. 6:12). Because of this spiritual nature of its struggle it recognized the spiritual nature of its weapons. "(For the weapons of our warfare are not carnal, but mighty through God to the pulling down of strong holds;) Casting down imaginations, and every high thing that exalteth itself against the knowledge of God, and bringing into captivity every thought to the obedience of Christ" (II Cor. 10:4, 5).

2. Christianity is Redemptive, not Reformative. The object of Christ's mission was human redemption, not reformation. He came to do a redemptive and regenerative work on the inside and not merely change the outward appearance or circumstance.

Jesus' accusation against the religion of His day was its superficial and shallow outwardness. He said, "Woe unto you, scribes and Pharisees, hypocrites! for ye make clean the outside of the cup and of the platter, but within they are full of extortion and excess . . . Woe unto you, scribes and Pharisees, hypocrites! for ye are like unto whited sepulchres, which indeed appear beautiful outward, but are within full of dead men's bones, and of all uncleanness" (Matt. 23:25, 27).

As for the efficacy of religious reformation He said, "No man putteth a piece of new cloth unto an old garment, for that which is put in to fill it up taketh from the garment, and the rent is made worse. Neither do men put new wine into old bottles: else the bottles break, and the wine runneth out, and the bottles perish: but they put new wine into new bottles, and both are preserved" (Matt. 9:16, 17).

The true nature of Christianity is found in its regenerative work in the heart and character of man. It is described by Paul in these words, "Therefore if any man be in Christ, he is a new creature: old things are passed away; behold, all things are become new" (II Cor. 5:17).

3. Christianity is Creative, not Destructive. Jesus was not an iconoclast. He did not come to destroy old systems and leave a vacuum created by these destructions. He did not come to destroy idolatry and leave men bereft of religious expression. Indeed, these things were to be done away with, but only for the sake of clearing a site on which to build a new and better order of faith and worship.

This new order would be *individual*. Jesus said to Nicodemus, "Ye must be born again." Here was something creative. He would bring in a new life, and make a new man, and create a new destiny, and establish a new purpose for life.

Jesus did not propose to begin with the goodness, character, religion, morality or Judaism of Nicodemus and build upon what might be good in these things. He would not take the best He could find in the worst of men, and make this the foundation of a new life. He would begin with something new, and whatever there was in Nicodemus and is in us that belongs to the old order of morality and religion must go. Christianity is a new thing.

This new order would also be *institutional*. Jesus did not continue the ceremonials of Judaism and make these the beginnings of Christianity. This idea was smashed at the house of Cornelius, and settled in the Jerusalem council, for Christianity was a new order of things through the church. Henceforth the church would be the divine agency through which God would accomplish His will and purpose in the world.

The church is not only God's voice to witness to truth; it is also by its new nature, the salt of the earth and the light of the world, and is to exert a righteous influence on the world. It should be concerned about such things as religious liberty, human freedom, war and peace, political corruption, greed, poverty and civic unrighteousness.

"Karl Marx was baptized as a Lutheran in Germany. Why did he forsake the faith to write the bible of communism, Das Kapital? History reveals that the church in Germany at Marx's time was nothing but an institution which approved whatever the state did. In Berlin there were eight hundred thousand people, but the churches had seats for only twenty-five thousand. And these were never filled. People brought their children for baptism, as a matter of course. The children returned for confirmation. Then came marriage and finally death. The church was not a part of the people. It had no concern for the needs and problems of its people. Marx turned from the Christian religion for one of his own making which he claimed had a concern for people's needs.

"The same was true with Stalin, who once prepared for the priesthood in the Russian Orthodox Church. He turned away from a church which was identified with a corrupt state. Never did the church, at that time, protest against the abuses of the people: the Jewish massacre, the Siberian camps, the terrible poverty, the machines of torture, the killing of peasants who came to protest their condition. One thing we can be sure of — the scourge of communism in our world today is God's judgment upon a world with too much of the wrong kind of religion."

To be revolutionary, redemptive and creative required a character in Christians which would be aggressive, bold, fearless, uncompromising, brave and sacrificial. It could not be done by proponents who were like the preacher who had preached with such unmanly and effeminate characteristics that after the service when he stood at the door, someone asked him his maiden name.

It was precisely because this first generation of Christians was courageous that it was effective and could turn the world upside down. Turning the world upside down was achieved by bringing an entirely new concept of life into being. This new concept had at least seven new ideas.*

---

* Identity of the source of these seven new ideas unknown

I. THE IDEA THAT THE INDIVIDUAL WAS MORE THAN THE STATE

In the oligarchies, monarchies and despotisms of the First Century the state was everything. People were taught to believe that they existed for the state, not the state for them. Christianity gave a new dignity to life. It made the individual the key person in society. The individual bore the image of God and not the state. For this reason Paul could defy kings, magistrates, governments and rulers.

England's Magna Charta and our own Bill of Rights are the direct descendants of this revolutionary idea. These documents respect the rights of the individual, guarantee due process of law and make the individual and his property sacred.

One of the recent princes of Wales came to a humble miner's cottage and knocked at its door, humbly asking entrance. "Come in, come in," said the miner. "You are my sovereign and you have right of access." "No," said the prince, "Your home is your castle and fortress and not even the king can enter without your permission.".

II. THE IDEA THAT GOD WAS COME DOWN AMONG MEN

This was revolutionary, for while the Jews looked for a messiah they expected one to come up from the nation and not down from heaven. The incarnation was a thing unbelievable, yet here was Immanuel in their midst.

The Romans had their Pantheon, and the Greeks had their temples and multiple gods in the form of animals, reptiles and birds. But here was something revolutionary. Here was God, not in angel form with fantastic bodily shapes, nor in marble or plaster; but in one who was born in a manger, working in a carpenter shop, living among men, and in all these ways revealing God to men.

III. THE IDEA OF SALVATION BY FAITH

When Judaism is rightly understood it is seen as a salvation by faith, for its sacrifices were a progressive picture of the coming salvation by Jesus, the great High Priest. It was perverted into a system of ordinances, observances and works, losing its essential meaning in deeds of merit. But Christianity reversed all this and salvation became something of faith. Their prophet, Habakkuk had said, "The just shall live by faith."

When the Philippian jailer saw his predicament he said, "Sirs, what must I do to be saved?" The answer was simply, "Believe on the Lord Jesus Christ and thou shalt be saved." Here was something new. The emphasis in salvation was what it always had been, on faith and not on works.

IV. The Idea of a Spiritual Perception of God Rather than a Physical One

Men's idea of God had been corrupted so that He expressed Himself in physical images rather than a spiritual fellowship. When Paul wrote to the Romans he said, "Because that, when they knew God, they glorified him not as God, neither were thankful; but became vain in their imaginations, and their foolish heart was darkened. Professing themselves to be wise, they became fools, And changed the glory of the uncorruptible God into an image made like to corruptible man, and to birds, and fourfooted beasts, and creeping things" (Rom. 1:21-23). When Paul arrived at Athens he observed this same tendency in the innumerable altars and images to the gods. But Christianity does away with the physical perception and introduces the spiritual, as Jesus said to the woman of Samaria, "But the hour cometh, and now is, when the true worshippers shall worship the Father in spirit and in truth: for the Father seeketh such to worship him. God is a Spirit: and they that worship him must worship him in spirit and in truth" (John 4:23, 24).

Jesus was the manifestation of God in the flesh that we might be able to worship God in the spirit. The church later corrupted worship and substituted the spiritual concept of God with liturgies, images, murals, candles, incense, and vestments so that it appealed to everyone of the five physical senses rather than to the spiritual senses.

V. The Idea of a Non-Racial Faith

The Jews had built religious fences around themselves for years, so that none dared enter who would know Jehovah. The Greeks made gods only for the Greeks, so that God had become the personal property of a few people who dared others to try and take Him from them. But Christianity is non-racial: it is for the world. John 3:16 is the Bible's great declaration of a non-racial faith. "For God so loved the world, that he gave his only begotten Son, that whosoever believeth in him should not perish, but have everlasting life."

VI. The Idea of a Bodily Resurrection

There had been many prior ideas in the world about what happened to life after death, if indeed anything happened at all. There were the ideas of transmigration, re-incarnation, and immortality. But into this agglomeration Christianity came with its bodily resurrection. It was an integral part of God's redemptive plan which conceived not only a new man, but also a new body in which to display this new man. Then there would be added, as the finale of the plan, a new enviroment in the form of a new heavens and earth in which man can have an adequate expression of his new life. These new things are on the celestial drawing boards, waiting for appropriate execution.

VII. The Idea that Life can have a New Beginning

The ancient world believed in possible new beginnings in various forms of life after death; but none believed in a new beginning in this life. Christianity was revolutionary at this point also for it offered man a new beginning through justification and forgiveness. Moreover, the work of God's grace in a human life would reverse the downward trend of that life; stop the process of self-destruction; introduce a new life-principle, the life of Christ; and provide man with a new direction and destiny of life. All of this would begin in this world when a person encountered Jesus Christ as his personal Savior.

43

THE UNKNOWN GOD

Acts 17:15-34

The most famous tourist ever to visit Athens was a man by the name of Paul. He visited this famous city about the year 51 A.D. and after landing at the port city of Piraeus, wandered about, looking at all the famous places such as the Acropolis. Here he saw the Parthenon, the Erechtheum, the Propylaea, and above all the Areopagus, built where it is said the war god, Mars, was tried by the other gods on the charge of murder.

Above all else the Areopagus was famous for the most venerable court of Athens, the Council on the Areopagus. Here sat a council of nobles to hear, consider, and judge the latest problems of Athenian life.

It had been at least five hundred years since the Acropolis and the Areopagus had been the seat of the highest culture known to man during the Periclean age, when such notables as Pericles, Demosthenes, Sophocles, Euripides, Socrates and Plato were the leading intellectual lights. Now it was different. The city of Athens was in ruins. The Acropolis and the Areopagus on Mars Hill had but a semblance of their former physical glory. But the council of the nobles still sat to consider "some new thing."

Paul was not a mere tourist come to satisfy his curiosity on the fading glories of the past. He was a man with a mission and when he had thoroughly surveyed the Athenian scene "his spirit was stirred in him, when he saw the city wholly given to idolatry." Then he went to work. His work was to bring the message of Christianity to bear upon the needs of men.

At Athens Paul's message would confront the cultivated mind

of the Greeks. Before it had confronted the Jewish mind, the pagan mind and the barbarian mind and in every case it was in conflict. What would it be like at Athens, continuing seat of the world's greatest intellectuality? Let us see!

Paul preached in three places in Athens: the synagogue, the market place or Agora and the Areopagus or Mars Hill.

I. THE SYNAGOGUE

It was always the strategy of Paul to preach in the synagogue. He would first go to the synagogue because his prior responsibility was to "the Jew first." He must bear witness to them, seeking to persuade them to accept Jesus as Messiah and become the proclaimers of the Christian gospel. Here he followed the usual custom of disputing or reasoning with them out of the Old Testament scriptures. Apparently his impact on the Jewish colony at Athens was without results for, unless some of the few converts he won at Athens were from the synagogue, his ministry here was fruitless.

II. THE MARKET

This was known as the Agora and was not in fact a market place as we understand it. It was more like a plaza in the center of the city, around which were grouped on four sides such buildings as the city hall, senate, lawcourts and other public buildings. Here it was the custom of civic leaders, magistrates and other functionaries to gather in one of the porches, and hear the latest philosophical discussion. It was customary for traveling teachers and philosophers to seek an audience among these Athenians and expound their philosophies. Observing this custom, Paul saw an opportunity to get a captive audience for his message.

After some days of this preaching, representatives of the two opposing schools of philosophy passed judgment on this itinerant preacher from Judea. One school was the Epicureans, the sensualists and lovers of pleasure. The other school was the

Stoics, or idealists and fatalists. Neither of them responded to Paul's preaching or became converts to his doctrine. Instead they ridiculed him and called him a "babbler" which in their vernacular was a "seedpicker," a sort of gutter-bird that picked up scraps of refuse from the street. They judged him as an "itinerant peddler of religion" who could not be taken seriously by the cultured minds of the Athenians. He had spoken of a strange god whom he called Jesus and about a resurrection from the dead. To the frequenters of the Agora these were unacceptable and Paul was ridiculed into silence.

Thus in the gospel's first meeting with the cultivated Grecian mind it was ignominiously rejected, to prove what Paul would later write to the Corinthians and say that "the world by wisdom knew not God" (I Cor. 1:21). This is not to say that wisdom, learning or philosophy have no place in Christianity. It is only a reminder that it is the wisdom of this world that cannot comprehend or understand the true nature of the Christian message. And because these Athenians were representatives of the highest form of this wisdom of the world, they rejected the preacher and his preaching with prejudice and emphasis.

Let it be said to all cultists of the mind that " . . . the preaching of the cross is to them that perish foolishness; but unto us which are saved it is the power of God. For it is written, I will destroy the wisdom of the wise, and will bring to nothing the understanding of the prudent. Where is the wise? where is the scribe? where is the disputer of this world? hath not God made foolish the wisdom of this world? For after that in the wisdom of God the world by wisdom knew not God, it pleased God by the foolishness of preaching to save them that believe. For the Jews require a sign, and the Greeks seek after wisdom: But we preach Christ crucified, unto the Jews a stumblingblock, and unto the Greeks foolishness; But unto them which are called, both Jews and Greeks, Christ the power of God, and the wisdom of God. Because the foolishness of God is wiser than men; and the weakness of God is stronger than men" (I Cor. 1:18-25).

III. The Areopagus

Paul was taken to the Areopagus on Mars Hill to stand before the council of nobles to give an account of his teaching. Here he gave a brilliant defense of Christianity. He had observed many altars to many gods on his way from Piraeus to Athens, and among them was an altar "To the Unknown God." The Athenians were very superstitious and thought their calamities were caused by the displeasure of the gods; and because they did not want to offend a god they had not noticed, they put up this all-embracing altar to "The Unknown God." This gave Paul his theme. He would talk about the Unknown God for He was the one Paul had found to his own satisfaction and was serving with all his vigor. He said to them, "Whom therefore ye ignorantly worship, him declare I unto you."

Paul said three of the most important things that are to be said about God. He is *Creator*, dealing with the past. He is *Redeemer*, dealing with the present. He is *Judge*, dealing with the future.

1. God as Creator (verses 24-26). In order to understand the universe we do not begin with the universe and reason back to God; we begin with God and reason out to the universe.

It was Hermes Trismegistus who said, "God is a circle whose center is everywhere and circumference nowhere."

Paul began where everyone must begin who hopes to solve the riddle of the universe and have a satisfactory answer to the problems of personal life — with God. There is no solution except that which considers God as the first, the last and the inbetween element of life.

What is important about the universe is not its stars, planets, land masses and oceans, but man whom God made in His image. And this man is one. God made all men of one blood and in His own image and likeness. This was a death blow to the Athenian idea that man sprang from the soil of Attica, when he was in effect the creation of God. Being the creation of God he had a responsibility to God. This also deals a death blow to the theory of a master race, propounded by the Kaiser before the first World War, and Hitler before the second World War. There are no superior peoples. There are no special races. All sprang from a single Creator and a common source.

We stand today in the light of man's greatest scientific achievements, yet man has learned little about man though he knows much about the universe. At the 1960 Chicago meeting of the American Association for the Advancement of Science, it was concluded that man is the product of evolution and is "a part of nature and not apart from it." It was also concluded that man "has a moral sense, including a sense of responsibility." But to whom is this man responsible? The post-Darwinian answer seems clear. It says, "Man is responsible to himself for himself." Here is the ignorance of the modern scientific mind. Paul would have condemned it as he condemned the Athenians for their idolatry. Man is responsible to God, first upon the basis of creation and second upon the basis of redemption.

2. God as Redeemer (verses 27-29). There is no doubt that all is not well with God's creation, a fact that is not God's fault but man's. Into the picture of human history we must put the ugly image of sin and its despoiling effects upon God's good and perfect creation.

God has revealed Himself to man through a Redeemer and not in the images of gold or silver or stone. Our image of God is the flesh and blood image of God's Son, the Redeemer. It is not the image of an idol or of religious artifact.

A created man is not a saved man. He is a sinner who needs to be saved. This salvation is not in his intellect so he can think his way out of the dilemma he is in. It is in Christ who is God's revelation to man.

The theory that children are born good and need only to use self-expression to evolve out of their problems into a natural completion of their destiny, is at the root of much of our modern dilemma. It certainly has a great deal to do with juvenile delinquency and everything to do with adult delinquency. Its only remedy is a reversal of thought and a submission to the regenerating grace of God.

3. God as Judge (verses 30, 31). If man is answerable to God he is answerable not only because God *made him* but also because God *redeemed him*. He is answerable not only in *time* for the life he is living, but he is answerable in *eternity* for the life he has lived. It is written that "it is appointed unto men once to die, but after this the judgment." To the cultured Athenians Paul preached the judgment of God. He said to these philosophers, "but now God commandeth all men everywhere to repent."

The Christian gospel is the gospel of faith in Christ for salvation: of repentance from sin and of judgment for sin. The certainty of this judgment is the resurrection. "Because he hath appointed a day, in the which he will judge the world in righteousness by that man whom he hath ordained; whereof he hath given assurance unto all men, in that he hath raised him from the dead" (verse 31).

This gospel of faith, repentance and judgment was preached to the cultured Athenians with the greatest history of intellectual culture the world has ever known. A person can just as easily go to hell from Athens as from Sodom and Gomorrah: just as easily from the Areopagus as from the brothel: just as easily from the Atheneaum as from the gambling casino.

An American traveler returning from abroad is confronted with a challenging question: "Have you anything to declare?" It is the question which the customs officer solemnly asks as you open your luggage at the port of entry. You are expected to declare all your purchases abroad and perhaps pay a customs levy. But the question is even more pertinent to life itself. What will we have to declare? At the port of entry to the next world we will be stripped of all our material possessions and although a man may have died opulent, his declaration value at heaven's gate is nothing. The only wealth we can carry to heaven is spiritual in nature. That is why Jesus said, "Lay not up for yourselves treasures upon earth, where moth and rust doth corrupt, and where thieves break through and steal: But lay up for yourselves treasures in heaven, where neither moth nor rust doth corrupt, and where thieves do not break through nor steal" (Matt. 6:19, 20). What will you have to declare as you stand before the celestial customs officer? Will it be the liability of a sinful life? Will it be the emptiness of a fruitless life? Will it be the poverty of a misspent life? Will it be the tragedy of a Christless life? My friend, have you anything to declare?

44

PAUL, HIS LIFE AND LETTERS
Acts 18:1-28

It is certain that the life and letters of no other individual have done more to influence the world than those of the Apostle Paul, excepting, of course, the life of our Lord. We have already witnessed enough of the life of Paul, since his conversion, to be convinced that this is true. Now we see the beginning of his letters. Both his life and letters loom large at this point where we have the writing of the first of these letters. Out of an abundance of miscellaneous incidents we observe Paul's life in terms of his companions, and Paul's letters in terms of the epistles which make up the major portion of the content of the New Testament. We reverse the order and consider the letters first.

I. HIS LETTERS

Paul wrote fourteen epistles out of a total of twenty-seven New Testament books. The writing of these fourteen epistles begins at this point with the First Epistle to the Thessalonians, being written at Corinth, just a few months following the founding of the Church at Thessalonica.

Intertwined with the events of the remaining chapters of Acts come the writings of the rest of the epistles, such as II Thessalonians and Romans, written also at Corinth on a later visit. Then, beginning his third missionary journey, Paul moved on to Ephesus where he wrote I Corinthians and Galatians. Then followed the writing of II Corinthians from Macedonia. During Paul's imprisonment at Rome he wrote Ephesians, Philippians,

Colossians and Philemon. In between his two imprisonments he wrote I Timothy, Titus and Hebrews, and after his second imprisonment he wrote II Timothy. This completes the letters of Paul, the incalculable influence of which continues to be made on mankind.

How impoverished we would be without such magnificent writings, we have only to reflect on such passages as the thirteenth chapter of I Corinthians on love, the fifteenth chapter of I Corinthians on the resurrection of the body, the book of Romans with its philosophy of Christianity, Galatians and its teaching of justification by faith, the eleventh chapter of Hebrews and its story of faith, and the rest of the great presentations of truth.

But if we think Paul's letters were influential it is only part of the story. The rest of it concerns his friends and companions.

II. HIS LIFE

If Paul's letters are intertwined with the events of Acts, Paul's life is interrelated with a lengthening roster of friends and companions, including those mentioned at this point in Acts, such as Aquila and Priscilla, Silas, Timothy and Apollos; then Barnabas, John Mark, Doctor Luke, Philemon, Tychicus, Trophimus and Epaphroditus.

Jonathan Swift was enticed to attend a dinner by being sent the menu to be served on the occasion, concerning which he wrote, "He showed me his bill of fare to tempt me to dine with him: pooh, said I, I value not your bill of fare; give me your bill of company." Paul's bill of company included all of the foregoing and many more who, with him, tell us of the principal parties in the establishment and extension of the church.

It is being suggested that the greatest challenge today to man's ascendency is not other men, but mechanical monsters of his own creation. Cybernetics is the science of control mechanism and man is being warned that computers and other educated machines may yet outgrow man's control. Machines have already been built that can learn by experience. Taught to play checkers, some modern computers have learned, after only twenty hours of play, to beat the man who programmed them. Once their human masters have set them to work, it is quite possible that an overeducated machine may sweep its masters to disaster before they realize what it is up to. But what is really important to understand in this machine age is that we cannot get along without men. There has never been a good society made up of bad men. And it is God's plan to build the Kingdom of Heaven with men, not machines. That is why we have God's redemptive plan for men in the Bible. Christianity does not propose to change the world by thinking or by doing but by being. It is going to produce better men. This is redemption's purpose and this is the church's business.

Notable among Paul's friends were the women in his life. We know, of course, that he was unmarried. The reason for his celibacy was not religious principles or scruples, but expediency. His pioneering life made it inadvisable to enter into marriage, for any wife of Paul's would have to endure inordinate hardship and heartaches. But there were women in his life, and this is brought to mind by the mention of Priscilla with whom Paul lived at Corinth. Added to her name were such illustrious women as Lydia of Philippi, Synteche and Euodius likewise of Philippi.

But Priscilla and the other women were more important to Paul than hostesses. They did more than provide comfortable lodging and prepare good food. They were important as fellow-workers in the gospel. Priscilla probably took a leading part in evangelistic work. In writing to the Philippians, Paul was careful to give them instructions to "help those women which labored with me in the gospel." These women had integral and important parts in the work of the gospel. Perhaps we will never fully know what the work of women has meant to the establishment and extension of Christianity. And perhaps we are in serious error in limiting woman to such secondary service for God as she now has, when her talents, devotion and sacrifice recommend her to the primary tasks of preaching and teaching along with other major aspects of Christian service.

The Bible is not only about faithful and noble women; it is about man as a whole and men in particular. Human life in all its spectral shades is fully portrayed in the scriptures. All the conditions of human life are found in the men who walk through the Bible. "What a book!" wrote William Lyon Phelps about the Bible. "You can learn more about human nature by reading the Bible than by living in New York City." Here are to be found the qualities, good and bad, that characterize all men. But in the life of Paul and his companions you find the qualities of redeemed life that made them so conspicuously important. What are some of these qualities?

1. Faith

This is the first and foremost quality. It is that quality which produces every important characteristic in life. All others proceed from faith, for faith links us with the source of life in God. Faith is both a way *to* life and a way *of* life. Men find salvation through faith, but they also discover that it is the motive power that creates the energy of success in life.

To search the records of Paul and his companions will be to discover this driving force behind all of their endeavors. These men were not afraid of life because with faith they could master all of life's situations and face everyone of life's conditions.

Like a dead soul out of Gehenna, a human figure rose out of a dung heap recently in the Ukranian village of Tsirkuny and rushed forth shrieking, "I want to live, I want to work!" Astounded neighbors found that the stinking, blinking sunken-jawed wretch was a fellow townsman they had all thought had died a hero's death fighting the Germans in World War II. But in truth, he had deserted the very night he marched away to war, sneaked home to a hiding place his parents made for him under the manure pile at the back of the family goat shed. For eighteen years he hid in this living grave, kept alive by the food his mother fed him twice a day. He was afraid of life,—a man without faith.

Akin to him was the American soldier who deserted his regiment in France during World War I and hid in a garret for forty years. And then there was the man in Finland who hid in a barn for twenty years. And more recently the Chinese student at the University of Michigan who hid in a church steeple for three and one half years because of bad grades. Here were men afraid of life. Many are like them but they have different hiding places than barns, dung heaps, church attics and garrets. But to all intents they are in hiding, surrounded by their own shame and shackled by their own fear. They never move onward or upward from one year's life to another. They are captives to their fears of life. Faith can liberate such captive souls and send them on glorious adventures of life.

2. Love

When Timothy arrived in Corinth from Thessalonica he reported to Paul the good news of the faithfulness of the Thessalonian Church. It filled Paul with joy and it says in this text that "Paul was pressed in the spirit" (verse 5). With this stimulation he redoubled his efforts to win the Jews of Corinth to Christ. The phrase "pressed in the spirit" really means "constrained by the word." Actually the force which was exerting itself upon Paul was the love of Christ. Love became the constraining, impelling, motivating force of the apostle's life and ministry. We will never become people of great lives without a great love. The greatest love is the love of Christ.

3. Courage

To backtrack over the missionary trails of the apostle and his companions, is to see a display of courage unequaled in the sagas of men. They faced hostile men, fanatical religionists, implacable functionaries, stern judges, cruel barbarians, and the cold-blooded military. In the face of these oppositions they exhibited unwavering loyalty and inflexible courage in their devotion to Christ.

It has been recently remarked that "our society no longer makes courage an ideal. We teach our children to protect their own rights, but we do not teach them that there are impersonal values which may be more important than their personal safety and comfort. In fact, we subtly communicate the idea that courage as an end in itself, is naive and foolish. We replace dedication to country, to democracy, to mankind, with dedication to oneself. Self-preservation becomes a primary, rather than a subsidiary, moral principle. And thereby we train our young men in a weakness of spirit that borders on cowardice."

Where is similar courage of conviction, sacrifice of life and daring to uphold principles in our modern society to that found in these pioneers of faith? We no longer know the meaning of the words "sacrifice" and "suffering" in the church. Harry Golden, who arose from the obscurity of a Jewish immigrant's background to national fame said, "If I were faced today with the decision my ancestors faced — become a Christian or die — I would pick a church fast. There is nothing to offend me in the modern church. The minister gives a talk on juvenile delinquency one week, reviews a movie next week, then everyone goes downstairs and plays Bingo. The first part of a church they build nowadays is the kitchen. Five hundred years from now people will dig up these churches, and wonder what kind of sacrifices we performed." Extreme we say, but there is a great measure of truth in this indictment.

4. Maturity

The failure to grow up physically, mentally or spiritually is one of the greatest tragedies of life. Its failure spiritually is particularly tragic, because it is in the realm of our relationship with God and is, in consequence, the most important growth area of all our development.

Paul knew its value and wrote later to this very Church of Corinth. "And I, brethren, could not speak unto you as unto spiritual, but as unto carnal, even as unto babes in Christ. I have fed you with milk, and not with meat: for hitherto ye were not able to bear it, neither yet now are ye able. For ye are yet carnal: for whereas there is among you envying, and strife, and divisions, are ye not carnal, and walk as men? For while one saith, I am of Paul; and another, I am of Apollos; are ye not

carnal? Who then is Paul, and who is Apollos, but ministers by
whom ye believed, even as the Lord gave to every man?" (I Cor.
3:1-5).

Queen Victoria was officiating in a dedication ceremony at the
Royal Academy of Sciences. Somewhat overawed by all the
brilliant scientists gathered for the occasion, she turned to her
Prime Minister, John Bright and whispered, "Where do all these
learned men come from?" "From babies, your majesty," was the
answer. Babyhood is the common source of all life both
physical and spiritual. There are "babes in Christ" as well as
other kinds of babies. But growth is expected and when we
see strong, virile, useful, fruitful, forceful people we see people
who have grown to maturity. It was this mature strength which
was the secret of Paul and his companions.

5. Action

When all the factors of life are considered it is what we do
that counts; not what we say we are going to do, or what we
hope to become. Paul was a man of action who demonstrated
his faith by his works and put that faith to work in a continuous
stream of deeds done for Christ. He opened new continents to
the gospel; he founded many churches; he wrote fourteen books
of the Bible and he preached with indefatigable zeal. To read the
Book of Acts is to read the story of unceasing action and
unending accomplishment. Here indeed is *life in action!*

"Oh, well," a husband remarked rather philosophically to
his wife, "when all is said and done. . . . " "When all is said
and done — what?" asked his wife. "When all is said and done,
there's a lot more said than done." So it is in the Christian
enterprise. We have our say, but we do not get it done. We
preach and preach, commit and commit, sing and sing, study
and study, but the job does not get done. We ought to declare
a moratorium on saying and have a time of doing. Paul and
his companions did it and then talked about it afterward.

Everytime the benediction is pronounced in a church service
it is the sign of a beginning and not an ending. It is to be the
beginning of action, doing and living. We are dismissed to put

into action what has been said to us. We are responsible to live and labor in the spiritual strength accumulated in worship. The benediction is: "The holiest moment of the church service is the moment when God's people — strengthened by preaching — go out of the church door into the world to be the church. We do not go to church; we are the church."

45

CHRISTIANITY AND THE UNUSUAL
Acts 19:1-20

One thing that must impress the reader of the Book of Acts is the presence of the unusual. It contains abundant evidence of divine acts through human instruments, such as healings, resurrections, speaking in tongues, deliverance from evil spirits, besides acts of divine providence in general.

If Christianity had always happened in terms of the usual or ordinary, it could always be interpreted and understood in terms of the usual and ordinary; but since we are observing it unusually and supernaturally we can then only understand it at these places on the level of the unusual and supernatural.

One great difficulty at this point lies in the fact that we undertake to interpret Christianity in terms of the modern experience of it, which in many respects is of a character unlike that found in the First Century. We practice a more inferior level of Christianity than that exhibited at its beginning. In one sense we cannot ever repeat much of the supernatural for the good reason that we are not expected to. But in another sense we are not reaching the high level of experience that is still available to the church through the Holy Spirit.

If Christianity is at times a display of the unusual it is certainly not a system of magic, superstition or legerdemain. It does not traffic in the freakish or fanatical. There is much of this that parades under the name Christianity, which has no semblance to the real thing.

There was an eventual departure from the simple elements of worship found in the early church to formalism, and from the genuinely unusual to the magical and superstitious. The reason for this is that instead of remaining the religion of the spiritual man, with genuine evidences of the unusual, it became the religion of the natural man, using relics, symbols, images, saints, pilgrimages and ceremonies to impress the five senses of the physical body. In doing this it ceased being the worship of the true church which Jesus indicated would be in "spirit and in truth," and not in magic and superstition.

Occasionally some religious personality crosses the horizon and attracts notoriety and money while practicing an extra-scriptural system of gaudy and magical religion which does not approach even the slightest facsimile of the real thing. Such a personality was the recent Bishop Charles Manuel (Sweet Daddy) Grace. He lived a bizarre life while attracting an immense following and amassing a fortune of twenty-five million dollars. He manufactured and sold Daddy Grace soap, writing paper, toothpaste, trans-continental tea and coffee, hair pomade and hair straightener, face powder and talcum powder, cookies and other products almost unlimited. He built houses of prayer in principal cities of America, painted red, white and blue. These were furnished with furniture upholstered in the same motif. He wore an ermine cape, had five inch finger nails and walked on a carpet strewn with roses. He was decked out in a green vest, a pure white cutaway, purple satin trousers or a black tail coat with gold lapels. He baptized people by using a fire hose at one hundred pounds pressure. He told audiences everywhere he went that the Kingdom of heaven was coming and that he was the General Builder and that, like everything else, building costs had gone up. In consequence he sold his products, lived his bizarre life, preached his peculiar doctrines and became fabulously wealthy. But none of this has a semblance of similarity to Christianity although it must be said it was unusual. None of this bizarre caricature of Christianity has any precedent in the unusual events described in the Book of Acts.

Prayer as practiced by the apostles was not magic. The Holy Spirit and the consequent speaking with tongues was not magic.

The healing of the sick and two instances of resurrecting the dead were not magic. These were all evidences of the unusual within the framework of the supernatural.

A fundamental objection to physical miracles is that if miracles by God's power are possible it makes God responsible for all bad things. But God could not abolish the existence of bad things without destroying the framework of the good. Nor could God abolish the power of doing evil, thus ridding the world of evil, because if He did He would have to abolish the power of doing good. We cannot have the good without the evil. We cannot have the usual without the unusual. We cannot have the seen without the unseen.

The presence of the unusual is to observed in the following incidents:

1. Speaking with Tongues (verses 1-7)

When Paul came to Ephesus he observed twelve disciples who had been taught by Apollos. Upon inquiring whether they had received the Holy Spirit "when" (not since) they believed, he was told that they had not even heard of the Holy Spirit. This aroused Paul's curiosity and he asked the nature of their baptism; and being told it was John's baptism, Paul concluded that these twelve men were not Christians in the true sense but disciples of John; whereupon they were presented with the gospel and were baptized as Christians.

Because of the nature of this event the validity of their experience was sealed by the same evidence the disciples had at Pentecost, speaking in tongues. And while the same abundant opportunity for preaching the gospel in many languages was not present at Ephesus as it was at Pentecost, this Ephesian speaking with tongues was of the same nature, namely speaking with different languages after which came the gift of inspired oratory (prophecy) in which they gave witness to the gospel.

Here was an unusual phenomenon. It is identical to the Pentecostal manifestation and similar to what happened at the house of the Gentile, Cornelius in Caesaria. It is evident that the Ephesian, Caesarian and Pentecostal speaking in tongues were identical, that is, the use of known and existing languages for the purpose of proclaiming the gospel. It is also, by the same token, evident that these occurrences were unlike the Corinthian phenomenon which involved the use of ecstatic speech, which was abused and prostituted by the Corinthian Church, bringing excess and disorder so that they were rebuked by the apostle.

It is our understanding that the occasion for the Pentecostal, Caesarian and Ephesian speaking in tongues no longer exists because these were manifestations solely and entirely associated with the coming of the Holy Spirit. He has come and the attesting manifestations are no longer necessary.

2. Special Miracles (verses 11, 12)

When the enemies of the gospel "spake evil of the way" Paul not only reasoned and disputed with them but, to give added force to his arguments, God wrought "special miracles by the hands of Paul." You will notice it says "special miracles" to indicate that this was an expedient procedure for the emergency at hand. This was not standard and usual but rather unusual and extraordinary. Christianity henceforth would be sustained and advanced by wisdom, reason, knowledge, faith, love and example, all through the Holy Spirit, rather than by unusual manifestations such as "special miracles."

As a result of these unusual manifestations a superstitious practice developed so that cloths, actually napkins for wiping off sweat and aprons worn by working men, which had been brought into contact with Paul's body, were carried away and applied with apparent efficacy to the sick. We are not to understand at all that Christianity involves the valid use of such means as this for the healing of the sick. It is true that the sick were healed by touching Jesus' garment and passing under Peter's shadow, but these were not in and by themselves the means of healing. Healing was by the direct power of God and using handkerchiefs became a superstitious and altogether unwarranted use of means to achieve what Paul could do by direct prayer and faith.

Here was the unusual employment of "special miracles" but

here also is man making an unwarranted use of physical objects that could and did develop into superstition and magic.

3. Evil Spirits (verses 12-19)

The New Testament gives wide evidence of the presence of evil spirits belonging to an unseen kingdom of evil described by Paul in Ephesians 6:12, "For we wrestle not against flesh and blood, but against principalities, against powers, against the rulers of the darkness of this world, against spiritual wickedness in high places."

Ephesus appears to have been the center of a widespread practice of the use of magic, and a considerable body of literature had been created to be used by both the magicians and the exorcists. Because of this local condition Paul's special gifts gave him power over these magicians and also the power to exorcise evil spirits from others. The net result of this unusual display was the conversion of a great number of magicians, who renounced their imagined powers and their league with Satan, and at a public ceremony burned vast and expensive quantities of this literature of magic and superstition.

4. Raising the Dead

While this does not occur at this point it is recorded in at least three places in Acts. Once in Chapter 9 where Peter raises Dorcas: once in Chapter 14 where Paul survives death by stoning at Lystra: once in Chapter 20 where Paul raises the young man named Eutychus from the dead as the result of a fatal experience of falling asleep in a church service.

It must be observed that here is an unusual experience which is found in only seven instances in the New Testament. Three of these instances were by the hand of our Lord, one was the resurrection of Jesus and three are these instances in Acts. No one today dares to profess the power to reproduce the unusual by raising the dead. It was for the times then existing and falls into the category of wonders that authenticate the divine nature of Christianity, rather than things to be repeated by the church today.

5. Prayer

All throughout the Book of Acts the disciples prayed and the unusual happened. There are notable instances of this as when the one hundred and twenty prayed for ten days and Pentecost resulted; also when the disciples prayed and Peter was released from prison.

Prayer produced the unusual but prayer itself is not unusual, because it is the divine provision whereby mortal and circumscribed man may have access to Almighty God for fellowship and communion, and for the accomplishment of those things beyond man's ability. Prayer is an expression of confidence in God. Prayer is an evidence of dependence upon God. With all of man's advancement and inventions he has not advanced beyond his use and need of prayer.

Scott Crossfield, the famous test pilot who took the X-15 in its first free flights into space, records his experiences with a remarkable testimony about prayer. He recalls the day when he was to make his first free drop from the mother ship. As he faced the critical moment he recalled that success or failure of the great enterprise now solely rested upon him. Some weeks afterward when he was replaying the tape of this flight a friend noticed a peculiar noise. He inquired about it. Crossfield replied by shrugging it off as noise from the breathing system in his pressure suit. "The truth was," he later confessed, "that I was quietly praying to God to help me not to let our team down. My sensitive mike had picked up the movements of my vocal cords in the act of praying." With all the fifty million dollars worth of equipment representing man's ultimate in science, this man in this place felt his need of God.

When Arthur Godfrey was ill and hospitalized with cancer he received more than two hundred thousand letters. His personal secretary commented, "I haven't picked up one piece of mail that hasn't mentioned prayer or the Lord. I didn't quite realize that we were such a God-fearing nation."

How did all these unusual things transpire? What powers did the early Christians possess that enabled them to do the unusual?

The answer is found in the provisions made by the Holy Spirit and these provisions are of two kinds, the gifts of the Spirit with which to present Christ and the graces of the Spirit with which to represent Christ. The gifts of the Spirit comprise nine such gifts including wisdom, knowledge, faith, healing, miracles, prophecy, discerning of spirits, tongues and interpretation of spirits.

It was through these gifts that the apostles manifested the powers that produced the unusual. Their use is still valid today but in a most limited sense because the church now has the written Word which it did not have in these beginning days. It also has the validated evidence of a faith authenticated and established by divine authority. Nevertheless a sovereign God has it in His power to bestow such powers and abilities as special needs arise.

Most of our lives will be lived in the drab monotony of the usual. It is in our power to change life into "days of heaven on earth" through the calculated use of the means of grace which God has placed at our disposal.

46

IS CHRISTIANITY THE ONLY WAY?

Acts 19:9

"But when divers were hardened, and believed not, but spoke evil of *that way* before the multitude. . . ."

When the apostles and disciples began their witness to Christ, they had no idea they were beginning a new body of people to be later known as the church. This thought or concept perhaps never entered their minds; but some such eventuality was inevitable for God was doing a new thing. When three thousand were added to the one hundred and twenty and other hundreds and thousands were added to this nucleus, some designation had to be made. What would these people be called?

Because they were known as believers in the name of the Lord Jesus they were ultimately called Christians. But the Jews, however, would not recognize a name which implied the truth of this faith, so they called the early Christians Nazarenes or Galileans, as an indication of their contempt. Later on when these Nazarenes became solidified into a considerable and formidable group which was winning converts all over Asia, they were known as those who were followers of "the way." If the sayings of Jesus were commonly known at this point, then it is conceivable that this was a direct reference to His own claims when He said, "I am the way, the truth and the life, no man cometh unto the Father but by me."

This designation of the new sect, as people of the way, was a natural change because as they grew stronger and more dominant and developed a society and a doctrinal constitution of scripture, they, as the people of "the way,"* took the place of the Jews who had been known as "the people." So here was a new people and a new way laying the foundations of a new society in an old world.

What were the characteristics of this way and where did it take those who took it? Let us walk its well-worn path and see what we shall find.

I. It Was a New Way

This had already been established at Caesarea and at Jerusalem. At Caesarea Peter discovered, while preaching to the Gentile members of the house of Cornelius, that "God is no respecter of persons" and "that through his name (Jesus) whosoever believeth in him shall receive remission of sins." The proof of this fact was that "on the Gentiles also was poured out the gift of the Holy Ghost."

But it took the Jewish converts to the Christian faith a long time to concede this fact for they, as yet, had not clearly seen that God was doing a new thing and founding a new society which was walking a new way. They thought that this was a continuation of Israel in all its old forms and practices, so they tried to Judaize Christianity and make it a Jewish sect like the Essenes. But this was settled at Jerusalem where the issue had been formally presented to the church and the judgment of this council was that no Gentile convert need be Judaized in order to become a follower of the way. This was a milestone in the history of the church for from this point on, though Judaizers still continued in the church, the message was that God was doing a new thing and founding a new society with a new doctrine leading to a new manner of life and a new destiny.

II. It Presented New Truth

This new society was not built upon the best things found in the Old Testament or in current religious systems. What was being formed now was a new body of truth to be known as the New Testament. This was in effect a new covenant or a new

---

*Acts 9:2; 18:25, 26; 19:9, 23; 22:4; 24:14, 22.

arrangement and contract between God and the new people of the new way. And from this point we see the progressive creation of this new body of truth to be known as the New Testament. By the time we have arrived at this place several segments of this new body of truth have already been brought into existence, including I Thessalonians.

The message of this new body of truth, known as the New Testament, is that God is building the Kingdom of Heaven. It is being builded on "the foundation of the apostles and prophets, Jesus Christ himself being the chief cornerstone" (Eph. 2:20).

The entrance into this new body has already been established for it is through Jesus Christ. Peter proclaimed the name of Jesus as the open sesame to the new kingdom and said, "Neither is there salvation in any other: for there is none other name under heaven whereby we must be saved" (Acts 4:12).

If one thing is certain and sure, it is that Christianity is not a compilation of the best that all the religions of the world have to offer. There are in it, to be sure, things that have been said and done before, but the new thing about this way is that Jesus Christ becomes the primary rallying point and the door of entrance into the Kingdom of God which is made up of a new society of people who have been made new by the new birth.

There have been courageous efforts made by men in repeated instances in which they have made monumental sacrifices to achieve some kind of religious aim. But no matter how great these efforts have been, Christianity is the way by which men are brought into the Kingdom of God.

III. It Led Men In a New Direction

Wherever proclaimers of this new way went in the ancient world they called upon men to repent and turn to God. We call this conversion and conversion means to turn about from one's natural course of life and go in a new direction. It called for an about-face position.

This new direction was at the same time toward God and away from the world.

1. It was Toward God

The natural direction of life is away from God. Men are born with their backs toward God. They are born with a natural bent toward evil and a native fear of God in their consciousness. Conversion turns their faces toward God so they walk in a new direction.

2. It was Away from the World

Jesus established this new direction when He said of His disciples, "They are not of this world, even as I am not of this world." Here is a new specie, a different breed, a new society. Here are people of a new way of life because they are walking in a new direction. They have purpose, a meaning, and are headed toward a sure and certain destiny. It may not always be plain what they are doing or where they are going, but God has given them a principle by which they are to walk: it is faith. In the meantime let us learn to live as we walk in the way. Santayana, the Spanish philosopher said, "Man is not made to understand life, but to live it." And when we learn to live life we learn not to expect consistency or harmony in all of life's events or even that we will get our just deserts out of life. Living life is living in spite of adversity, injustice, disappointment and suffering.

IV. It has a New Purpose

The purpose of this new way was to elevate the individual man to a new level of life. He was to become a part of the divine plan of life and the beginning of this was to make the individual disciple a witness. He was to be an integral part in the plan to build a new society, and it was to be done by witnessing to Christ on the basis of change in the witnesser's own life.

In Egypt they killed off a million stone carriers to insure the proper burial of a single human being, an Egyptian king. Life was cheap then and it is cheap now, for today we have the instruments to destroy fifty or sixty million free people with the war head of a single intercontinental ballistic missile. But Christianity puts a new value on life in terms of the individual. Christ died for that individual that he might be freed from the shackles of sin and become a possessor of eternal life.

The new way not only gave a new purpose for the individual but also for history. When history comes to its climax it will have concluded the divine plan and produced a new society, a race of on-going people, who will inhabit a new world consisting of new heavens and a new earth.

The end of this purpose in history will not be the gradual evolution of society into the roll of super men who have made the world into a Shangri-La. The end will be catastrophic for the prophetic content of the new message of the church predicts a catastrophic end to human history. But the church will rise, phoenix-like (II Peter 3) out of the fires of its new purification to live on as the people of God.

V. Its End is Eternal Life.

The direction in which this way leads is heaven. Its ultimate end is eternal life. This eternal life is not only a state to which we shall be brought, but a condition in which we are to live; for the moment one becomes a follower of the way that moment he becomes a possessor of eternal life. Jesus said, "I am come that they might have life and that they might have it more abundantly" (John 10:10). He also said, "Verily, verily I say unto you, He that heareth my word, and believeth on him that sent me, hath everlasting life, and shall not come into condemnation; but is passed from death unto life" (John 5:24).

It is impossible to imagine the incalculable comfort of this fact to those who are followers of this way and who, from time to time, lay away their loved ones in death. This is particularly true of the untimely and unfortunate death of youths. Speaking of these matters let us be reminded that when our obituaries will be read they will be about the things we were and did; not about what we said. In this sense we are all writing our own obituaries. There was a man who twice announced his own death just for the fun of reading the obituaries. But when he really did die some newspapers, having been fooled twice, did not carry any obituary notice. But each day we live we are unconsciously writing the ultimate content of our own obituary. The most significant sentence any obituary could carry is the words, "he was a follower of the way." This encloses a multitude of truths for it ensures content to life and destiny for its end.

The question is now properly asked, is this way exclusive of all others or is it inclusive, embracing the best that can be found in the most? The Bible says, "There is a way which semeth right unto a man, but the end thereof are the ways of death." There are many ways that seem right to many people and they have been walked through many centuries of time. This is no proof that they are right.

If the Bible is to be taken at face value it must be concluded that Christianity is not one way among many, but the only way. Jesus indicated this when He said, "I am the way . . . no man cometh unto the Father but by me." Peter had said the same thing following Pentecost, "Neither is there salvation in any other: for there is none other name under heaven given among men, whereby we must be saved."

This seems pretty conclusive, but if more conclusiveness is required then we have some of the concluding statements of the Bible to fall back upon, for it says, "And there shall in no wise enter into it any thing that defileth, neither whatsoever worketh abomination, or maketh a lie: but they which are written in the Lamb's book of life" (Rev. 21:27). And again, "Blessed are they that do his commandments, that they may have right to the tree of life, and may enter in through the gates into the city" (Rev. 22:14).

A man was traveling in a distant country. His destination lay over high mountains. It was a difficult and dangerous journey, and he needed a qualified guide. One man offered his services. The traveler asked, "Have you ever been to the village to which I wish to go?" "No," the man replied, "but I have been part of the way, and I heard others tell of the rest of the way." The traveler answered, "You will not do." Another volunteered to serve as his guide. He, too, was asked, "Have you ever been to the village?" His answer was, "No, but I have been to the top of the mountain and have looked down on the village." The traveler replied, "You will not do." A third man came and offered his services. He was asked the same question as the others. "Sir," said he, "the village to which you are going is my home." Jesus' qualification to be our life-guide lies in the fact that His way leads us to His home.

47

CHRISTIANITY'S CONFLICT WITH RELIGION
Acts 19:21-41

To say that Christianity is in conflict with religion per se, sounds like a conflicting statement; but it is not, for Christianity and religion are not necessarily synonymous. While Christianity is a religion in the broad sense, not all religions are of the same nature, or on the same level as Christianity. We understand Christianity in terms of the divine, religion in terms of the human. One is revealed, the other natural.

There are many things in common between Christianity and other religions, for God has made use of many modes of revelation. But Christianity is unique in its revelation of God through Jesus Christ. "The Son of God became a man to enable men to become sons of God."*

Christianity and religion came into conflict at Ephesus which was a great religious center.** Here a serious incident took place which might have led to ugly consequences. It arose out of the threat which the gospel presented to the cult of the great goddess Diana (Artemis), and to those trades which were largely dependent on the cult. Diana's temple at Ephesus was one of the seven wonders of the ancient world and her image, enshrined in the temple, was believed to be of heavenly workmanship. It appears to have been a meteorite in which the semblance of the many-breasted female was discerned. Her worship was marked by the traditional features of nature-worship and was presided over by eunuch-priests and three grades of priestesses.

---

*C. S. Lewis
**F. F. Bruce

The silversmiths of Ephesus regarded their guild as being under the special patronage of Diana, in whose honor so many of their wares were manufactured. Among these wares were miniature silver shrines containing an image of the goddess, which her votaries brought to dedicate in her temple. The sale of these small shrines was a source of considerable profit to the silversmiths, and they were alarmed at the fall in the demand for them, caused by the spread of Christianity.

In consequence of this crisis, created by the conflict between Christianity and religion, Demetrius, a prominent member, and perhaps head of the guild or union of silversmiths, called a meeting of their union and persuaded them to stage a mass public protest against Paul and his colleagues.

The conflict of interest arose because the Christian preachers denied the existence of deities "made with hands" and were thus threatening the livelihood of the silversmiths who carried on such a profitable business in the manufacture of these shrines and their images. But more than this, they were challenging the divine majesty of the great goddess herself—a goddess venerated not only in Ephesus and Asia, but over the whole civilized world.

Aroused by the inflammatory speech of Demetrius, the guild members rushed into the open streets, invoking their goddess with the loud cry, "Great is Diana of the Ephesians." This in turn aroused the populace and an estimated twenty-five thousand demonstrated in the open-air theatre of the city and laid hands on two of Paul's companions, Gaius and Aristarchus. Finally the town clerk intervened. He was in effect the city manager, who calmed the multitude with sobering arguments and dispersed the assembly.

This was the end of the crisis but not the end of the conflict. It has gone on with continuous passion and persistent zeal. It manifests itself in many forms and has even entered the ranks of Christianity itself and corrupted its worship and paganized its practices. When true Christian devotion comes into conflict with the economic interests of religion, anger is aroused and trouble is on foot.

What would happen today if certain elements of the Christian religion would divest itself of its religious artifacts and cease its business and gambling operations? If it did it would have to close up half of its hospitals, monasteries, churches, seminaries and secondary schools, for it could not long exist without the economic assistance of its business enterprises. I refer to the manufacture of shrines, images, statues and creches. I refer to the superstitious wearing of medals, the placing of statues on automobile instrument panels.

There is a great similarity, as you have undoubtedly noticed, between the pagan worship of Diana and its use of images and patron saints and the modern use of the same devices in certain religious circles. There is today this same practice in statues, images, niches, patron saints and their superstitious and magical employment. It is fast crowding out the true worship of God in this system that parades under the name Christian, but is in effect pagan and political.

Recently a church was raided by the police in Philadelphia where the practice of bingo games was violating city laws. The budget of that church was ninety thousand dollars a year, with fifty thousand dollars of it coming from the illicit use of gambling devices. This is what we mean by the conflict of Christianity and religion. There is a church in the French Quarter of New Orleans to which one may go to inspect its ancient and historic building, and where he will be amazed to find shelves, counters and tables in the narthex filled with all kinds of religious trinkets and artifacts for sale. Here is Christianity and religion in conflict.

Christianity is not merely competitive to religion, as if it were one form of religious expression among many forms of religious expression; and as though all of these forms were equally efficacious; and as though ultimately all forms of religious expression lead to the same gracious end in heaven. No, Christianity is not competitive; it is in conflict and opposition. It is opposed to and at war with religion in its many forms.

There is Zoroastrianism, the religion of ancient Persia and practiced currently by the Parsees of India. One is to be saved by a morality of pure thoughts, pure words and pure deeds. There is Buddhism, the religion of Japan. One is to be saved by annihilation of self through sacrifice, torture and denial. There is Hinduism, the religion of India. One is to be saved by achieving nirvana or a state of nothingness and final absorption into deity. There is Islam, the religion of the East. One is to be saved by keeping the five requirements of Mohammed. These five requirements are to repeat the creed, observe prayer five times daily, keep the thirty-day fast of Ramadan, give alms and make a pilgrimage to Mecca.

Martin Luther came into conflict with religion in the church he served as priest. He rebelled and revolted against its pagan and extra-scriptural practices and found salvation in the simple exercise of faith on the Scala Santa. The Scala Santa consisted of twenty-eight white marble slabs, brought to Rome during the Crusades. They were believed to have been, originally, part of the Roman praetorium in Jerusalem, and, in fact, to have been the steps leading to the judgment seat of Pontius Pilate. They were, it is said, the very steps upon which Christ stood while Pilate considered His case. Waiting upon them He heard His doom pronounced. Thorn-crowned and tied with thongs, Christ is pictured as standing there silently before being led away to his death. These were sacred steps, therefore, and no one could ascend save upon his knees. At the top of these steps was the golden Bambino in its delicate shrine. Through the lattice one peered at the sacred figure purported to have the power of curing sick children. On these steps Martin Luther heard Habakkuk's words, "The just shall live by faith." From that time on he was in conflict with religion.

The prophet Micah speaks of Jehovah being in conflict with religion when he said, "The Lord hath a controversy with his people" (Micah 7:2). Jesus was in conflict with the religion of His day. He pronounced a series of unrelenting and unmitigating woes upon the religious leaders. He began by saying, "But woe unto you, scribes and Pharisees, hypocrites! for ye shut up the kingdom of heaven against men: For ye neither go in yourselves, neither suffer ye them that are entering to go in" (Matt. 23:13). The apostles, without exception, were in conflict with religion during the period of the founding of the church. This controversy began with Judaism and extended to all the forms of paganism that existed. This controversy continued down the intervening years and arrays Christianity in battle against every religious system devised by man. And the one consistent characteristic which marks the difference between Christianity and religion, per se, is that religion without exception offers salvation by works as against Christianity's justification by faith through grace.

Christianity is essentially the story of man's redemption enacted historically at the crucifixion and expressed by a single word — the gospel. When we define the gospel we are defining Christianity and the essential difference between it and religion.

When the New Testament tells us that Jesus Christ is the lamb "slain from the foundation of the world," it is saying that God created the world on a redemptive basis. This is evident at the very beginning when human sin became a fact, for God immediately introduced the evangel of the gospel and says to Satan, "I will put enmity between thee and the woman, and between thy seed and her seed; it shall bruise thy head, and thou shalt bruise his heel" (Gen. 3:15). From this moment the revelation of God in the Bible becomes the story of the evangel. It is unfolded in the sacrifice of Abel, the offering of Isaac, the story of Abraham and the redemptive history of Israel. Then one day, in the fulness of time, John the Baptist stands with two of the disciples of Jesus and says, "Behold the Lamb of God that taketh away the sin of the world." The age-long question is answered and the age-long quest is over for salvation has now come.

What is the gospel? Of what does Christianity consist that marks it off from religion as something totally different and forever irreconcilable? The answer is in what Paul had by this time written to the Church at Corinth. "Moreover, brethren, I declare unto you the gospel which I preached unto you, which also ye have received, and wherein ye stand; by which also ye are saved, if ye keep in memory what I preached unto you, unless ye have believed in vain. For I delivered unto you first of all that which I also received, how that Christ died for our sins according to the scriptures; and that he was buried, and that he rose again the third day according to the scriptures" (I Cor. 15:1-4).

The gospel centers in Jesus Christ.

1. Christ Is the Fulfillment of Old Testament Prophecies.

This is what Paul and Peter had consistently preached to congregations of Jews and Gentiles alike. This is what they had argued from the scriptures in the synagogues and proclaimed in the market places.

The gospel has continuity. It began at the foundations of the earth; is revealed in the promise of redemption in Genesis 3:15; is found at the altars of Israel and was consummated at the cross and is to be experienced in the heart and life of man.

2. Christ was Born of the Seed of David.

This, too, reveals the continuity of the gospel for it identifies the Savior as the Messiah. He is indeed the seed of the woman and here is the miracle of heredity that preserved the redemptive line from the beginning of the promise down to Mary.

3. Christ Died for Our Sins.

Christ was born to die and when the record of His life and ministry is written, two-thirds of it deals with His passion and death and only one-third is concerned with His deeds and words.

4. Christ was Buried.

This was to signify the doing away of all the corruption of human sin. It was to be forever buried and removed from sight and memory.

5. Christ was Raised.

Life was victorious in the Savior. His coming meant the fulfillment of the promise of eternal life. The mission of Jesus was to bring life without which the forgiveness of sins was without meaning.

6. Christ Will Come as Judge and Sovereign.

This will constitute the climax of history. It will be attended by cataclysmic events that will shatter the dreams of man's paradise on earth and bring to pass the millennial aspects of the Kingdom of God on earth.

In the final reduction of all life, the problem of personal salvation involves but two persons. One is the person of Jesus Christ for "there is none other name under heaven, given among men whereby we must be saved." The other is the person of the sinner. If there is no other name there is likewise no other way, and each person is confined to the personal necessity of a personal faith in Jesus Christ. Thus the person of the sinner must meet the person of the Savior and embrace in an act of personal faith.

Again let us say, "The Son of God became a man to enable men to become sons of God."

48

IS SUNDAY THE RIGHT DAY OF WORSHIP?

Acts 20:1-2

The question is often before us whether Saturday, as the Sabbath, or Sunday, as the Lord's Day, is the right day of worship. Much, if not most, of the confusion comes because we miss the meaning of the original Sabbath regulation which required man to set aside the last day of the week for rest and worship.

I. THE MEANING OF THE SABBATH

God divided time into units of seven days, six days to labor and one day to rest. The rest was not merely for physical relaxation and recuperation but for a higher purpose, namely, the remembrance of God and spiritual things. In this regulation the important thing was not the day, whether the seventh or the first, but what was to be done on that day. The important thing was not even what was *not* to be done on that day, because the negative restrictions of the Sabbath day were not for the purpose of restricting activity for restriction's sake: but solely because inactivity in physical and material things would emphasize spiritual and divine things.

This restriction made the Sabbath day a means to an end and not an end in itself. Therefore, the important consideration was not which day but what was done on the day. Observing this day took man out of a physical environment and atmosphere and put him into a spiritual environment and atmosphere. It took his eyes off man and put them on God. It reminded man that life was not merely an animal's existence, but primarily a relationship to God with spiritual implications. It told him that man did not live by bread alone but rather by the words that proceeded from God.

In other words, the purpose of the day was bigger than *a* day. It went beyond a day to embrace the total meaning of life as a partnership with God. Jesus affirmed this when the religious literalists took Him to task for His liberal attitude to the Sabbath, by healing the sick and gathering corn on that day. He said, "The Sabbath was made for man and not man for the Sabbath." He is saying that God never intended us to be bound to or become slaves to a day. Instead, it was meant that the day was an avenue of benefit to man.

II. The Sign of the Sabbath

The Sabbath, or seventh day, was given as a sign of God's perpetual covenant to the Jews (Ex. 31:13-17); as such it was a sign given to the Jews alone and not to other people. In other words, it is not a perpetual sign to Christians.

Moreover, when the first, or old covenant, gave way to the second, or new covenant of the New Testament, the Sabbath as a sign has neither validity nor significance. What good is the sign of a covenant if the covenant is no longer in existence? The only covenant that concerns the Christian is the covenant of the New Testament. It also follows that with the new covenant of grace we have the new day of grace — the first day of the week. To this day we transfer all the spiritual and moral significance of the old day, whose purpose as a day of rest and worship was to give us a spiritual framework in which to remember God and spiritual things. On the other hand, the purpose of the old day as the "sign" of a covenant between Jehovah and Israel has long since passed away.

Much is made by Sabbatarians of the fact that the Sabbath is called the sign of an "eternal" covenant, as if the sign were to last forever. But exactly how eternal was it? Was it eternal in the sense of lasting *forever*, even into heaven and eternity? We think not. It was eternal only in the sense of the accomplishment of the divine purpose. That purpose included the cross and the cross marked the bringing in of a new covenant which is called "a better covenant." Better than what? Why, better than the covenant of the law and its Sabbath sign. Thus when the new covenant came the old covenant went, and when the old covenant went the new day came. This new day is the first day of the week in contrast to the seventh day of the week. This leaves us in the position of having a better covenant than the old covenant, and a better day than the old day. (Heb. 8:6-13).

All of this means that we have a change from an old covenant to a new covenant and from an old day to a new day. The definite time of the change was the cross. This is made plain by the resurrection which was on the first day of the week and became the chief item of preaching in the new message of the New Testament. The change, in other words, came when Christ came. He took away the first covenant with its laws, ordinances and signs, in order that He might establish the second covenant with its new day and spiritual implications. The place of the change was the cross.

For those of us who are on this side of the cross it is neither law, ordinances, days, feasts, nor sacrifices. These things are for those who were or are on the other side of the cross. For us it is grace or the new law of the heart and mind. For us it is the new day with its libertarian philosophy as opposed to the Sabbatarian philosophy.

The sign of the old covenant was the Sabbath and since the old covenant has been superseded by a new covenant, the old day has been superseded by a new day and a new philosophy of life.

Although the Sabbath, as a day of rest and worship, existed from creation it never became a sign to any other nation than to Israel. The reason for this was because the Sabbath was a symbol of redemption; for the seventh day was the redemptive day, and as such it can only be kept by those who are regenerate in nature.

It is absurd and spiritually illogical to ask men without a

spiritual viewpoint to keep the Sabbath. That is why Sunday laws and legislation intended to regulate conduct according to Christian principle are illogical and wrong.

The Sabbath is likewise not commanded for the church. The Sabbath is law; the church is under grace. The Sabbath is the day of the dead Christ for He lay in the tomb on the Sabbath; the church has a risen and living Christ. The Sabbath is a memorial to an old creation which is now under condemnation and doom; the church stands for a new creation. The Sabbath is a part of the law associated with an earthly priesthood; the church is under a new law, the "law of the spirit of life in Christ Jesus," and a new priesthood of believers.

The basic principles of the Sabbath day were two fold: First, there was the human side. On this side the Sabbath was a day of physical rest from physical labor. This applied to cattle as well as men and even extended to the land, for in the Sabbatical year, which was once in every seven years, the land was to lie fallow. This provision for land and animals has been proven wise in our industrial age because man produces more in six days than if he labors continuously for seven days without rest. Second, there was the divine side. On this side the Sabbath was a day of worship as a reminder of man's obligations to God. On this day man was to turn from the labor of making a living to the consideration of making a life. Man was to stop work for one day to remember that the labor of six days was only possible by divine help. Both life and the things that make life possible are from God and do not come from our own creation or invention.

The real purpose of the Sabbath was to enable man to pay his tithe; to meditate and contemplate; to orient himself to another world while he lived in this world. In this sense the Sabbath belonged to God.

Now, to legalize this day and transpose it into the sphere of the new covenant under which the Christian lives is not only unscriptural, it is illogical and unreasonable. This is so because it puts the Christian under the law where he is not intended to be, because God has placed him under grace. Under the law, if a man was found gathering sticks on the Sabbath day in order to make a fire to cook some food, he was put to death. But under grace, there is the broad base of Christian liberty such as is expressed in Romans 14:5, 6, 10, 12, 13.

The Sabbatarian claims obligation to one part of the Sabbath law and exemption from another part. He, for example, is obliged to break such scriptures as Exodus 35:2 in the middle; at a mere punctuation mark. He arbitrarily teaches that the first part of the verse, which speaks of Sabbath keeping, is binding now; but the second part which requires the putting to death of anyone doing work on the Sabbath day is not binding.

III. THE CHURCH'S NEW DAY

We observe in the Book of Acts that the seventh day gives way to the first day as the Christian day of worship. This was both immediate and gradual. It was immediate in the sense of principle, because recognition of the new day stemmed from the resurrection. It was gradual from the standpoint of practice, because for a long time Christians continued worshipping in the synagogues on the seventh day, while observing the breaking of bread and communion on the first day.

The observance of the first day by the apostolic Christians began immediately after the resurrection so that when you get to Acts 20:7, you read, "And upon the first day of the week. . . . " This spans a period of twenty-four years during which the apostles and disciples had been observing Sunday as the Christian day of worship.

The change to this new day was not commanded by God; it was instinctive. It was a Spirit-led recognition of a new dispensation. The change was not the arbitrary change of a church council. Nor was this an act of the state, for while Constantine later recognized Sunday as the day of worship by establishing it by law; he did not either start Sunday worship or change the day of worship. This was changed by the apostles and the

Christians who had been doing it for three hundred years. All Constantine did was to legalize and recognize it as such.

IV. THE ABSENCE OF NEW TESTAMENT REFERENCE TO THE OLD DAY

There is a total absence of reference in the New Testament, following the gospels, concerning the Sabbath as a day of worship. While everyone of the moral principles of the Decalogue is reaffirmed in the New Testament, the fourth commandment, or Sabbath commandment, is not reaffirmed. Although lists of sins are found in the New Testament which cover every kind of disobedience to the law, not once is Sabbath breaking alluded to as a sin or breach of any kind. Not once in the New Testament is any Christian ever commanded to keep the seventh day. Not once is anyone ever commended or rewarded for keeping the seventh day. Not once is the keeping of the seventh day listed in any of the doctrines enumerated in the New Testament.

Moreover, on the positive side we have some plain teaching about the proper day of worship. In I Corinthians 16:1, 2 we are told to observe the first day of the week as the day to bring our offerings to the Lord. In Colossians 2:14-17 we are told that since the ceremonial law was nailed to the cross we are not to observe feast days or sabbath days.

When the apostles met in the first Christian council at Jerusalem, they rendered a significant decision against efforts being made to Judaize and legalize the Christian church and identify it with Old Testament practices. That decision was against legalism in any form, but perhaps its greatest significance was in what it omitted. It said nothing about Sabbath worship which was a significant omission if Sabbath worship was the proper thing for the Christian.

Against the absence of any reference to Sabbath keeping we have the definite command against it; and beside this we have the historical precedent of the disciples' observance of the first day of the week as the Christian day of worship. Not once in the twenty-one epistles of the New Testament is the Sabbath regarded as holy or sacred. Paul rebuked the Galatians for returning to the observance of "days, and months, and times and years" (Gal. 4:9-11). Paul declares that anyone who puts himself under the law is "fallen from grace" (Gal. 5:2-6). The keeping of the Sabbath is declared to be nonessential (Rom. 14:5, 6; Col. 2:16).

If the law sets apart one day in seven as sacred, grace declares that all seven days of the week are equally sacred. As for the importance of the first day of the week, note these facts:

1. On a Sunday the Lord Jesus arose from the dead (Matt. 28:1).
2. On a Sunday He appeared to His disciples (Luke 24:1, 36).
3. On a Sunday the Holy Spirit came from heaven (Acts 2).
4. On a Sunday the believers got together to break bread (Acts 20:7).
5. On a Sunday they gave to God their offerings (I Cor. 16:2).
6. On a Sunday the first Christians were in fellowship together (John 20:26).

There is an incontrovertible contrast between the seventh day and the first day which establishes the first day as the proper day of worship:

The Sabbath was the seventh day; Sunday is the first day.

The seventh day was associated with creation; the first day is associated with redemption.

The seventh day was a memorial to God's work; the first day is a memorial to Christ's resurrection.

The seventh day marked an unfinished redemption; the first day marked a finished redemption.

The seventh day was based upon law; the first day is based upon grace.

The seventh day looked back upon an old week; the first day looked ahead upon a new week.

The seventh day was rest at the end of a week; the first day was preparation at the beginning of a week.

The seventh day was reward for work done; the first day was preparation for work yet to do.

The seventh day was obligatory; the first day is voluntary.

On the seventh day God said, "Give me this day and I will bless you"; on the first day the Christian says to God, "Because thou hast blessed me I will give Thee this day."

The seventh day was a shadow of things to come; the first day is the substance of things that have come.

The seventh day was a sign of God's old covenant with His earthly people, the Jews; the first day is a confirmation of God's new covenant with His heavenly people, the church.

The seventh day had to do with the first man, Adam; the first day has to do with the Second Man, Christ.

The seventh day stands for the earth; the first day stands for heaven.

The seventh day is on the other side of the cross and the grave; the first day is on this side of the cross and the grave.

Let us then say, "This is the day which the Lord hath made; we will rejoice and be glad in it." In our search for the right day let us be sure we have found the Lord of all the days.

49

THE IDEAL CHRISTIAN SERVANT

Acts 20:13-38

As the founder of many churches, Paul appears before us in the image of the ideal Christian servant. He is at the sea coast city of Miletus to which he has come by ship from Troas on his way to Jerusalem. Because it was Paul's intention to reach Jerusalem by Pentecost, some twenty-four years after the first Pentecost, it was necessary to move with all haste. It appears, since a large party was involved, that they had chartered a coastal vessel to take them as far as Lycia. And because they had only thirty days to get to Jerusalem for the day of Pentecost, they decided to by-pass Ephesus and take the shorter route to Miletus.

Although Paul had passed by Ephesus, he was very anxious to see the leaders of that church and give them his final charge; consequently he sent for them to meet him at Miletus. And while the ship lay at anchor for three or four days, on the south shore of the Latonian Gulf, at the mouth of the Meander River, he held his rendezvous with the church leaders from Ephesus.

Before leaving Troas Paul had preached to the Troasian Church on the first day of the week. But here his message is to the church leaders and it is the only one of Paul's sermons delivered to Christians which is recorded. Because it is recorded it affords us an opportunity to see the self-painted portrait of the ideal Christian servant.

I. THE SERVANT'S MOTIVES. "And when they were come to him, he said unto them, Ye know, from the first day that I came into Asia, after what manner I have been with you at all seasons, serving the Lord with all humility of mind, and with many tears, and temptations, which befell me by the lying in wait of the Jews: And how I kept back nothing that was profitable unto you, but have shewed you, and have taught you publickly, and from house to house, testifying both to the Jews, and also to the Greeks, repentance toward God, and faith toward our Lord Jesus Christ" (verses 18-21).

There was a transparency of motive in Paul's ministry which was observable to the Ephesians from the first day of his service to them and throughout all the whole two years he remained with them.

He describes himself as a servant and to do so he uses a word which indicates a slave. He was not a cheap hireling, working for day wages, but a committed, purchased slave, whose only occupation was serving his heavenly Master.

He specifically mentions humility as one of the characteristics of his ministry. Who dares to speak of himself as being humble, save he who is really humble and can do it without affectation? Humility forbids of boasting, taking personal credit and speaking of oneself in laudatory terms. Humility is no doubt the greatest virtue to be found in a servant of Christ. He may be forgiven anything and everything else, but to profess to serve Christ in terms of self-esteem and personal glory is an unforgivable crime against Christian propriety.

Paul never went to lower depths of self-abnegation than when he wrote to the Corinthians two years prior to this Milesian incident and said, "And I, brethren, when I came to you, came not with excellency of speech or of wisdom, declaring unto you the testimony of God. For I determined not to know any thing among you, save Jesus Christ, and him crucified. And I was with you in weakness, and in fear, and in much trembling. And my speech and my preaching was not with enticing words of man's wisdom, but in demonstration of the Spirit and of power: That your faith should not stand in the wisdom of men, but in the power of God" (I Cor. 2:1-5).

It is well to inspect our motives to see what really prompts us in our Christian service. Is it the glory of God that prompts us, or is it personal glory that seeks to build big churches and large denominations? Is it to serve the Kingdom of God, or is it to serve our own sectarian interests so that personal fame or personal gain may accrue to us?

When Paul speaks of tears and temptations, we can be sure that no more bitter tears were shed than those of discouragement and disappointment; and no more enticing temptations were felt than those that sought to vitiate his high-minded motives with intentions of personal gain and credit.

This is a Christian servant's greatest temptation: the surrender of his motives to serve Christ without personal gain in that service.

II. THE SERVANT'S SUFFERINGS. "And now, behold, I go bound in the spirit unto Jerusalem, not knowing the things that shall befall me there: Save that the Holy Ghost witnesseth in every city, saying that bonds and afflictions abide me. But none of these things move me, neither count I my life dear unto myself, so that I might finish my course with joy, and the ministry, which I have received of the Lord Jesus, to testify the gospel of the grace of God" (verses 22-24).

Paul's sufferings were of many kinds. He suffered from an incurable physical disease. He suffered from bodily abuse, which in one instance brought stoning at Lystra and in other instances beating with stripes. He suffered the perfidy of friends. He suffered the ridicule of his motives. He suffered the questioning of his apostleship. And when he wrote his second letter to the Corinthian Church he gave them an auto-biographical account of himself in these terms, "Are they ministers of Christ? (I speak as a fool) I am more; in labours more abundant, in stripes above measure, in prisons more frequent, in deaths oft. Of the Jews five times received I forty stripes save one. Thrice was I beaten with rods, once was I stoned, thrice I suffered shipwreck, a night and a day I have been in the deep; In journeyings often, in perils of waters, in perils of robbers, in perils by mine own countrymen, in perils by the heathen, in perils in the city, in perils in the wilderness, in perils in the sea, in perils among false brethren; In weariness and painfulness, in watchings often, in hunger and thirst, in fastings often, in cold and nakedness. Beside those things that are without, that which cometh upon me daily, the care of all the churches. Who is weak, and I am not weak? who is offended, and I burn not? If I must needs glory, I will glory of the things which concern mine infirmities. The God and Father of our Lord Jesus Christ, which is blessed for evermore, knoweth that I lie not" (II Cor. 11:23-31). Again he writes in the same letter, "Giving no offence in any thing, that the ministry be not blamed: But in all things approving ourselves as the ministers of God, in much patience, in afflictions, in necessities, in distresses, in stripes, in imprisonments, in tumults, in labours, in watchings, in fastings; by pureness, by knowledge, by long-suffering, by kindness, by the Holy Ghost, by love unfeigned, by the word of truth, by the power of God, by the armour of righteousness on the right hand and on the left, by honour and dishonour, by evil report and good report: as deceivers, and yet true; as unknown, and yet well known; as dying, and, behold, we live; as chastened, and not killed; as sorrowful, yet alway rejoicing; as poor, yet making many rich; as having nothing, and yet possessing all things" (II Cor. 6:3-10).

We are often prone to wonder and quick to question God when adversity, in its many human forms, strikes us. But, bear in mind, it is common to all men, and in the life of a Christian it is permitted providence which results in richer character, higher good and more profitable service.

A friend of some years' acquaintance sent us a Christmas card and, in a personal comment, adding to the season's sentiment she wrote, "Did I say last year that it started to rain in my life? Yes, but one thing I forgot to say is that when it rains it makes something grow." It is necessary for rain to come in every life, but rains mean stormy days, overcast skies and a dreary outlook. There is a place in Patagonia where it never rains and is always sunny; but nothing ever grows to make it lush and green. Do not despise the rain; it is necessary for the harvest of good things in your life.

To read Paul's autobiography is to read the experience of almost perpetual crisis. He moved from one crucial situation to another. A minister must live his life, raise his family and perform his work of preaching, counseling, administering, studying, marrying and burying, in the atmosphere of continuous crisis. Sometimes it is personal crisis,—the crisis of temptation, discouragement or personal inadequacy. Sometimes it is family crisis; for he does not escape any of the situations and conditions which confront his people. But always it is crisis in the lives of his people. Not a day dawns but what he must help someone facing a crisis; the crisis of sickness, sorrow, marriage or a hundred similar life situations that daily confront people in the experience of living. Unless God's servant learns to live and work in crisis with poise and purpose, he never lives or works with any measure of competence or success.

III. THE SERVANT'S FAITHFULNESS. "And now, behold, I know that ye all, among whom I have gone preaching the kingdom of God, shall see my face no more. Wherefore I take you to record this day, that I am pure from the blood of all men. For I have not shunned to declare unto you all the counsel of God" (verses 25, 26).

We touch here at the most vital point of any servant's work. What are the criteria of success? Is it bigness? It is busyness? Is it numbers? Is it the world's standards of success? None of these fit the case of service for Christ, because here it is faithfulness above everything else.

No servant of Christ is guilty of the blood of any man so long as he has declared "all the counsel of God." If men are lost because they have rejected the gospel, it is no fault of the preacher of the gospel. It is their own fault and he is "pure from the blood of all men."

Superficially minded observers, pew-side superintendents and Monday morning quarterbacks count converts as though this were the criteria. Who knows who is really converted? Only God knows this and only God has the last source of evaluation.

Let a man's work stand the test of faithfulness and he can be content with the proper judgment.

Paul gave the right criteria when the Corinthian Christians were dividing themselves into cliques and coteries around men whom they thought were more successful than others. He said, "For while one saith, I am of Paul; and another, I am of Apollos; are ye not carnal? Who then is Paul, and who is Apollos, but ministers by whom ye believed, even as the Lord gave to every man? I have planted, Apollos watered; but God gave the increase. So then neither is he that planteth any thing, neither he that watereth; but God that giveth the increase. Now he that planteth and he that watereth are one: and every man shall receive his own reward according to his own labour. For we are labourers together with God: ye are God's husbandry, ye are God's building" (I Cor. 3:4-9).

IV. THE SERVANT'S RESPONSIBILITIES. "Take heed therefore unto yourselves, and to all the flock, over the which the Holy Ghost hath made you overseers, to feed the church of God, which he hath purchased with his own blood. For I know this, that after my departing shall grievous wolves enter in among you, not sparing the flock. Also of your own selves shall men arise, speaking perverse things, to draw away disciples after them. Therefore watch, and remember, that by the space of three years I ceased not to warn every one night and day with tears. And now, brethren, I commend you to God, and to the word of his grace, which is able to build you up, and to give you an inheritance among all them which are sanctified" (verses 28-32).

The emphasis turns from Paul to the elders of the Ephesian Church who were given shepherding responsibilities over the local flock. To have amplified this into a bishopric over many flocks is a development of later church history. Whether this was right or wrong only the full record of history will reveal; but the intent of the original charge was apparently to leaders over the local church at Ephesus.

The need for this charge was "the imminent peril of false teaching coming both from without and within."* From without there was the danger of "grievous wolves." From within would be the danger of false teaching, "speaking perverse things, to draw away the disciples after them." That this development took place is a matter of record from Paul's later epistles, where he enumerates numerous instances of the depredations of wolves and the machinations of false teachers. Such men as Alexander, Hymenaeus and Philetus are named as false teachers.**

"Of all the dangers to which the Church is subject the greatest is from within. Last year bank robbers in the United States took $1,300,000 in holdups. During the same period of time, however, the employees of banks walked out with $9,500,000. The enemy within can be greater than the enemy without. Paul told the Ephesian elders that after his departure there would be bank bandits and embezzlers who would cause great loss to the Church. He said, 'I know that after my departure fierce wolves will come in among you, not sparing the flock; and from among your own selves will arise men speaking perverse things, to draw away the disciples after them' (Acts 20:29, 30). There are many ways of embezzling, and there are many methods of speaking perversity. It can come through the open denial of Christ, and this would be the bandit approach, but it can come through men who are fundamental in all the great essentials but who steal through putting legalism in place of grace, and who put the emphasis on the human will instead of on sovereign grace. The ratio of such perversity, like that in bank robberies, is also 9 to 1."***

V. THE SERVANT'S MATERIAL REWARD. "I have coveted no man's silver, or gold, or apparel. Yea, ye yourselves know, that these hands have ministered unto my necessities, and to them that were with me. I have shewed you all things, how that so labouring ye ought to support the weak, and to remember the words of the

---

* Rackham
** II Tim. 2:17; I Tim. 1:20
*** Eternity Magazine

Lord Jesus, how he said, It is more blesssed to give than to receive" (verses 33-35).

This is perhaps the most delicate subject of all for it is here where the greatest imbalance can come. The justification of great material reward may seem to be a logical consequence for rendering great service.

Paul sets down the principle that giving rather than getting is the servant's primary goal. It is to do good and not merely to receive good. It is to follow the example of our Lord who said that He "came not to be ministered unto but to minister and give His life a ransom for many."

Paul established his own ideal for service when he quoted a variant of one of the sayings of Jesus, "It is more blessed to give than to receive."

Paul was careful, because of his vulnerable position, to set a good example and declare that with his own hands he ministered to his own "necessities and to them that were with me." His avocation as a tentmaker, or leatherworker, supported his vocation as a servant of Christ.

While sheer economic necessity requires some form of support, either from one's own labors or from the support of those who receive the benefits of a spiritual ministry; it is important to remember that those who take care of the work of God must do so without the thought of material reward as the reason for their labor.

The greater satisfactions of life are not in the realm of rewards but in the realm of service. To selflessly serve is to achieve some of the greatest rewards in life.

A man was once impressed by the courtesy of the conductor toward the passengers on a streetcar. After the crowd had thinned out, he spoke to the conductor about it. "Well," the conductor explained, "about five years ago I read in the paper about a man who was included in a will just because he was polite. 'What in the world?' I thought. 'It might happen to me.' So I started treating passengers like people. And it makes me feel so good that now I don't care if I never get a million dollars."

This is both an example and a picture of the life that assures rewards. Ours is a faith that goes beyond rewards as a part of a bargain, or rewards as a lure to virtue, to rewards as the satisfying experiences that follow Christian living.*

This incident of the ideal Christian servant presumably transpired in the home of some Milesian believer, ends with a display of affection that should be the normal reaction of all believers. Paul had told them that they would not see his face again. It filled their hearts with grief and their eyes with tears. They bade him a tearful farewell with characteristic early Christian affection. What they surely knew was that God's providences would overrule all human events and bring this separation to a happy conclusion.

---

* Rolland W. Schloerb

50

DIVINE PROVIDENCE AND HUMAN EVENTS
Acts 21:1-17

By this time twenty-six years have elapsed since the founding of the church at Pentecost. Paul has been a Christian for some twenty-two to twenty-four years, during which time he has founded many churches; made three missionary journeys; carried the gospel into Europe and endured unprecedented opposition and persecution in the process. By this time Paul has written six of his fourteen New Testament epistles. Now he stands at the crossroads of his career, and begins the final phase of his life when he undergoes numerous trials at the hands of both Jews and Romans; is taken a prisoner to Rome where he finishes his writings; carries the gospel to the capital city and finally dies as a martyr to the cause of Christ.

When one surveys these facts he must consider the relation of divine providence to human events. Where in the course of such a turbulent life can one find room for such a thing as providence? How can one say that it was an act of providence that so necessary an instrument and so important a servant in the work of the kingdom of God should endure such unspeakable adversities and finally die an untimely death in prison? Let it be said at the very beginning of such an inquiry that Paul himself believed in divine providence. Before he became a prisoner, and after a fully tested experience in adversity, Paul wrote to the Romans and said, "And we know that all things work together for good to them that love God, to them who are the called according to his purpose" (Romans 8:28). When he was in prison at Rome he wrote to the Philippian

Church and remarked about the providential working of God, even in his imprisonment at Rome. "But I would ye should understand, brethren, that the things which happened unto me have fallen out rather unto the furtherance of the gospel; So that my bonds in Christ are manifest in all the palace, and in all other places; And many of the brethren in the Lord, waxing confident by my bonds, are much more bold to speak the word without fear" (Phil. 1:12-14).

Although it does not occur at this point, the Book of Acts contains the only use of the word "providence" to be found in the entire Bible. It is in Acts 24:2, where it is used without any reference to God, but rather to a pagan Roman emperor. Here it means "forethought" or a provident planning of one's affairs. But when it is applied to God it refers to divine forethought and care of His creatures. In another and larger sense it refers to the divine economy or management of the affairs of this world, so that history will come to a good end.

Paul used another expression which has the same meaning as providence. When he wrote his second letter to the Corinthians, in which he recounted the great extent of his personal sufferings for Christ, he said, "For our light affliction, which is but for a moment, worketh for us a far more exceeding and eternal weight of glory" (II Cor. 4:17). The Revised Standard Version translates the word "worketh" more properly when it used "is preparing." This is an example of the divine economy of God which is preparing a more glorious end than that which is apparent in our current sufferings, ignominy and shame.

God has a working purpose so that Paul could say, "all things work together for good."

The reason this matter of divine providence and its relation to human events is brought to our notice at this time is the impending imprisonment of Paul, first at the hands of the Jews and then the Romans; first in Jerusalem, then in Caesarea, and finally in Rome where Paul is martyred.

Paul was on his way to Jerusalem for the twenty-sixth observance of the day of Pentecost. On the way, at the city of Tyre, he and his companions found disciples who "said to Paul through the Spirit that he should not go up to Jerusalem" (verse 4). Then arriving at Caesarea they stayed at the home of the evangelist Philip, of previous gospel fame, where they came in contact with a prophet named Agabus. Agabus, like an Old Testament prophet, gave a physical demonstration of his prophecy by taking Paul's girdle and binding his hands and feet, saying. " . . . So shall the Jews at Jerusalem bind the man that owneth this girdle, and shall deliver him into the hands of the Gentiles" (verse 11). But Paul was convinced that it was the will of God that he should complete his journey and fulfill his intention by going to Jerusalem. After spending several days in Caesarea he made ready for the sixty-four mile journey to Jerusalem and the imprisonments that awaited him there.

Here we observe a remarkable example of divine providence in human events for as a result of the transpiration of the events at Jerusalem and Rome, the gospel is furthered and the cause of Christ extended in a manner that would not have been possible in any other way.

We must of reasonable necessity believe that God is capable of the management of the events of life and being able, is willing to do so; for how can we conceive of a God who has created a world such as this and then has left it to its own uncertain devices? We are led by this reasoning as well as the experiences of Paul to the assurance that this present world is under divine management; that it has a destined end and that that end is good. We are led to the assurance that through all the maze of human events a divine purpose is at work; that behind the movements of history there is a divine plan which will ultimately be fulfilled, according to the pattern of God's forethought.

But some say, how can you reconcile human events such as war, crime, disease and suffering to such a divine plan? As far as the plan is concerned God is not responsible for these things. None of these things are of His planning. All of them are here as the result of human transgression and are permitted to exist because of the freedom of human will. But in the ultimate arrangement war, crime, disease and death will be eliminated. In the meantime, God is ruling in heaven and over-ruling on earth.

"Why doesn't God do something about the tragedies of the world?" someone asks. Let it be answered that God has done something about these tragedies. He has made full redemptive provision for changing the hearts of men without which there cannot be a changed world.

Another question is often asked: Does the record of human events in general, and human experience in particular, lead us to believe that such a divine management is actually taking place? In other words is there a providence in force now, and does it guide and govern the events of my life? We are familiar with many classic expressions of faith in this respect both in and out of Holy Scripture. Shakespeare said, "There's a divinity that shapes our ends, Rough hew them as we will." And a common proverb assures us that "man proposes and God disposes." Beecher said, "There seems to be no order in the movement of the bees of a hive, but the honeycomb shows that there was a plan in them all." And there may not seem to be any order in the life you live, but the finished product will reveal a plan.

Providences may be divided, for explanation's sake, into three categories such as general, ordinary and extraordinary. They may be described in their purpose as permissive, preventive and punitive. They operate in physical nature, human history and human nature.

General providences are seen in the creation and preservation of the world. Ordinary providences are seen in the history of mankind as a race of human beings. Extra-ordinary providences are seen in individual men, guiding and intervening in their lives.

Just how are these providences executed? General providences are executed by divine law in nature. What God created by direct act is sustained by indirect act, such as natural causes or laws. These are the laws of cause and effect, gravity, conservation of energy, wind movements and rainfalls. This means that when there is an earthquake, cyclone, flood or drought it is not necessarily an act of God in divine judgment.

Ordinary providences are executed by the directive and determinative acts of divine intervention. These acts direct or govern the course of human history and fulfill the divine purpose. Perhaps the most outstanding example of this kind of providence is found in the birth of Jesus. It had been predicted by God that the Messiah should be born at Bethlehem, the town of David. The angel Gabriel appeared in a home in Nazareth and announced to Mary that she would become the virgin-mother of "the Son of God" (Luke 1:26-35). After that, Mary went into the hill country of Judea, where Bethlehem was located, and greeted Elizabeth, her cousin. She stayed with her some months, and then hastened back to Nazareth, to be there at the time of the birth of Jesus. Jesus would have been born there but for the interposition of divine providence, for there went out a decree from the emperor that all must be enrolled, each in his own city. Mary, with Joseph, must go at once to Bethlehem. And so it came to pass that Jesus was born in Bethlehem, and not in Nazareth. Behold then the fact that God kept Mary and Joseph ignorant of the prediction that the Christ was to be born in Bethlehem (Micah 5:2), where, as devout persons, they would have of themselves gone. Behold also the providence of God in causing the emperor just at that time (note Luke 2:2) to issue his decree of enrollment!

The art of Bezaleel is another evidence of this kind of providence. The remarkable art of Bezaleel in constructing the tabernacle; the architectural genius of Solomon as well as the great wisdom and military strategy of Joshua, Gideon, Barak and David and the legal acumen of Moses were all due to divine inspiration.

The permanence of the Jew also bears out this providence. A Jew domiciled in America is an American Jew; he remains a Jew. On the other hand a German domiciled in America is a German American; he is assimilated into American life. Let an Arab get domiciled in any other land and in a few generations his Palestinian origin is forgotten. But the Jew has always been a Jew and always will be a Jew. No matter how widely dispersed or how viciously persecuted or generously killed he remains a Jew. This is undoubtedly an act of divine providence to maintain the permanent identity of this people.

This providence appeared in the life of Abraham Lincoln who was destined to save the Union from permanent dissolution. Lincoln was a man of whom Herndon said, "melancholy dripped from him as he walked." He had no home life, and he never invited even his most intimate companions to dine with him. He avoided his wife, Mary, as much as possible and spent his nights at the law library. If Lincoln had married Ann Rutledge, the fiancee of his early years, in all probability he would have been happy, but he would not have been president. Mary Todd, obsessed with a determination to live in the White House, was no sooner married to Lincoln than she had him running for Congress.

Extraordinary providences are executed by miraculous intervention, such as the case of Elijah, the destruction of Sodom and Gomorrah, the crossing of the Red Sea, the virgin birth of Jesus, the miracles of Jesus, the resurrection of Jesus, and the present experience of Christians in answered prayer.

The important question is, what is your relation to this providence? It is not a matter to be generalized as if it were a blanket to cover everyone, for providence that is individual is not general.

The working of providence is only true of those whose lives are in the purpose and plan of God. Nowhere but in the Bible do we have a revelation of the purpose and plan of God and of those who share it. It is stated in Romans 8:28 that "all things work together for good to them that love God, to them who are the called according to his purpose." It does not say that all things are good things, but rather that "all things work together for good." It does not say that all men are in God's plan and purpose, but that this providential working is only for "them that love God" and those "who are the called according to his purpose."

The most difficult thing to account for in viewing our lives as the objects of God's providential management is the presence of the things that are tragic and difficult. We are apt to say with Jacob when he was about to see Benjamin go to Egypt, "all these things are against me," when as a matter of fact they were for him instead of against him; because Benjamin's going to Egypt meant salvation for Jacob and his family.

We are apt to take our apparent misfortunes as the happenings of chance, when they are a part of the divine management of our lives. "Our light affliction, which is but for a moment, is preparing for us a far more exceeding and eternal weight of glory."

A friend once showed Ruskin a costly handkerchief on which an accidental blot of ink was made. "Nothing can be done with that," the friend said, thinking the handkerchief ruined and worthless. But Ruskin took it away with him and afterward sent it back to his friend. In a most skillful and artistic way he had made a beautiful design in India ink, using the blot as its basis. Instead of being ruined, the handkerchief was made more beautiful and valuable than ever. So God providentially improves the blemishes, sins and mistakes of our lives to make our lives more valuable and beautiful.

51

CHURCH AND STATE

Acts 21:18-40

The Apostle Paul now faces the last five years of his life. These years are not spent in continued missionary effort or in the quiet contemplation of a fruitful life. They are spent in the turbulance of mob riots, court scenes, and a succession of incarcerations in prison, which are climaxed with his death. These turbulent years begin at Jerusalem to which Paul and his companions have returned. These companions include Doctor Luke, the narrator, and an Ephesian Greek by the name of Trophimus.

By this time, some twenty-six years after Pentecost, the Church at Jerusalem has grown from the original one hundred and twenty to what is described here as "many thousands" or more properly perhaps, several thousands. They are cordially welcomed by James, one of the three pillars of the church still remaining in Jerusalem, and the elders to whom they rehearsed the mighty movement of God among the Gentiles.

In spite of the decision of the Jerusalem council (Acts 15) not to impose legalistic requirements on Gentile converts, while at the same time acting with conscience and liberality toward Jewish believers, a complication arises over the fact that Paul is under suspicion of the Jewish party in the church. He is accused of taking an arbitrary attitude against these conclusions and of being openly hostile to ancestral customs and temple practices. It was decided that Paul would sponsor four Jewish believers in assuming the Nazarite vows in temple ceremonies. He did this in an effort to allay any suspicions of his animosity to the Jews. This went amiss for some Asian Jews who had seen Paul in

Jerusalem in the company of the Greek Trophimus, falsely assumed that Paul took Trophimus with him into the temple and thus polluted the sacred place. For this they seized him for being a teacher of treason against the people, the law and the temple.

When the news of Paul's seizure reached the city a multitude of people converged upon the temple and Paul was dragged out of the sacred precincts to prevent further pollution, and to be punished. The mob was about to kill Paul when he was rescued by the intervention of a strong detachment of Roman soldiers from the Antonia. This rescue at the hands of the Romans is the beginning of five years of bondage under the Gentiles and his ultimate imprisonment and death in Rome.

This incident marks the beginning of the history of the relationship of the church and the state. In this case the church is represented by Paul and the state is represented by the Roman government in Judea.

There have been three principal views of the relationship between church and state:

1. That the Church should be Supreme.

Thomas Aquinas was the champion of the supremacy of the church. He contended that the church aids man to attain eternal salvation while the state aids him to attain temporal happiness. Eternal salvation is the highest goal and therefore the temporal authority of the state should be subject to the spiritual power of the church.

2. That the State should be Supreme.

Thomas Hobbes, the Eighteenth Century English political philosopher was the champion of state supremacy. He contended that the state rules over all spheres of human life. He said that the head of the state should be the head of the church.

3. That the Church and the State should be Separate.

The modern doctrine of church-state separation comes to us through John Locke, the Seventeenth Century English philosopher who contended that religion is a purely spiritual matter and hence the church should have no secular power at its disposal to interfere in religious matters. This principle of separation and of the rights of individual conscience became the governing rule for church-state relations in this country. It is expressed in the American principle of separation of church and state as found in the basic American documents on religious freedom by Roger Williams, Thomas Jefferson and James Madison. It is explicitly stated in the First Amendment to the Constitution which forbids Congress to "establish" any religion as a state church on the one hand and to prohibit religious freedom to worship on the other hand. The First Amendment prohibits the federal government from interfering in religious matters, promoting or prohibiting religious beliefs and practices, or favoring one religious body over another.

The scriptural basis for separation of church and state is found in such Biblical passages as the following:

John 18:36, "Jesus answered, My kingdom is not of this world: if my kingdom were of this world, then would my servants fight, that I should not be delivered to the Jews: but now is my kingdom not from hence."

Matthew 22:21, ". . . Render therefore unto Caesar the things which are Caesar's; and unto God the things that are God's."

The beginning of the struggle for religious freedom in America began with the arrival in this country from England in 1631 of a Puritan minister of Baptist persuasion by the name of Roger Williams. Within a short time Williams found himself in such complete disagreement with the Massachusetts Colony on church-state relations that he was exiled from the colony. In 1636 he fled from Salem, Massachusetts in a violent snowstorm and settled in the wilderness in what is now Rhode Island where he founded the settlement of Providence. There he put into practice the beliefs he had taught in Salem.

Williams argued that there are two areas in life, both ruled by God but in different ways. In one, the area of natural life, of society and of government, man lives according to the laws and customs of that life. In the other, the area of grace, man lives only by the direct call from God. He argued that you cannot enforce the second area by laws from the first area. But, also you cannot leave God out of the first. These views of the relations between the powers of the state and the religious beliefs of the citizens was the forerunner, by more than one hundred and fifty years, of the American ideal of separation of church and state.

Where are we today in relation to religious liberty and the wall of separation between church and state? Theoretically we are at the same place as when the Constitution was framed and the First Amendment was added. But actually we have gone a long, long way down the road to the loss of freedom. This is done by breeching, compromising and circumventing the wall of separation. It is being done by school bus transportation subsidies for non-public school children, by free text books and by the teaching in public schools by garbed religious teachers.

Separation of church and state does not mean separation of religion and state. This nation was founded upon religious principles; it was the result of man's search for religious freedom. All this nation's genius lies imbedded in its religious heritage and it must never allow separation of church and state to be the occasion for separating religion and state.

There are areas where there can be a proper recognition of this relationship and a cooperation between church and state to maintain the religious character of our nation. It is proper for police to protect the property of churches. It is proper for the fire department to come to the aid of churches when fire strikes their buildings. To this extent it is proper for churches to pay taxes on its property for the payment of these and other services which it cannot render to itself. It is proper for the armed forces to provide the services of chaplains. When the government removes a young man from his home and community and places him in an alien environment of its own choosing, it is duty bound to meet his spiritual as well as physical needs. This service is provided in the best way by the government since under direct church provision it would be too competitive. It is proper to hold religious baccalaureate services in public schools since public school children are meeting together on a non-sectarian basis to consider the ideals of life. It is not the case of one group using public facilities to exploit its own sectarian doctrine. It would likewise seem proper to use the Bible in the public schools as a means of teaching the moral and spiritual values which are found in the Word of God. While it may remain true that the main thrust of Christian education belongs to the church and the family, yet the Bible can have a legitimate and appropriate place in public education.

It seems strangely anomalous in Christian America that the attorney general of the state of California should rule that God cannot be mentioned in the public school classroom. As a result of this ruling, one school has directed its librarian to remove from circulation all books in the library in which mention of God is made. God is proclaimed on our national currency, in our national anthem and in at least forty-seven state constitutions. But in our schools God is unconstitutional. In the famous McCollum case the plaintiff, an atheist, sought to eliminate all forms of religious instruction, including the Bible. But the supreme court completely ignored these extreme and distasteful aspects of the case.

As Roger Williams pointed out there are two areas of life, both ruled by God, but both are intended to be separate from each other and laws from the state should not interfere with the church. But while these are independent spheres the state cannot long exist without the supporting moral and spiritual force of the church. The Bible is specific about these spheres. The church is a society of twice-born people who are members of the Kingdom of God and under the direct supervision of the Holy Spirit. It is bound in both faith and practice to the principles spread upon the pages of the Word of God. It is to keep itself separate from the world in order that it may maintain its prophetic ministry to the world. The state is made up of its constituent citizens who unite in government for their mutual welfare and protection.

While the Bible nowhere prescribes the form of government

it does set down the principles of government. This is done in Romans 13:1-7, "Let every soul be subject unto the higher powers. For there is no power but of God: the powers that be are ordained of God. Whosoever therefore resisteth the power, resisteth the ordinance of God: and they that resist shall receive to themselves damnation. For rulers are not a terror to good works, but to the evil. Wilt thou then not be afraid of the power? do that which is good, and thou shalt have praise of the same: For he is the minister of God to thee for good. But if thou do that which is evil, be afraid; for he beareth not the sword in vain: for he is the minister of God, a revenger to execute wrath upon him that doeth evil. Wherefore ye must needs be subject, not only for wrath, but also for conscience sake. For for this cause pay ye tribute also: for they are God's ministers, attending continually upon this very thing. Render therefore to all their dues: tribute to whom tribute is due; custom to whom custom; fear to whom fear; honour to whom honour."

52

CHRISTIANITY'S BEST APOLOGETIC
Acts 22:1 — 23:35

An apology is something said or written in defense or justification of the Christian faith. Its best apology, in this sense, is its product.

The Gospel of John carries the account of a blind man whose healing by Jesus brought a great deal of contention and controversy. The people could scarcely believe it because it happened to a common street beggar. The Pharisees objected to it because the healing was performed on the Sabbath day and therefore transgressed tradition. Finally the parents of the healed man were appealed to and they said, "He is of age; ask him." And when they asked him he said, "One thing I know, that, whereas I was blind, now I see." Here was the greatest testimony of who Jesus was and what He was able to do. It remains as Christianity's best apologetic.

This form of apologetic appears now in Paul as he presents a series of defenses before hostile crowds and courts.

First, there was Paul's defense of himself before a great crowd of Jews from whom he had been rescued by soldiers from the Roman Antonia. They had threatened to kill Paul because of his supposed desecration of the temple. Then there was Paul's defense before the Sanhedrin to whom he appealed as a Pharisee. Then there was his defense before Felix, procurator of Judea, at Caesarea, before whom Paul reasoned of righteousness, temperance and judgment to come with such power and persuasion that Felix trembled. Then there was Paul's defense before Agrippa, or Herod Agrippa II, whom he almost persuaded to become a

Christian. Before these courts and in these scenes Paul gave a defense of Christianity. But the most persuasive element in these defenses was not what Paul said so much as who he was. He was Christianity's best apologetic,—its finest product.

At one time Paul said of himself, "Christ Jesus came into the world to save sinners, of whom I am chief" (I Tim. 1:15). Knowing the nature of his own sinful heart, and knowing the extent of his own sinful activities, he classified himself as the chief of sinners. From this position he was elevated to the greatest of the apostles and a great saint of the church.

One of the earliest developments in the early church was a succession of apologists who arose to defend Christianity against its attackers. Among these were powerful writers like Justin, Athenagoras, Clement, Origen, Irenaeus, Tertullian. These men left a massive amount of literature in which the Christian position was brilliantly defended.

But while these men were adding their contribution to Christian truth there was a vast company of Christians who were both living and dying for the defense of the faith. The rapid progress of Christianity resulted, not so much from the brilliant defenses of the faith by the apologists, as it did from the magnificent manner in which the rank and file of disciples were willing to live and die for their faith. These examples of faith's nobility left an indelible impression upon contemporary generations.

A series of ten vicious persecutions broke out within the first two hundred years of the church's existence. These came under the Emperors Trajan, Nero, Marcus Aurelius, Decius, Valerian, Diocletian, and others, who determined to exterminate the Christian religion and reinstate the ancient system of pagan worship. During this succession of persecutions, which came to an end with the accession of Constantine to supreme power and his adoption of the Christian faith, there were uncounted multitudes of Christians who submitted to imprisonment, torture and death.

"This is what is known as the heroic age of the Church, when with no aid from an arm of flesh, the whole might of the Roman empire was victoriously encountered by the unarmed and un-resisting adherents of the Christian faith. Imperial Rome, the conqueror of the world, was herself conquered and overcome by the bands of Christian disciples, whose weak but dauntless courage was more than a match for all her power."*

There are innumerable examples of heroism in martyrdom, but perhaps the best known of these was that of the venerable Polycarp, bishop of Smyrna, who had sat at the feet of John the Apostle. It was at the time of the Christian Easter festival, when the heathen were having their races and other games in the presence of the Proconsul Titus Anadratus. The aged saint was arrested in a house in the neighborhood of a city, where he had taken refuge. Polycarp declined to avail himself of another opportunity to escape. When he was required to curse Christ, he answered: "Six and eighty years have I served him, and he has done me nothing but good; and how could I curse him, my Lord and my Savior." Refusing to renounce his faith, he was burned at the stake.

When Paul wishes to refer to the most persuasive element in his defense of Christianity, he describes his own conversion. He describes at great length his experience on the Damascus road when he was arrested by the Spirit of God, and changed from a hater of Christians into a lover of all men. He tells about his conversion, his baptism and his subsequent work for Christ. This, concludes Paul, is the greatest evidence he can present to support and substantiate the truth of the Christian religion.

Just before Jesus' ascension He gave this promise to His disciples, "But ye shall receive power, after that the Holy Ghost is come upon you: and ye shall be witnesses unto me . . . " (Acts 1:8). This power was to be the power of the Holy Spirit. The witnessing was to be "unto me." It was witnessing to a person: not a creed, or a proposition, or a principle, or a system

---

* George P. Fisher

of ritual. This constituted the secret and source of power in the lives of such apologists as Paul and Polycarp, for the strength of their lives and the quality of their witness arose from their identification with Jesus Christ.

Now Paul is witnessing before the mob that had threatened to kill him, and his defense in the face of death is his Christian witness to the power of Christ to change human life. He could appeal to nothing greater, more powerful, and more persuasive. There is no greater apologist for Christianity than a saved sinner who is a living witness to the grace of God.

The prospects of facing a hostile mob demanding our life because we are Christians seems exceedingly remote. Yet the need of being a witness to our faith is a daily necessity. This need is not so much the need of dying as martyrs for our faith, as proper as that may be under critical circumstances; it is the need of living for our faith. It is the need of living as Paul lived, a born again, dynamic, vocal witness of the grace of God.

In Hebrews 12:4 it says, "Ye have not yet resisted unto blood, striving against sin." This is the case of most of us, for few of us have the likely prospect of facing a bloody martyrdom. But this statement is preceded by an exhortation for living an apologetic life: "Wherefore seeing we also are compassed about with so great a cloud of witnesses, let us lay aside every weight, and the sin which doth so easily beset us, Looking unto Jesus the author and finisher of our faith; who for the joy that was set before him endured the cross, despising the shame, and is set down at the right hand of the throne of God" (Heb. 12:1, 2). And it is followed by an equally important reminder about the daily chastening process of God's dealings with His children: "And ye have forgotten the exhortation which speaketh unto you as unto children, My son, despise not thou the chastening of the Lord, nor faint when thou art rebuked of him: For whom the Lord loveth he chasteneth, and scourgeth every son whom he receiveth. If ye endure chastening, God dealeth with you as with sons; for what son is he whom the father chasteneth not?" (Heb. 12:5-7).

1. Christians by their example and life need to set up new standards of values in the society in which they live.

This was done by the Christians of the First Century, who were willing to surrender their lives to support their witness to the gospel as God's power to change not only the life of the individual, but society itself.

The values of life today are being perverted by contemporary literature, movies and television. A popular rock-and-roll singer recently received no less than one hundred and twenty-five thousand dollars for one night's appearance on a television network program. He did two wiggles and sang two songs, and for this received more than the yearly salary of the President of the United States and three times the yearly salary of the Chief Justice of the Supreme Court. An identical sum of money would pay the salaries of twenty-five school teachers, forty-two ministers, or sixty-three farm hands in many of our states. It would provide a year's training for thirty or more nurses, would give one hundred twenty-five American young people a year in college, would stock ten mission hospitals with elemental tools and drugs, would feed three thousand refugee children for a whole year. Here is a flagrant example of our perverted values. So long as we permit this perversion of values we can blame no one but ourselves when we witness the degradation of our society.

Peter, who had followed the fortunes of a large group of Jewish-Christian refugees who had been forced to flee their homes and countries because of the violence of persecution, writes to them and us to say: "Beloved, think it not strange concerning the fiery trial which is to try you, as though some strange thing happened unto you: But rejoice, inasmuch as ye are partakers of Christ's sufferings; that, when his glory shall be revealed, ye may be glad also with exceeding joy" (I Pet. 4:12, 13).

2. Christians by their example of life need to be effective witnesses to win others to Christ.

The mission of the Christian is that of a witness. He fulfills this mission not only in the vocal expression of his faith but in the vocational expression of his life.

3. Christians by their example of life need to reveal the true nature of the Christian life.

The true nature of Christianity is not merely theological. It is by its very nature a certain kind of life that has a theological definition, but, what is more important, has a practical explanation through example.

4. Christians by their example of life need to be effective witnesses in order to counteract the secularism in modern society.

We need to be in the best sense leaven in the lump of life, so as to reveal that life is essentially a spiritual relationship with God. It is something which has to be lived with God's help and God's blessing, or else it is a vain exercise, for "man doth not live by bread alone."

5. Christians by their example of life need to be effective witnesses in order to prove that the ordinary sufferings, disappointments and sorrows of life are God's appointed ways to develop and improve character.

Paul was such an example in his own life. His second epistle to the Corinthians is an autobiographical account of his personal experiences as a Christian. In this account he tells of the almost innumerable instances of personal difficulty and adversity. He said upon one occasion, "We are troubled on every side, yet not distressed; we are perplexed, but not in despair: Persecuted, but not forsaken; cast down, but not destroyed; Always bearing about in the body the dying of the Lord Jesus, that the life also of Jesus might be made manifest in our body. For we which live are alway delivered unto death for Jesus' sake, that the life also of Jesus might be made manifest in our mortal flesh" (II Cor. 4:8-11). On another occasion he said, "But in all things approving ourselves as the ministers of God, in much patience, in afflictions, in necessities, in distresses, In stripes, in imprisonments, in tumults, in labours, in watchings, in fastings; by pureness, by knowledge, by longsuffering, by kindness, by the Holy Ghost, by love unfeigned, by the word of truth, by the power of God, by the armour of righteousness on the right hand and on the left, by honour and dishonour, by evil report and good report: as deceivers, and yet true: As unknown, and yet well known; as dying, and, behold, we live; as chastened, and not killed; As sorrowful, yet alway rejoicing; as poor, yet making many rich; as having nothing, and yet possessing all things" (II Cor. 6:4-10).

It was by these various means, through experience and the daily example of life, that Paul became Christianity's best apologetic.

While the defense of our faith by the surrender of our lives seems to most of us a remote possibility, the defense of our faith with our lives and example is an everyday imperative.

53

WHEN IS THE BEST TIME TO BE SAVED?

Acts 24:1-25

It is a false assumption that we are automatically given time enough to do the things we ought to do. It is on this basis that most people live their lives, presuming that they can use time as they please and have enough left over for the all-important matter of their relationship to God. Presuming this to be true, many people adopt the Epicurean philosophy propounded by the rich fool who said, "Soul, thou hast much goods laid up for many years; take thine ease, eat, drink and be merry." Presuming this to be true, many people squander their useful and productive years and then expect to turn over wasted lives to God, falsely assuming that there will always be time enough to make the transition.

We do not have the promise of unlimited time. We are not promised time to live as long as we want to. We are not promised time to achieve our ambitions. We are not promised time to realize our hopes and dreams. We are not promised time to mature our plans. There is no such thing as Felix expressed it, of a more "convenient season."

The true assumption at this point is that the present time is the best time to be saved. In fact, it is the only time, because we do not have promise of a more convenient or more advantageous time. The Bible counters with this word, "Behold, *now* is the accepted time: behold, *now* is the day of salvation."

We have already witnessed Paul's bold defense of his faith before the Jerusalem mob in the temple, where he was rescued from imminent death by the soldiers of the Antonia. Then we witnessed Paul's courageous and stirring defense of his faith before the Sanhedrin. Now we see him before Felix in Caesarea.

Felix is the Roman procurator, or governor of Judea, before whom Paul was taken because his life was not safe in Jerusalem. Before Felix he argued his case so eloquently in terms of righteousness, temperance and judgment to come that the tough, calloused governor "trembled" and said, "Go thy way for this time. When I have a convenient season I will call thee."

Paul spent two years in Roman custody at Caesarea, during which time Felix sent for Paul many times and listened to him as he expounded the Christian faith. Although there were many such occasions when Felix, and his wife Drusilla, listened to Paul's explanations, they never found an occasion to become Christians. No, because there is never a more convenient season for salvation. The best time, the only time, the appointed time is *now*.

Time is one of the most valuable commodities we have. The value of time arises from the following things that are true of it:

1. Its Brevity. At the longest, time is brief. It goes by and we scarcely know we have existed.

2. Its Uncertainty. The scriptures tell us, "Boast not thyself of tomorrow." There is no such thing as tomorrow. The only thing we have or know anything about is today. Tomorrow is an unknown quantity.

3. Its Irrevocability. We never, never reverse time. It cannot be turned back. We can turn back the hand on our watch but we cannot reverse time.

4. Its unchangeability. Time never changes but the times do. There is progressive or retrogressive change in the times, but not with time. It remains brief, uncertain and irrevocable.

What is the chief value of time?

1. It is given us to do the things we must do for the world of which we are a part. We are in this world but once and what contribution we must make has to be made while we are in it, for we are never to do anything for it when we are out of it.

2. To prepare for the eternity into which time inexorably moves us. Eternity can only be prepared for in time. There is no such thing as a second chance for eternity any more than there is a second chance for time. The scriptures say, "It is appointed unto man once to die, but after this the judgment."

Time is a relative thing. In some situations it moves swiftly while in others it drags heavy feet. Albert Einstein said, "When you sit with a pretty girl for two hours, you think it's only a minute. But when you sit on a hot stove for a minute, you think it's two hours. That's relativity."

The relativity of time is apparent to the youth to whom time moves slowly and to the aged to whom time moves swiftly.

You cannot kill time without injuring eternity, because "we must all appear before the judgment seat of Christ; that every one may receive the things done in the body." This refers to the things that are done in time.

There are many kinds of clocks but they all measure the same kind of time; the time that leads to eternity.

The first clock was the sun clock or sundial which consisted of a stile or piece of metal made parallel to the earth's axis and pointing toward the pole. As the sun hit the stile its shadow struck the dial plane on which were the markings of the hours of the day. Next came the water clock, and after this in succession, the sand clock or hour glass, the weight clock, and the spring clock. More recently we had the electric clock, and then the atmos clock powered by changes in the atmosphere. Then we have had the solar clock with energy directly from the sun, operating mechanism that moves the hands across its time-telling face. Most recent of all time measuring devices is the atomic clock which consists of a small quartz crystal enclosed in a vacuum tube which oscillates some one hundred thousand times a second. These rhythmic vibrations control an electric current which drives the motor clock movement and also counts the number of vibrations which are shown on a dial to the last fraction of a second. This clock, checked by the stars, does not vary over a week's period more than one-one thousandth of a second per day.

However time is measured, it is all the same time which is measured and the more accurate our means of measurement becomes, the more responsible we are made for the right use of time.

I have a friend in New Jersey who has a most unique collection of antique clocks. There are over sixty of them hanging on walls all over this remarkable house. But the significant thing about these sixty clocks is that my friend does not have any more time for his responsibilities than if he had only one clock.

Clocks tell us what time it is but the Bible tells us what to do with time.

When is the best time to be saved?

1. When the gospel is first heard.

This is by far the best time. There is no such thing as "any time" to be saved. No one can be saved at his own pleasure. He is not at liberty to choose his time to be saved. It is not when he pleases, but rather when God wills, because the only time we can be saved is when the Holy Spirit moves upon our heart, making it possible for us to believe. We are naturally incapable of faith because we are spiritually dead; and faith and its use is something God must make available to us.

There was a time when God said, "My spirit shall not always strive with man," indicating that the time may come when God forsakes the soul and leaves it to its own consequences.

Do not make the mistake of Felix who wanted to find a more convenient time. The most convenient time to be saved is when we first hear the gospel, when the first sweet influences of the Holy Spirit move across our emotions to incline our hearts to believe. After this may come indifference, hardness and callousness which preclude belief.

2. At the earliest possible time of life.

This means youth. This is by far the best time to be saved. It comes at a time when life is not soiled by grievous and heinous acts of sin. This is the time when we are most sensitive and responsive to the appeal of the gospel. This is the time when we can employ our youthful talents and energies, to the fullest effect of their use, in the service of God instead of waiting to turn over the worn out facilities of a wasted and misspent life to God.

The wise man said, "Remember now thy creator in the days of thy youth, while the evil days come not, nor the years draw nigh, when thou shalt say, I have no pleasure in them" (Eccles. 12:1).

3. At the immediate moment.

The Bible uses the word "now." This, in fact, is the only time of which we have any promise. We do not have promise of tomorrow or even the next breath, and we are enjoined to accept the overtures of God when they are available. This means "now."

Satan's most effective weapon against the soul is procrastination. He is constantly advising delay as if to suggest that there is a more convenient season for salvation than the present time.

You will.discover that you will never find a better time than the present. There will never be a better time emotionally, because the first emotions that sweep across the soul are the sweetest and the most compelling. Repeated resistance and rejection make them less compelling and urgent.

There will never be a better time opportunity-wise, because the best time is the present time. The circumstances now are better than they will ever be.

There will never be a better time intellectually, because to assume we need a better understanding is a false assumption. It is not intellectuality we need so much as disposition and action. "If any man will do his will, he shall know of the doctrine, whether it be of God, or whether I speak of myself" (John 7:17).

What the fate of Felix was is not indicated in the account which tells of his search for a convenient season; but it is presumed that he did not find one and because he did not find one he was not saved. Thus his search for a better season became a tragedy, as it does so often with modern people who think some other time is a better time to be saved.

Are you going to make the mistake of Felix or will you improve the present moment?

What men actually do in seeking a better time is not really the search for a better opportunity as much as an excuse to postpone the crisis of decision. It is a dodge rather than a desire. It is delay rather than decision. They want to put off what they know must be done; but they will find either to their regret or ultimate sorrow that they will never find a better time than the present time.

54

ALMOST OR ALTOGETHER
Acts 25:1 — 26:32

King Agrippa was the last reigning sovereign of the House of Herod and under Caesar was King over the Judean area of the vast Roman dominions. While a nominal Jew so far as rites were concerned, he was not a blood-born Israelite.

At the historical moment recorded at this point in Acts, Agrippa had come to Caesarea to congratulate Festus upon his ascendency to the procuratorship of Judea. While Agrippa was at Caesarea, Festus took opportunity to refer Paul's case to him, because Festus was at a loss about the report he would need to make to the emperor concerning Paul (verses 24-27). Accordingly he relates the history of the case to Agrippa who agrees to hear the accused prisoner. The day of the hearing has now arrived and Agrippa, in company with his sister, Bernice, comes to the governor's audience chamber where the hearing is to be conducted. They are escorted in pomp to their assigned places, followed by the royal entourages, the military, and the principal men of Caesarea, including Festus. It all makes an imposing company before whom one man must plead his case.

When the details of arrangement are ready, Paul is brought in and introduced to Agrippa who bids him speak for himself. There then follows the remarkable address of defense by Paul. It is one of the gems of literature. He commences with a statement of his rigid Jewish loyalty as a Pharisee, and declares that the thing for which he is brought into judgment, namely the resurrection, is the very promise God made to Israel. He follows with an account of his zeal in persecuting members of the

Christian sect and of his subsequent conversion. And then he gives a statement of the gospel message and concludes with a dramatic appeal to Agrippa regarding his personal relationship to Jesus Christ. The result is a sweeping acquittal by Agrippa whose judgment is — "this man doeth nothing worthy of death or of bonds."

The climax of the whole trial, and its most important moral value for our day, is when the emboldened apostle challenges Agrippa with this question, "Believest thou?" To which the king answers, "Almost thou persuadest me to be a Christian." Whereupon Paul says, "I would that not only thou, but also all that hear me this day were both almost and altogether."

There is a relationship of circumstance to that of Agrippa which confronts all men and women of this present day. Like Agrippa we may assume the position of kings in our own personal realms and demand the right to adjudicate our fate. We may revolt against the Word of God and challenge the gospel's call to our conscience. But sooner or later the question of faith will be demanded of us, "believest thou?" And when the final assessments of life are made some will be "altogether" and some will be "almost."

I. WHAT WAS IT THAT ALMOST PERSUADED AGRIPPA?

In Phillip's translation, Agrippa is heard to say, "Much more of this, Paul, and you will be making me a Christian." He had "almost" believed. He was on the thin edge of capitulation. It was only one step to the other side of the line. The balances of the scale of decision were almost even, and although he was "almost," yet he was not "altogether"; and being weighed he was found wanting.

Why should Agrippa have been more than "almost"?

1. Because he had just heard the gospel declared (verse 18).

This is sufficient reason for any man, king or otherwise, to be a Christian. The hearing of the gospel immediately constitutes a moral obligation to the hearer. The moment he hears the gospel, that moment he stands under the most solemn obligation to become a Christian in the totality of experience.

You often hear people speak of the state of the heathen as justification for their own inaction. They say, what about the heathen who have never heard the gospel? That is not our problem; it is God's. Our problem is a more serious one; we have heard. What are we going to do with what we know? If we troubled less about the heathen and more about ourselves there would be more converts to the Christian faith. We are responsible for what we know.

2. Because he had the example of Paul's conversion (verses 13-15).

Agrippa not only had the advantage of having heard the gospel preached, but he had the further advantage of having the evidence of the power and efficacy of the gospel in the example of Paul's conversion.

If a chemist declares that he can produce the yolk of an egg from a Puerto Rican sweet potato, and also produce in addition one hundred useful products such as rubber, coffee, candy, dye, paint, paste, starch, vinegar, ink, shoe blacking and molasses from the humble peanut; and then puts the proof of his production before your eyes you cannot gainsay him. Neither can anyone gainsay God when He proposes a gospel which will regenerate life, and then gives proof of this salvation in men and women who have become new creations. On the basis of such proof both Agrippa and you should be Christians.

3. Because this thing was not done in a corner (verse 26).

Paul refers to the crucifixion of Jesus as something more than a local affair of the Jews; something more than an isolated happening. Indeed it had not been done in a corner. It was something that belonged to the world. It soon became common knowledge in all the world and men were without excuse.

Agrippa was therefore without legitimate argument for historical reasons, since he had every reason to believe the claims of Jesus and the abundant evidences of His true Messiahship.

Like Agrippa, men today have abundant historical evidences

and proof of the claims of Jesus and are bound by these evidences to a decision.

In Marie Corelli's "Barabbas" she tells of a conversation between Barabbas, lately released from prison, and Melchior, the dark skinned mystic. Barabbas is telling him he is going with the multitude to see the death of the condemned Nazarene; to which his companion responds: "Thou shalt most assuredly behold that death: — for will not all the world be there?" Yes, all the world was there. For the death of the cross is as if it happened yesterday. Its crime is as well known as any which appears daily in our newspapers. And "all the world was there."

II. Why Did Not Agrippa Become a Christian?

Agrippa, as we have just seen, had three compelling reasons to become a Christian. They were (1) The preaching of the gospel; (2) The proof of its saving power in Paul; (3) The historical evidences of the crucifixion. Why was he not a Christian? We can only leave the answer to conjecture, for Agrippa gives no intimations why he did not become a Christian.

There are these conjectures that we may assume were behind his lack of decision:

1. Agrippa may have feared public opinion.

Agrippa had calculated the consequences of a decision for Christ and concluded they were too great. What would Caesar say? What would Bernice say? What would friends and courtiers say? No, he could not pay the price. Like many another person he feared the cynical, criticizing tongue of man more than he desired the approval of God.

When it comes to a decision for Christ many are like Festus, who rudely interrupted Paul's speech and said, "Paul, thou art beside thyself; much learning doth make thee mad." That defense of indecision has been made many times. "Why, you are out of your reason"; "You are insane." But we can well believe that the only right minded man in Caesarea that day was Paul, because he was right with God.

2. Agrippa may have postponed a decision.

He might have said, I will decide this matter under less public circumstances. When I get back to my palace it will be time enough. When age forces me out of the public eye I will decide, but not now. But so far as we know, he never came to a decision. He was "almost" but not "altogether" because of delayed decision. There are more people who are "almost" because of delay than for any other single or combined reason.

> "There is a tide in the affairs of men
> Which, taken at the flood, leads on to fortune;
> Omitted, all the voyage of their life
> Is bound in shallows, and in miseries.
> On such a full sea are we now afloat;
> And we must take the current when it serves,
> Or lose our ventures."
>
> - Shakespeare in "Julius Caesar"

III. How Could Agrippa Have Become a Christian?

Had Agrippa followed the facts presented to him and been agreeable to the dictates of his conscience, he would have found the remedy not far from hand, for the apostle had already given the formula of faith and salvation (verse 20).

1. Repent

If there is any price to pay for salvation repentance is that price. Either way you choose to look at it, it will cost you something. To remain "almost" exacts the tremendous and incalculable price of a lost salvation and to be "altogether" is not without its payment, for it demands repentance from all known sin.

2. Turn to God

Salvation is a matter of right direction. It is not so much "how" shall I find God, but "where." God is to be found in a certain direction and Agrippa was told to "turn to God." God is in the opposite direction from what man is going. Men need to "turn" for conversion is life's "about face." It is a change of direction. It is going in the opposite way.

IV. WHAT DID IT COST AGRIPPA TO REMAIN "ALMOST"?

It cost him many things.

1. The Pardon of Every Sin

The gospel promises the pardon, forgiveness, cleansing of every sin, either imputed or acquired. It was this cost that Agrippa had to pay.

2. The Peace of a Pure Heart

Religious experience can be a cultural whitewash that is as Pharisaical as that of the First Century. Outwardly there may be the appearance of beautiful edifices while inwardly there is the reality of sepultured bones.

Peace comes from being washed white but not from being whitewashed. One is a thorough going purification of the inward impulses of life, while the other is a surface change.

3. The Pleasure of a Christ-Blessed Life

Pleasure is more than emotional fun. It is an inwardly satisfying experience of real joy that springs from a genuine experience with God.

4. The Prospect of a Heavenly Home

Heaven is in the desire of every man and is the instinctive goal of all the race; but it is a place to be prepared for. It is not the birthright of our first birth. It comes only with the second birth.

Did it pay Agrippa to stop at "almost" and not go on to "altogether"? If loss is gain and tragedy is romance then it paid and paid well, for Agrippa suffered much loss and involved himself in great tragedy. But by all the computations of right and reason it did not pay. And it does not pay today any more than it did then. In spite of the fact that one may live in prestige, be good and sincere, and otherwise commendable, "almost" will never spell "altogether."

Here are the consequences of a lost life. Where is "almost"

Agrippa and where is "altogether" Paul? Agrippa has vanished from the memory of man except for the brief notations of history. Paul is remembered wherever men call themselves Christians. Oblivion is the price of being "almost." Eternal remembrance is the reward of being "altogether."

Under the tremendous persuasion of these truths the scripture is very pertinent to this moment. It says, "I would to God, that not only thou, but also all that hear me this day, were both almost and altogether such as I am, except these bonds" (verse 29).

55

THE CONTRARY WINDS OF LIFE
Acts 27:1 — 28:10

The story of Paul's journey to Rome is one of the most interesting chapters of the entire book. It contains a document of unusual detail regarding the art of ancient seamanship. It furthermore tells of the enormous contest with physical forces against which the mariners had to battle. It describes the efforts of Paul's official party to survive great hazards in order that they might reach Rome, where Paul expected to present his case before Caesar. But beyond these things we see in it an allegorical story of the struggles of human life. Since human life is often compared to a voyage across a stormy sea, there is in this story a symbolic picture of the struggles of men against the contrary winds of life.

There is specific mention in this account of numerous instances involving adverse winds. In verse 14 — "But not long after there arose against it a tempestuous wind called Euroclydon." The Hebrews, who did not define directions with the minuteness customary in modern times, recognized four winds: the east, the west, the north and the south winds. Euroclydon was so regular in its blow that it was given this name perhaps to indicate its tempestuous, violent and destructive character. It was this wind that brought the vessel, in which Paul was sailing to Rome, to shipwreck.

In this sense Euroclydon is symbolic of some of the adversities of life and indicative of the fact that when launched upon the great business of life one is bound to face adversities and difficulties.

In verse 18 there is a continuation of their nautical struggle with Euroclydon and it says, "And we being exceedingly tossed with a tempest. . . ." In verse 20 it says, ". . . and no small tempest lay on us. . . ." And prior to this in verse 4 where they had hardly embarked upon their sea voyage, it says, " . . . the winds were contrary." And again in verse 7, " . . . the wind not suffering us. . . . "

But not all the winds that blow are contrary. In one instance the log of the journey says, ". . . the south wind blew softly . . . " (verse 13). Thank God for those times of life when the south wind blows softly, and life is tranquil and peaceful and we are able to have surcease from struggle and trouble and our spirits relax in the calm enjoyment of living.

But the tempest is also a part of life and we must understand it, be willing to face it, and have enough of the mariner of life in us to know what to do to meet it.

There are a number of practical lessons which appear in this prolonged incident involved in Paul's voyage to Rome.

1. One should have a proper concern for the end of life.

Paul, although he is not altogether aware of it, is nearing the end of his life. We say, not altogether, because he has already had several intimations of the serious things that face him when he goes to Rome.

It is fitting that we be concerned about the end of life. One wants it to end in successful endeavor. He would like to spend the golden years in contemplating a successful life; to be able to look back upon years of labor and struggle and see it finish in victory. There is great danger that the golden years may be filled with cynicism, skepticism, remorse and regret. This is so because the idealism and exuberance of youth is not always fitted with a perspective or philosophy which understands the true meaning and purpose of life.

What we will enjoy in the golden years of life are the things we do in the earlier years of conquest and struggle. How important it is that we understand what life is all about and live it for what it is worth.

It is far from true that the golden years necessarily mean years of gold in terms of financial success. Amassing a fortune is not to be the lot of most people. Only a comparatively few do this. What then constitutes success in the golden years? It lies in the symbolic picture of a voyage on the sea of life. It means success in terms of facing Euroclydon with faith, courage, faithfulness, tenacity and bringing one's ship of life to port intact although it may be scarred and marred by the struggle.

I have in mind a friend who saw a fortune slip from him through force of circumstances, yet to the very end of the struggle of life he has fought on with a faith and courage that has been a great source of inspiration to me. This I think is success for the golden years.

2. One presumes when he is in the will of God he will have smooth sailing on life's sea.

This was not true of Paul. Take a look at his turbulent life and you see in it almost every kind of adversity imaginable. First of all, he acquired a considerable number of personal enemies who were jealous and envious of his position and success. Then, he was the victim of a personal physical disability which would have ordinarily hampered his success. But God permitted this to come to Paul as a means to great excellence and usefulness. And besides these there appears three lists of things which Paul was faced to endure. One of these is II Cor. 4:7-11; another is II Cor. 6:4-10; and another is II Cor. 11:23-30.

About five years prior to the time spoken of in this narrative of Paul's journey to Rome, while he was in the City of Corinth, he wrote his now famous letter to the Romans. He addressed this letter as follows: "To all that be in Rome, beloved of God, called to be saints; Grace to you and peace from God our Father, and the Lord Jesus Christ." And then he goes on to say, "Making request, if by any means now at length I might have a prosperous journey by the will of God to come unto you . . ." (verses 10-17).

Paul prays for a prosperous journey by the will of God. But what kind of a journey did he get? Was it "prosperous" in the sense of freedom from adversity? Not at all. It was prosperous in its end results and from the standpoint of what it accomplished, although it was beset by hazards, hardships and danger. Was it in "the will of God"? Indeed it was, and what he experienced in the way of hazards and hardships were likewise in the will of God.

It is not necessarily true that when we are in the will of God we will be free from adversity and difficulty. This is borne out very clearly in Paul's voyage to Rome for, although he went to Rome by the will of God after he had prayed for a prosperous journey, he encountered everything short of death.

3. Here is proof of a supervising providence in the affairs of a Christian's life which guarantees the right and righteous ends of life.

Paul stated this in his letter to the Romans. He said, "For we know that all things work together for good . . ." (Rom. 8:28).

4. These adversities reveal the true nature of our character.

All during the immense struggles encountered in the voyage to Rome Paul stands out as the hero. He is looked to by his fellow voyagers for help and advice, although he was not a seaman. He has poise and strength in the midst of crisis. He was able to meet every situation with assurance because of his strength of character. In every situation Paul dominated the scene as the man of courage and faith. In their fierce struggle with Euroclydon which lasted for a number of days, Paul addressed the ship's company and spoke of his assurance from God that they would complete their voyage. This is what he said: ". . . Sirs, ye should have hearkened unto me, and not have loosed from Crete, and to have gained this harm and loss. And now I exhort you to be of good cheer: for there shall be no loss of any man's life among you, but of the ship. For there stood by me this night the angel of God, whose I am, and whom I serve, Saying, Fear not, Paul; thou must be brought before Caesar: and, lo, God hath given thee all them that sail with thee. Wherefore, sirs, be of good cheer: for I believe God, that it shall be even as it was told me" (Acts 27:21-25).

"When Abraham Lincoln was a young man, he ran for the legislature in Illinois and was badly swamped. He next entered business, failed, and spent seventeen years of his life paying up the debts of a worthless partner. He fell in love with a beautiful young woman to whom he became engaged — then she died. Entering politics, he ran for Congress and was badly defeated. He then tried to get an appointment to the United States Land Office, but failed. He became a candidate for the United States Senate and was badly defeated. In 1858, he was defeated by Douglas. But in the face of all this defeat and failure he eventually achieved the highest success attainable in life, and undying fame to the end of time."

It has already been observed that the Hebrews did not define directions with the minuteness of modern times but recognized direction in terms of four winds. Combined with this is an incident of Paul's voyage near the Island of Melita. Here they were driven so violently by the wind that they were in danger of being driven on the rocks and dashed to pieces when it is recorded, "they cast four anchors out of the stern, and wished for the day."

Put the four winds of adversity and the four anchors together and look at life's adversities and life's defenses.

I. THE FOUR WINDS OF ADVERSITY

Man is a creature of three parts, body, soul and spirit. Here is the physical, the mental and the spiritual. Add to these the natural (environment) and you have the four sources of adversity.

1. The Physical.
Much of life's adversity is physical in nature. We possess bodies which are subject to many ills and disabilities. They can cause us much of our adversity.

2. Mental.
In a recent article entitled, "Keeping Sane in a Crazy World,"

it pointed out the fact that one out of ten persons in the United States is in need of some sort of treatment for an emotional or mental disorder. One out of twenty will spend some part of his life in a mental institution. A quarter of a million persons every year are hospitalized as the result of mental breakdowns. One family in five has direct experience with mental illness.

How can one keep sane in a crazy world? The answer — by being a normal person.

What are the characteristics of being a normal person?

    1st — Maintaining give-and-take relations with others.
    2nd — Meeting one's problems as they arise.
    3rd — Being realistic about the future.
    4th — Having a grip on one's self.
    5th — Having self-respect.

3. Spiritual.

The Bible teaches the existence of a world of spiritual evil which is the source of many of life's adversities. It is put in this language by Paul: "Put on the whole armour of God, that ye may be able to stand against the wiles of the devil. For we wrestle not against flesh and blood, but against principalities, against powers, against the rulers of the darkness of this world, against spiritual wickedness in high places. Wherefore take unto you the whole armour of God, that ye may be able to withstand in the evil day, and having done all, to stand" (Eph. 6:11-13).

4. Natural (our environment)

This is physical adversity such as comes to us through natural consequences like that experienced by Paul at sea. It can be adverse winds, destructive earthquake, raging fire, devastating flood and many other natural and material adversities.

II. THE FOUR ANCHORS OF DEFENSE

1. Faith.

Faith is "the substance of things hoped for, the evidence of things not seen." It is our anchor to the great rock of reality which is God.

2. Prayer

This is not a coward's refuge in the time of fear, but the Christian's access to the presence of God in every time and condition of life. It is the climate in which he lives and therefore he is unafraid in the time of crisis.

3. Revelation

The Bible is the source of immeasurable courage and strength in the time of human adversity and difficulty. It can sustain and help when all other sources fail.

4. Use of Means

Paul was a man of faith, but also works. He was a man of prayer, but also action. He not only used the spiritual means of defense that were available, but he went to work.

We read the account of the crew's contest with the elements in terms of action. They used every nautical skill at their command. They worked fiercely and intently.

While conducting a Bible conference in the mountains near Prescott, Arizona, we had just finished the morning message when one of the camp workers rushed into the auditorium and shouted, "fire." Fire in the forest is an awful thing. There were two hundred and fifty men, women and children in a camp which was in the midst of the forest, and a fire with flames twenty feet high raged just behind the dining hall. The auditorium was evacuated in orderly fashion and men were soon armed with fire fighting equipment. They deployed around the fire and at the command of a leader went to work clearing a fire-break around the burning timber. In about thirty minutes the fire burned out and the danger of a holocaust was over. I took particular notice that, while everyone fervently believed in prayer— and prayed—yet men went to work, undergirded by both faith and prayer, and used the means at their disposal to put out the fire.

Upon one of D. L. Moody's journeys across the Atlantic there was a fire in the hold of the ship. The crew and some volunteers stood in line to pass buckets of water. A friend said to Moody: "Mr. Moody, let us go to the other end of the ship and engage in prayer." The evangelist with common sense replied, "Not so, sir; we will stand right here and pass buckets and pray hard all the time." How like Moody that was! He believed that prayer and work were like the two hands of the one person, in that they should never be separated.

These are the four winds of adversity and these are the four anchors of defense.

56

THE TRIUMPH OF A WELL-LIVED LIFE
Acts 28:11-31

The setting is a Roman prison. The prisoner is the Apostle Paul. The occasion is his coming to Rome by a hazardous sea voyage that had taken from August to March. The result is Paul's martyrdom, but with contingent effects that far exceed his death, so that we see in Paul's death the triumph of a well lived life.

Here we note two things: First, the conclusion of the Book of Acts; second, the triumph of Paul's well lived life.

I. THE CONCLUSION OF THE BOOK OF ACTS

This book concludes with a great climax. It is the climax of the gospel being brought from its cradle at Jerusalem to the capital of the Gentile world at Rome where its witness will be borne to the palace of Caesar.

This book tells us of the founding of the church. It is preceded and followed in the New Testament canon by the gospels and the epistles which also bear a vital message about the church. In the gospels you have the founder of the church. In the Acts you have the founding of the church. In the epistles you have the foundations of the church.

The purpose of the Book of Acts is to record the establishment of Christianity. This establishment unfolds in a record of life which is properly described as life in action, for here is an action book. It is the story of the acts and deeds, living and dying, of the proponents of the Christian faith.

It begins with the last interview of Christ with His apostles, which lasted for forty days, during which He reiterated His promise of the coming of the Holy Spirit and commanded His disciples to preach the gospel in all the world. Then follows the account of the founding of the church at Pentecost. Next, we see the transition of Christianity to a missionary faith in which the church becomes catholic. Then follows the establishment of Christianity in the principal centers of the empire through the three missionary journeys of Paul. Finally Paul is arrested and, after successively defending himself before the Jews, Felix, Festus and Agrippa, he is taken, on his own appeal, by sea voyage to Rome where he remains domiciled in a private prison from which he preaches and writes for two years.

This, briefly, is the story of the book which is the record of life in action. But Christianity is something more than history and a record written in a book. It is something personal. It is life and experience, contest and conquest, trial and triumph, pageant and perfume.

II. The Triumph of a Well Lived Life

None of us in the usual categories of life could possibly expect the degree of success and accomplishment which was true of Paul; but, notwithstanding this fact, all of us can experience the triumph of a well lived life, for the reason that success in life is based upon principle rather than things.

Let us consider this triumph of the well lived life.

1. Its Beginning.

Jesus gave us life's most familiar starting place when He said, "But seek ye first the kingdom of God and His righteousness and all these things shall be added unto you."

This is not a starting place identified with any particular age in life. It may be in adult years or in youth; but it is well considered when it is the starting place of youth, for then the immense advantages of God's means of grace all lie in our favor.

It is to be doubted that we would ever have heard of Paul

apart from his encounter with God on the Damascus Road. Up to this time Paul's chief distinctions were his scholarship and his religious zeal. Paul's notoriety would have been in the field of religion, but would have extended no further than the limits of his provincial Jewish faith; whereas, in his new beginning, his life became world-wide in its scope and influence. He influenced more people for good than any other person save Jesus Christ.

2. Its Purposes.

Every well lived life must have a purpose. This purpose must extend beyond the limits of personal selfishness to the fields of service and accomplishment in the cause of righteousness. It must extend beyond ceremonial righteousness to creative righteousness. It has been suggested that many young people are turning away from organized religion because churches emphasize "easy psychological adjustments rather than creative religious behavior."

It is told of a dentist who suffered periodically from what his family politely called "spells," that when these periods came upon him he went about frantically asking everyone, "Where am I?" The question did not concern his geographical location, since he knew precisely where he was with reference to his home and physical surroundings. What troubled him was a far deeper matter: "Where am I after sixty years of living? What have I accomplished? What have I done with my possibilities? Where am I spiritually?" He was haunted by the feeling that he had been going nowhere. There can be no triumph unless there is a well lived life and there can be no well lived life unless we have gone somewhere in our lifetime.

A thoughtful man put it this way, "I feel as if I had lived through everything but life." It is possible to pass through the motions of religion without experiencing the promotions of life.

3. Its Principles.

These are life's guidelines. They are necessary and important or else we will become involved in the minutiae of the unimportant or find ourselves beset by destructive forces.

Paul had numerous guidelines. "For I determined not to know anything among you, save Jesus Christ and Him crucified" (I Cor. 2:2). No doubt his greatest guideline was justification by faith. This was the foundation of his gospel. It was not new to Paul nor unique with Christianity. He borrowed it from Habakkuk. "Therefore being justified by faith, we have peace with God through our Lord Jesus Christ" (Rom. 5:1). Galatians 2:20 is the expression of another important guideline. "I am crucified with Christ: nevertheless I live; yet not I, but Christ liveth in me: and the life which I now live in the flesh I live by the faith of the Son of God, who loved me, and gave himself for me."

Relating to his own progress as a Christian he took a very positive stand. He said, "Not as though I had already attained, either were already perfect: but I follow after, if that I may apprehend that for which also I am apprehended of Christ Jesus. Brethren, I count not myself to have apprehended: but this one thing I do, forgetting those things which are behind, and reaching forth unto those things which are before, I press toward the mark for the prize of the high calling of God in Christ Jesus" (Phil. 3:12-14).

One of the dominating guidelines was his utter abandonment to Jesus Christ and his determination to make his life a great witness to Christ. He says: "Wherever I go, thank God, he makes my life a constant pageant of triumph in Christ, diffusing the perfume of his knowledge everywhere by me. I live for God as the fragrance of Christ, breathed alike on those who are being saved and on those who are perishing, to the one a deadly fragrance that makes for death, to the other a vital fragrance that makes for life" (II Cor. 2:14-16).

While he is a prisoner in Rome one of his ankles is chained to the wall of his dreary, damp dungeon. One of his wrists is fettered to the Roman soldier detailed to guard him. With the other hand he is writing a letter to a few fond friends in Philippi who had thoughtfully sent him a gift with which he was able to pay for his private lodgings. To these friends he says, "I can cope with everything by Him Who strengthens me. . . I have indeed enough and to spare. I am fully supplied, having received from Epaphroditus what your means allowed, a sweet-smelling perfume, an acceptable sacrifice, well-pleasing to God. . . ." But how does he react to his distressing confinement? He writes to his Philippian converts this philosophic reaction: "I have learned to be content, whatever the circumstances may be. I know how to live when things are difficult and I know how to live when things are prosperous. In general and in particular I have learned the secret of facing either poverty or plenty. I am ready for anything through the strength of the One who lives within me" (Phil. 4:11-13, Letters to Young Churches).

4. Its Qualifications.

Paul possessed the qualification of a triumphant life because it was his determination to "live for God."

Undoubtedly there were other qualifications. He had a good education and a fine family history. He had acquired a wide experience. He was a man of courage, fortitude, patience and faith.

A member of the pastoral relations committee in a certain church read a letter purporting to have come from an applicant. The letter was as follows: "I have many qualifications. I've been a preacher with much success and also had some success as a writer. Some say I'm a good organizer. I've been a leader most places I've been. I am over 50 years of age. I have never preached in one place more than three years. In some places I have left town after my work has caused riots and disturbances. I must admit I have been in jail three or four times, but not because of any real wrong doing. My health is not too good, though I still get a great deal done.

"The churches I have preached in have been small, though located in several large cities. I've not got along too well with religious leaders in towns where I have preached. In fact, some have threatened me and even attacked me physically.

"I'm not good at keeping records. I have even been known to

forget whom I have baptized. However, if you can use me, I shall do my best for you."

After reading the letter, the committee member looked at his fellow members and said, "Well, what do you think? Shall we hire him?" The others were aghast. Hire an unhealthy, trouble-making absentminded ex-jailbird? Was the man who read the letter crazy? Who was the applicant, anyway? Who would have such colossal nerve? "Oh," said the man who had just read the letter, "it's just signed, 'The Apostle Paul'."

5. Its Companions.

In the letter Paul wrote to the Romans a few years before he came to Rome he said, "For none of us liveth to himself, and no man dieth to himself" (Rom. 14:7). We are not capable of living a life of triumph as an isolated soul. We need the help of like-minded companions. Paul had these companions. The record of Acts is filled with innumerable friendships and com-radeships. He had many faithful friends working with him and sharing his busy life and arduous labors. Among these were Timothy, Tychicus, Aristarchus, John Mark, Doctor Luke and others.

These friends, mind you, were found within the context of the Christian faith and more particularly in church. The church is the best place to develop your friendships. Here are to be found the common bonds of faith and life which we can share with others who are likeminded. This is not to say that there are not good people outside the church, or that the church is a faultless society, or that its conditions of life will be unending perfection. As Jaroslav Pelikan points out in *The Riddle of Roman Catholicism*, ". . . membership in any church body in-volves the necessity of compromise and of settling for a great deal less than one would like. As one Protestant theologian has been heard to observe, the church may be likened to the ark of Noah because the only reason one can stand the stench inside is on account of the deluge outside. Only the most extreme organiza-tion man will seriously try to give the impression that everything is satisfactory in his own communion; and even he will do it only when he is defending his communion against outsiders. A certain amount of compromise belongs to membership in an organized church, but the question is how much compromise must one be prepared to stomach for the sake of peace and unity."

6. Its Providences.

A person's life is not a mass of protoplasm cast upon the sea of life and subject to the fatalistic forces of an impersonal nature. The Christian's life is constantly subject to the providences of God. This is why Paul could write to the Philippians and say, "But I would ye should understand, brethren, that the things which happened unto me (his imprisonment) have fallen out rather unto the furtherance of the gospel: so that my bonds in Christ are manifest in all the palace and in all other places; and many of the brethren in the Lord, waxing confident by my bonds, are much more bold to speak the word without fear" (Phil. 1:12-14).

God used the seeming adversity of Paul's imprisonment for an advantage, and Paul heralded the gospel from a prison-pulpit so that it was heard in all Caesar's palace and ultimately throughout the entire Roman empire.

We cannot live a life of triumph without the providences of God working in our favor, for the God who rules in heaven also over-rules on earth.

From this disadvantageous prison circumstance Paul wrote some of his most eloquent and effective epistles, in which he ascended to lofty heights of revelation and gave some of his most eloquent teachings. These prison-born epistles included Colossians, Ephesians, Philippians and Philemon.

7. Its Accomplishments.

It is impossible to detail all the accomplishments of this man's fabulous life, but it includes among other things fourteen epistles, the establishment of an unknown number of churches, the immense preaching results of three extensive missionary tours which extended Christianity into Europe and Asia, the conversion of a mass of converts, the contribution of his influence upon a large circle of friends, and the continuing effect of his written ministry upon untold millions of people.

All of these accomplishments stem from a man who went through a revolutionary conversion from a fanatical Jew, whose business was persecuting Christians, to become the most conspicuous follower of Jesus Christ. He is the living proof of one of the axioms of the Christian faith which says, "Therefore if any man be in Christ, he is a new creature: old things are passed away; behold, all things are become new" (II Cor. 5:17).

Paul was both a sower and a reaper. This is not true of all. Most people are sowers; few are reapers. Most people will never see the visible fruits of their life's accomplishments because they lie hidden in the gestating conditions of grace. We ought therefore to be encouraged to continue the faithful exercises of Christian life and service because the greatest reward that can come to a soul is the Lord's approval when He says, "Well done thou good and faithful servant; enter thou into the joy of thy Lord."

A farmer once said that when he engages a new worker for his farm he does not ask, "Can you reap?" but, "Can you sow?" because sowing is far the most difficult, tedious and taxing operation of the farm. This ought to be a comfort to those whose work seems chiefly of the seed scattering nature. Do not be discouraged if you are not a reaper; it is important to be a sower.

Although the Book of Acts leaves Paul a prisoner at Rome, there is abundant reason to believe that he was released after two years confinement and resumed his missionary work. During this period he went to Spain among other places and visited Crete, Ephesus and Macedonia. During his absence from Rome the great conflagration broke out and Nero satisfied his anger on multitudes of Christians who were slaughtered to justify a rumor that Christians were responsible for the destruction of Rome.

Meanwhile Paul returns to Rome and to his martyr's fate. He knows the end is near and conscious that he is writing his last words, he says to Timothy, "For I am now ready to be offered, and the time of my departure is at hand. I have fought a good fight, I have finished my course, I have kept the faith: Henceforth there is laid up for me a crown of righteousness, which the Lord, the righteous judge, shall give me at that day: and not to me only, but unto all them also that love his appearing" (II Tim. 4:6-8).